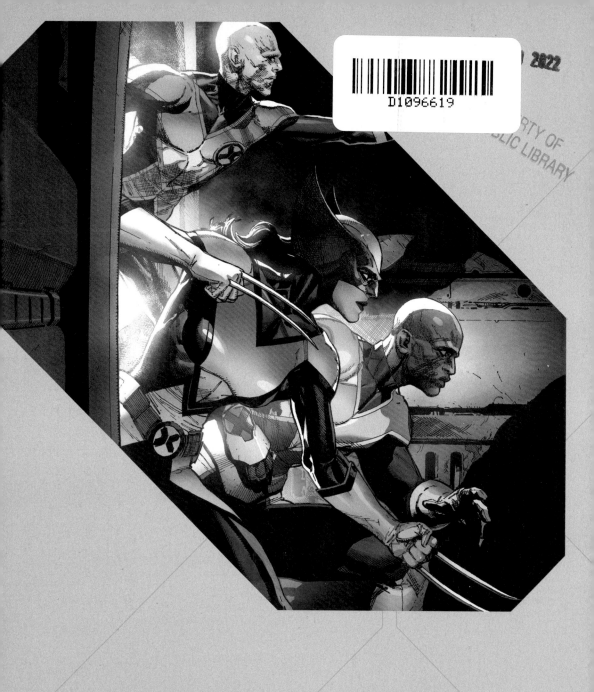

This gift provided by:

The Seattle Public Library Foundation

SUPPORTSPL.ORG

REIGN OF X VOL. 6. Contains material originally published in magazine form as S.W.O.R.D. (2020) #4, X-MEN (2019) #18-19, MARAUDERS (2019) #18-19 and X-FORCE (2019) #17. First printing 2021. ISBN 978-1-302-93185-8. Published by MARVEL WORLDWIDE, INC., a subsidiary of MARVEL ENTERTAINMENT, LLC. OFFICE OF PUBLICATION: 1290 Avenue of the Americas, New York, NY 10104. © 2021 MARVEL No similarity between any of the names, characters, persons, and/or institutions in this magazine with those of any living or dead person or institution is intended, and any such similarity which may exist is purely coincidental. **Printed in the Canada.** KEVIN FEIGE, Chief Creative Officer; DAN BUCKLEY, President, Marvel Entertainment; JOE QUESADA, EVP & Creative Director; DAVID BOGART, Associate Publisher & SVP of Talent Affairs; TOM BREVOORT, VP, Executive Editor; NICK LOWE, Executive Editor, VP of Content, Digital Publishing; DAVID GABRIEL, VP of Print & Digital Publishing; JEFF YOUNGQUIST, VP of Production & Special Projects; ALEX MORALES, Director of Publishing Operations; DAN EDINGTON, Managing Editor; RICKEY PURDIN, Director of Talent Relations; JENNIFER GRÜNWALD, Senior Editor, Special Projects; SUSAN CRESPI, Production Manager; STAN LEE, Chairman Emeritus. For information regarding advertising in Marvel Comics or on Marvel.com, please contact Vit DeBellis, Custom Solutions & Integrated Advertising Manager, at vdebellis@marvel.com. For Marvel subscription inquiries, please call 888-511-5480. **Manufactured between 9/10/2021 and 10/12/2021 by SOLISCO PRINTERS, SCOTT, QC, CANADA.**

10 9 8 7 6 5 4 3 2 1

REIGN OF X

Volume 6

X-Men created by Stan Lee & Jack Kirby

Writers:	**Al Ewing, Jonathan Hickman, Gerry Duggan & Benjamin Percy**
Artists:	**Valerio Schiti, Mahmud Asrar, Stefano Caselli, Matteo Lolli & Joshua Cassara**
Color Artists:	**Marte Gracia, Sunny Gho, Edgar Delgado & Guru-eFX**
Letterers:	**VC's Ariana Maher, Clayton Cowles, Cory Petit & Joe Caramagna**
Cover Art:	**Valerio Schiti & Marte Gracia; Leinil Francis Yu & Sunny Gho; Russell Dauterman & Matthew Wilson; and Joshua Cassara & Dean White**
Head of X:	**Jonathan Hickman**
Design:	**Tom Muller**
Assistant Editor:	**Lauren Amaro**
Associate Editor:	**Annalise Bissa**
Editors:	**Jordan D. White & Mark Basso**
Collection Cover Art:	**Leinil Francis Yu & Sunny Gho**
Collection Editor:	**Jennifer Grünwald**
Assistant Editor:	**Daniel Kirchhoffer**
Assistant Managing Editor:	**Maia Loy**
Assistant Managing Editor:	**Lisa Montalbano**
VP Production & Special Projects:	**Jeff Youngquist**
SVP Print, Sales & Marketing:	**David Gabriel**
Editor in Chief:	**C.B. Cebulski**

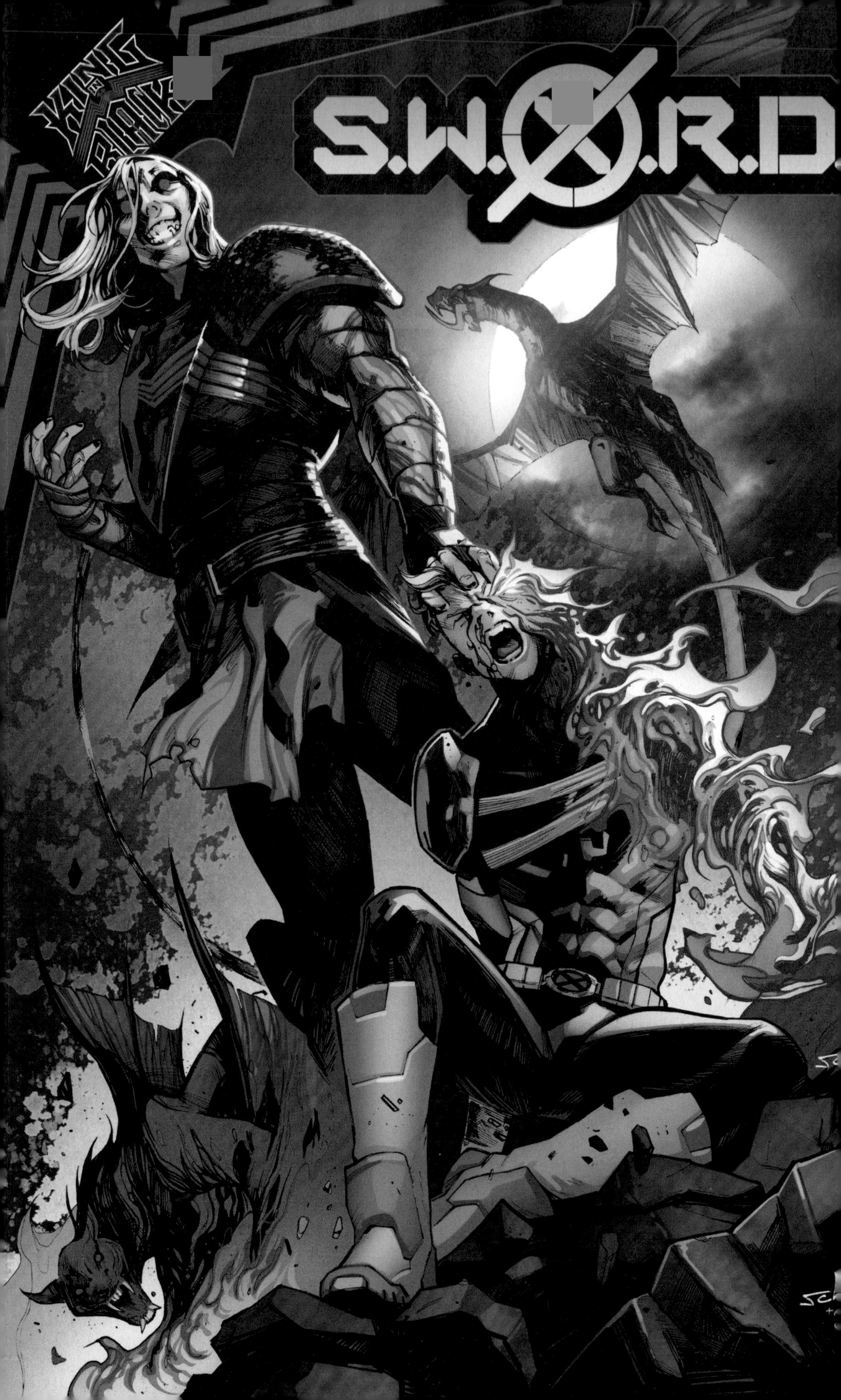
KING IN BLACK
S.W.O.R.D.

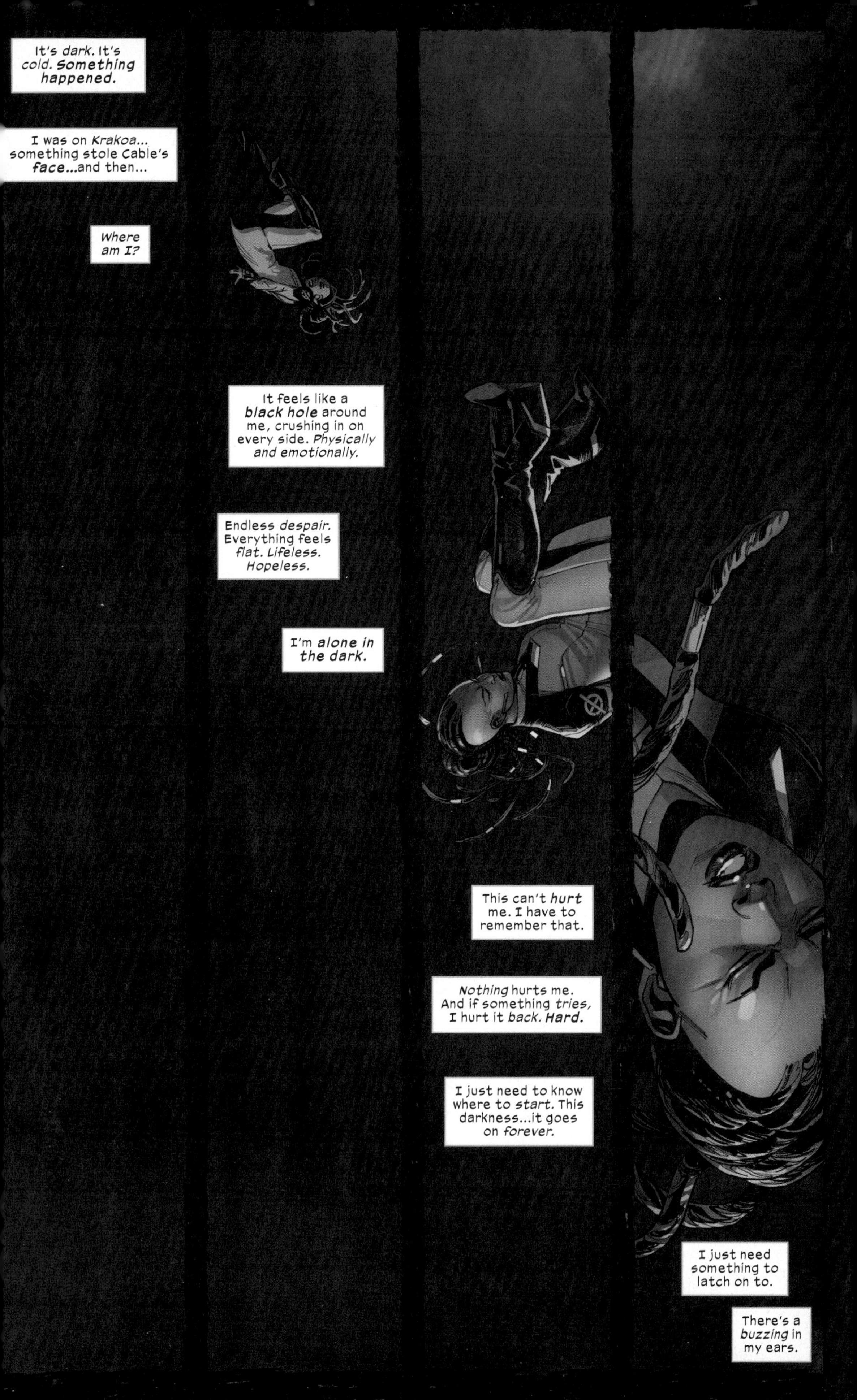
It's dark. It's cold. Something happened.
I was on Krakoa... something stole Cable's face...and then...
Where am I?
It feels like a black hole around me, crushing in on every side. Physically and emotionally.
Endless despair. Everything feels flat. Lifeless. Hopeless.
I'm alone in the dark.
This can't hurt me. I have to remember that.
Nothing hurts me. And if something tries, I hurt it back. Hard.
I just need to know where to start. This darkness...it goes on forever.
I just need something to latch on to.
There's a buzzing in my ears.

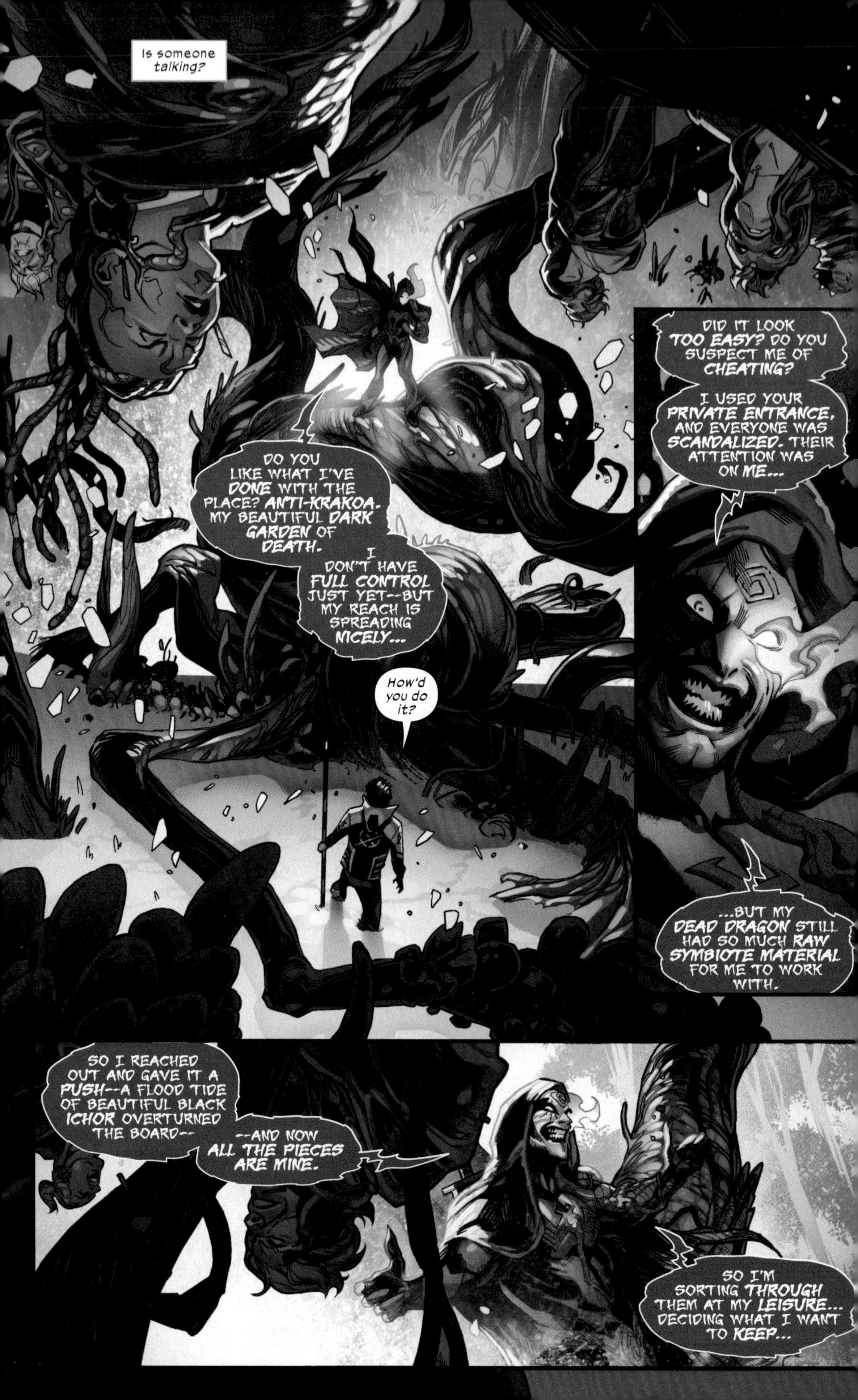
Is someone talking?
DO YOU LIKE WHAT I'VE DONE WITH THE PLACE? ANTI-KRAKOA. MY BEAUTIFUL DARK GARDEN OF DEATH.
I DON'T HAVE FULL CONTROL JUST YET--BUT MY REACH IS SPREADING NICELY...
How'd you do it?
DID IT LOOK TOO EASY? DO YOU SUSPECT ME OF CHEATING?
I USED YOUR PRIVATE ENTRANCE, AND EVERYONE WAS SCANDALIZED. THEIR ATTENTION WAS ON ME...
...BUT MY DEAD DRAGON STILL HAD SO MUCH RAW SYMBIOTE MATERIAL FOR ME TO WORK WITH.
SO I REACHED OUT AND GAVE IT A PUSH--A FLOOD TIDE OF BEAUTIFUL BLACK ICHOR OVERTURNED THE BOARD--
--AND NOW ALL THE PIECES ARE MINE.
SO I'M SORTING THROUGH THEM AT MY LEISURE... DECIDING WHAT I WANT TO KEEP...

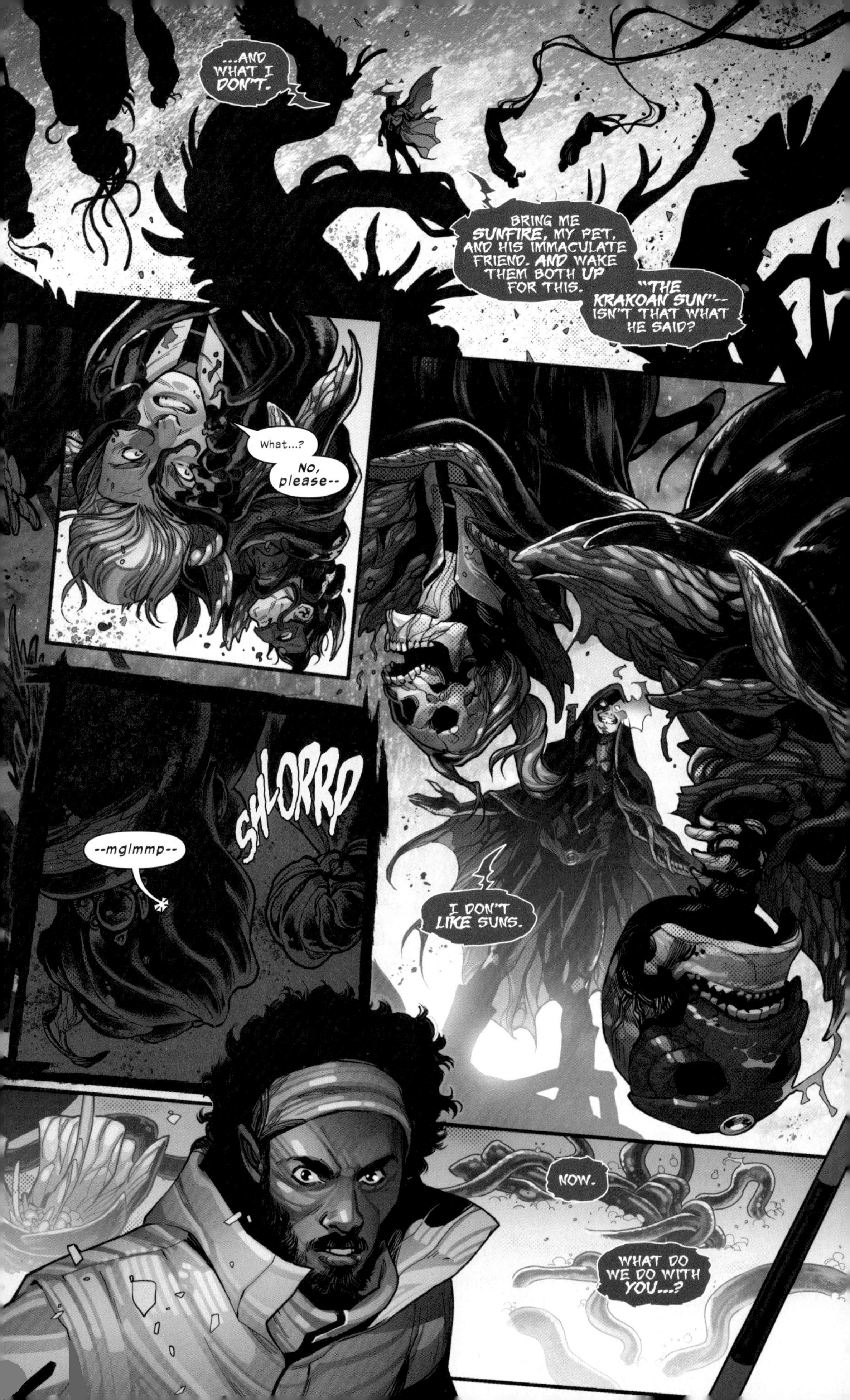
...AND WHAT I DON'T.
BRING ME SUNFIRE, MY PET, AND HIS IMMACULATE FRIEND. AND WAKE THEM BOTH UP FOR THIS.
"THE KRAKOAN SUN"-- ISN'T THAT WHAT HE SAID?
What...?
No, please--
SHLORRP
--mglmmp--
I DON'T LIKE SUNS.
NOW.
WHAT DO WE DO WITH YOU...?

NO LIGHT BUT RATHER DARKNESS VISIBLE

Knull -- the symbiote god of the Void -- has invaded the Earth with a complement of space dragons and formed a symbiote shell around the Earth that's cut off all communication with the Peak. Station technologist **Wiz-Kid** is working to solve the problem. Meanwhile, Manifold has gone to Krakoa to check the status of S.W.O.R.D.'s away team -- only to find them dangling in symbiote cocoons at the mercy of a possessed **Cable**...

Frenzy

Manifold

Cortez

Brand

Wiz-Kid

Mentallo

Hope

Egg

Tempus

Elixir

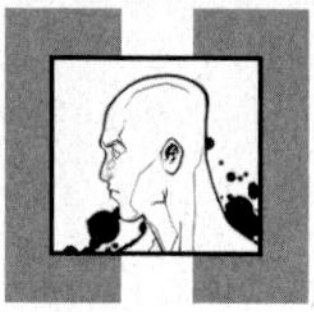

Proteus

Magneto

Cable

S.W.O.R.D.

[X_04]

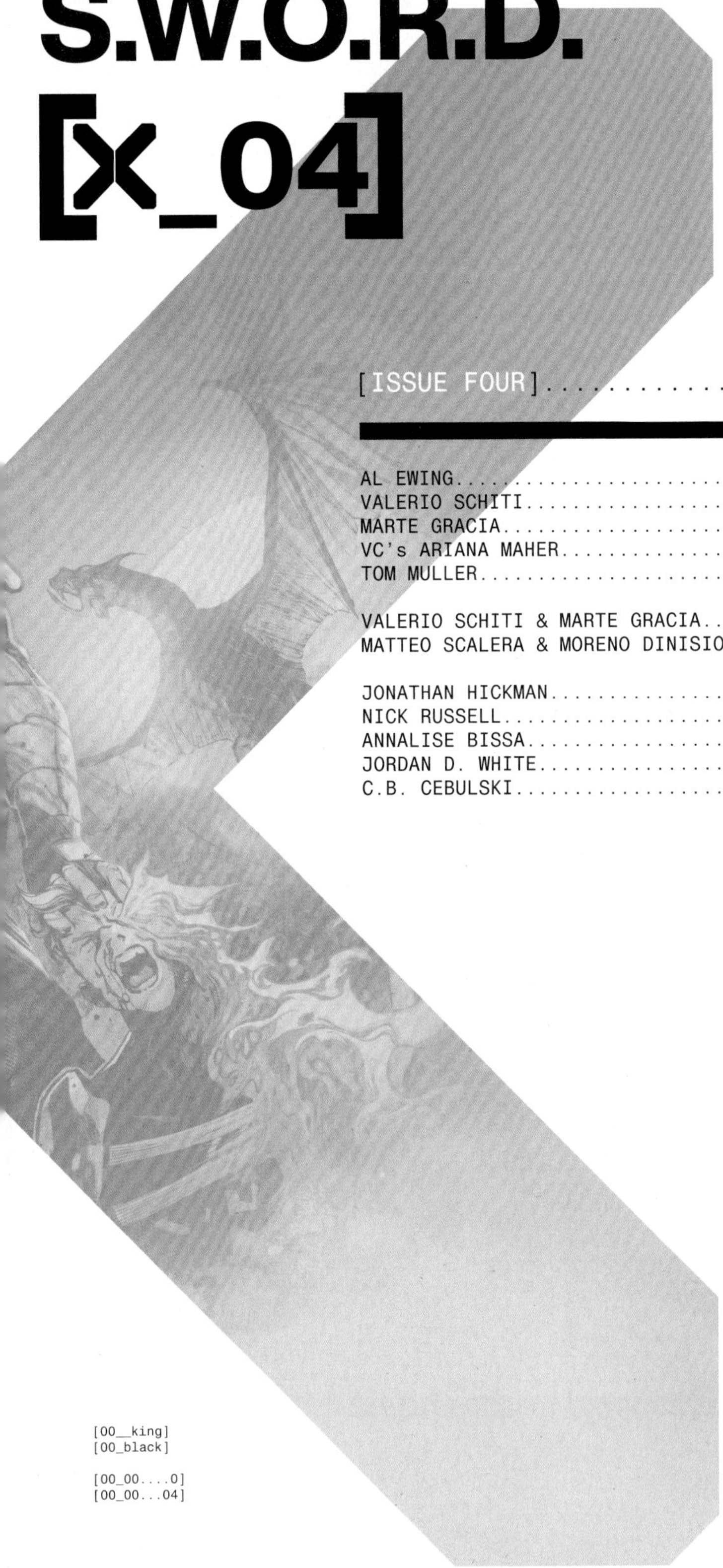

[ISSUE FOUR]..................THE KRAKOAN SUN

AL EWING..[WRITER]
VALERIO SCHITI..................................[ARTIST]
MARTE GRACIA..............................[COLOR ARTIST]
VC's ARIANA MAHER..........................[LETTERER]
TOM MULLER......................................[DESIGN]

VALERIO SCHITI & MARTE GRACIA...............[COVER ARTISTS]
MATTEO SCALERA & MORENO DINISIO.....[VARIANT COVER ARTISTS]

JONATHAN HICKMAN..............................[HEAD OF X]
NICK RUSSELL..................................[PRODUCTION]
ANNALISE BISSA.........................[ASSOCIATE EDITOR]
JORDAN D. WHITE.................................[EDITOR]
C.B. CEBULSKI............................[EDITOR IN CHIEF]

[00__king]
[00_black]

[00_00....0]
[00_00...04]

[00_knull_]
[00______]

[00______]

[00_____X]

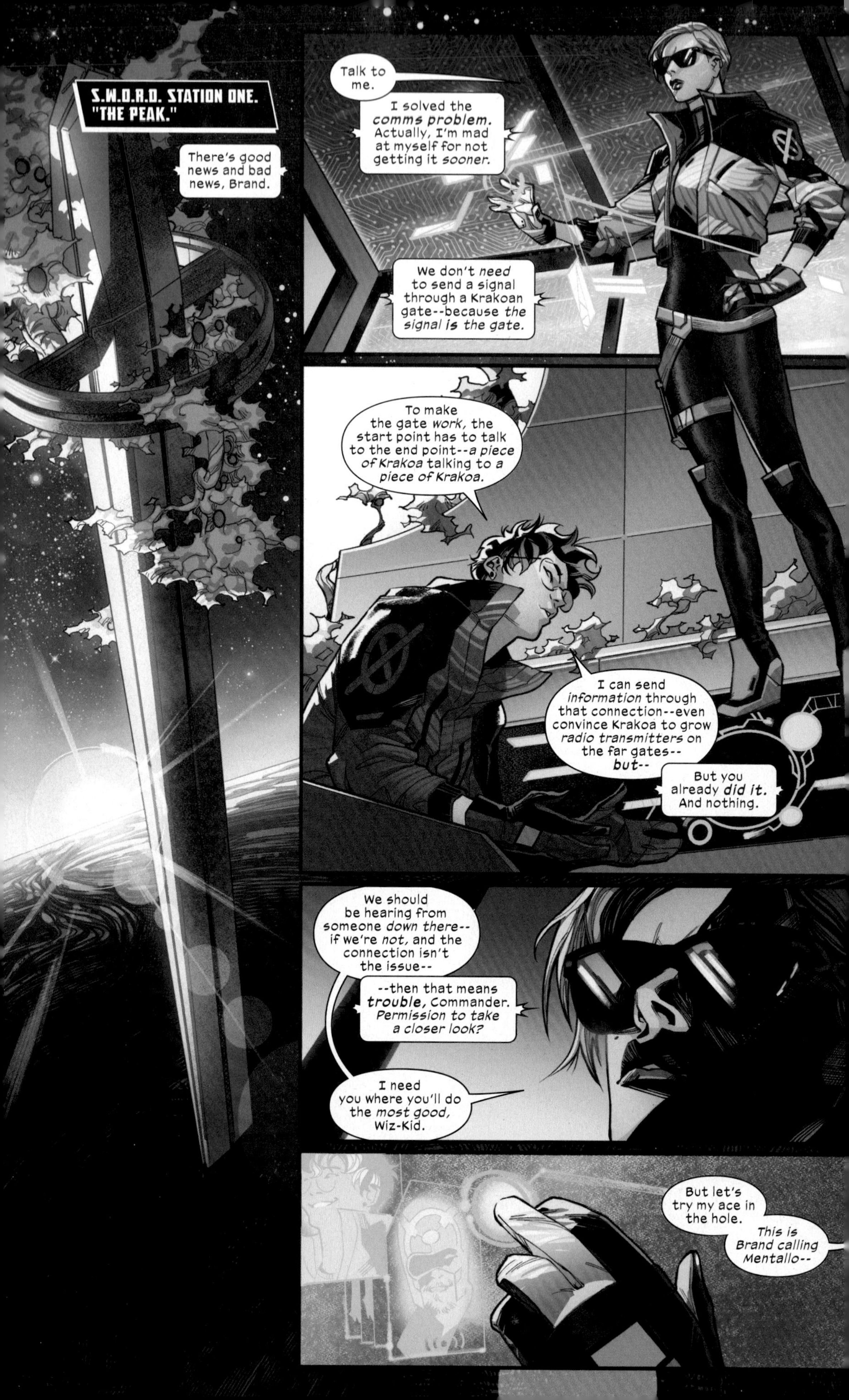
S.W.O.R.D. STATION ONE. "THE PEAK."
There's good news and bad news, Brand.
Talk to me.
I solved the comms problem. Actually, I'm mad at myself for not getting it sooner.
We don't need to send a signal through a Krakoan gate--because the signal is the gate.
To make the gate work, the start point has to talk to the end point--a piece of Krakoa talking to a piece of Krakoa.
I can send information through that connection--even convince Krakoa to grow radio transmitters on the far gates--but--
But you already did it. And nothing.
We should be hearing from someone down there--if we're not, and the connection isn't the issue--
--then that means trouble, Commander. Permission to take a closer look?
I need you where you'll do the most good, Wiz-Kid.
But let's try my ace in the hole.
This is Brand calling Mentallo--

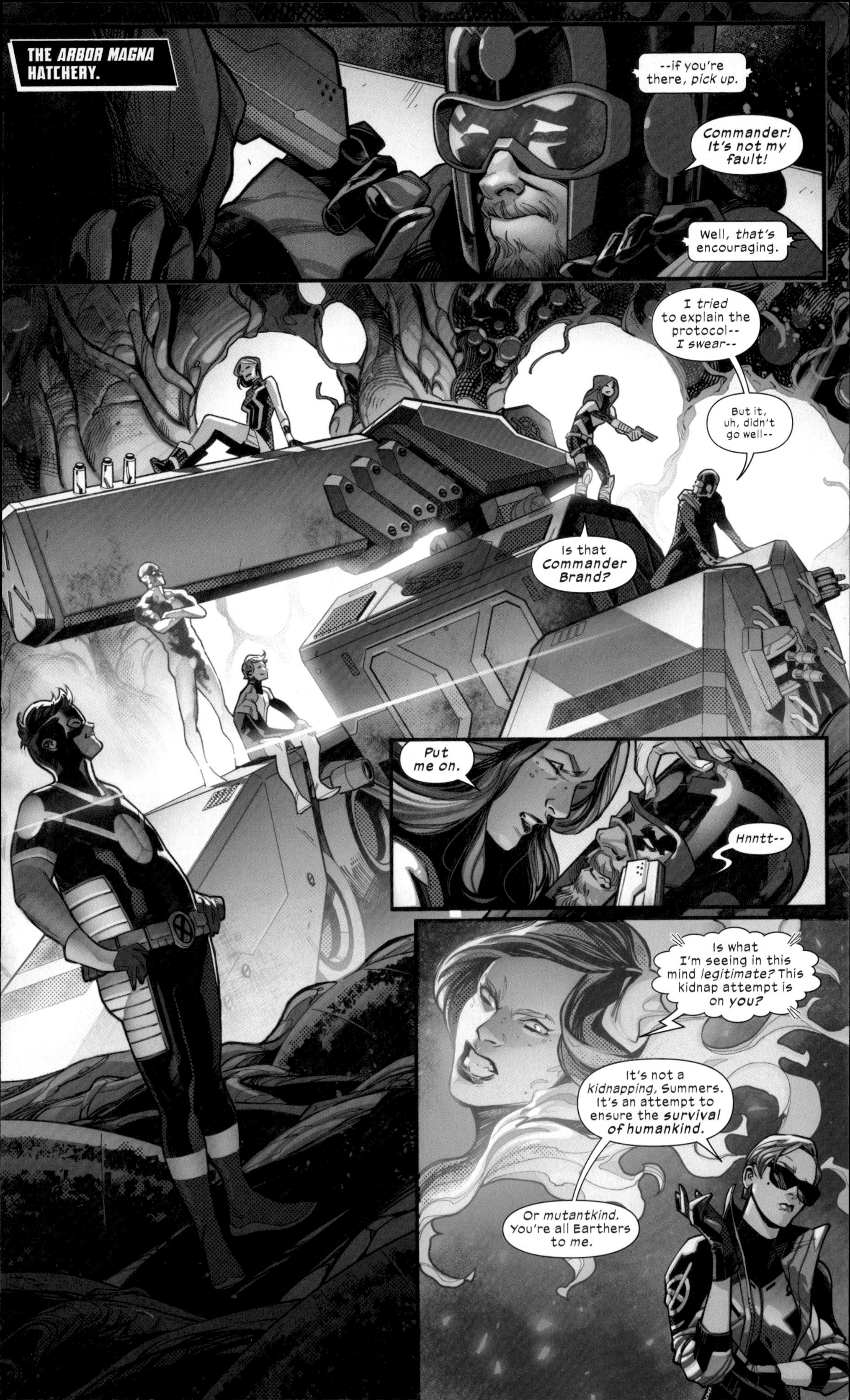
THE ARBOR MAGNA HATCHERY.
--if you're there, pick up.
Commander! It's not my fault!
Well, that's encouraging.
I tried to explain the protocol-- I swear--
But it, uh, didn't go well--
Is that Commander Brand?
Put me on.
Hnntt--
Is what I'm seeing in this mind legitimate? This kidnap attempt is on you?
It's not a kidnapping, Summers. It's an attempt to ensure the survival of humankind.
Or mutantkind. You're all Earthers to me.

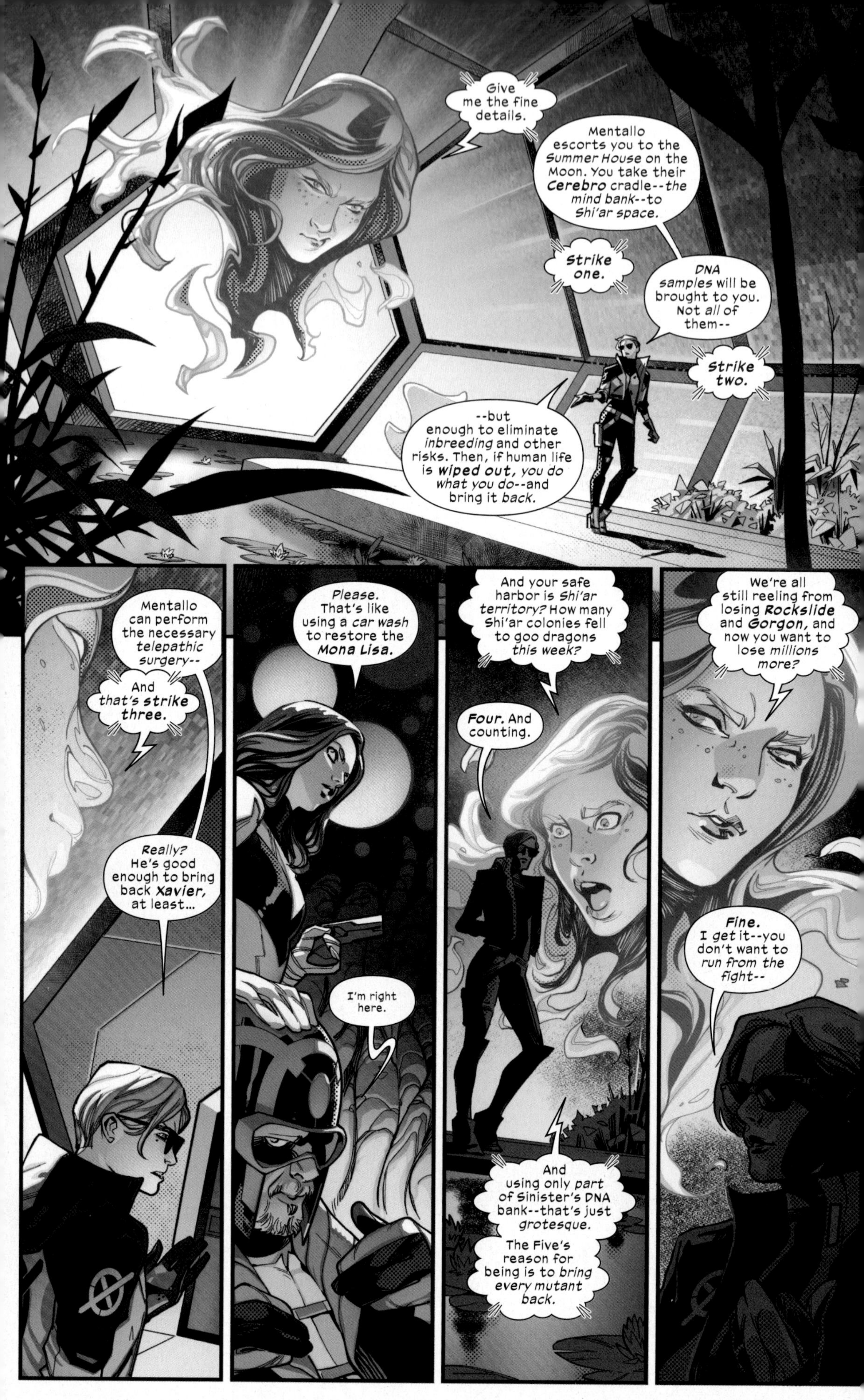

Give me the fine details.
Mentallo escorts you to the Summer House on the Moon. You take their Cerebro cradle--the mind bank--to Shi'ar space.
Strike one.
DNA samples will be brought to you. Not all of them--
Strike two.
--but enough to eliminate inbreeding and other risks. Then, if human life is wiped out, you do what you do--and bring it back.
Mentallo can perform the necessary telepathic surgery--
And that's strike three.
Really? He's good enough to bring back Xavier, at least...
Please. That's like using a car wash to restore the Mona Lisa.
I'm right here.
And your safe harbor is Shi'ar territory? How many Shi'ar colonies fell to goo dragons this week?
Four. And counting.
And using only part of Sinister's DNA bank--that's just grotesque.
The Five's reason for being is to bring every mutant back.
We're all still reeling from losing Rockslide and Gorgon, and now you want to lose millions more?
Fine. I get it--you don't want to run from the fight--

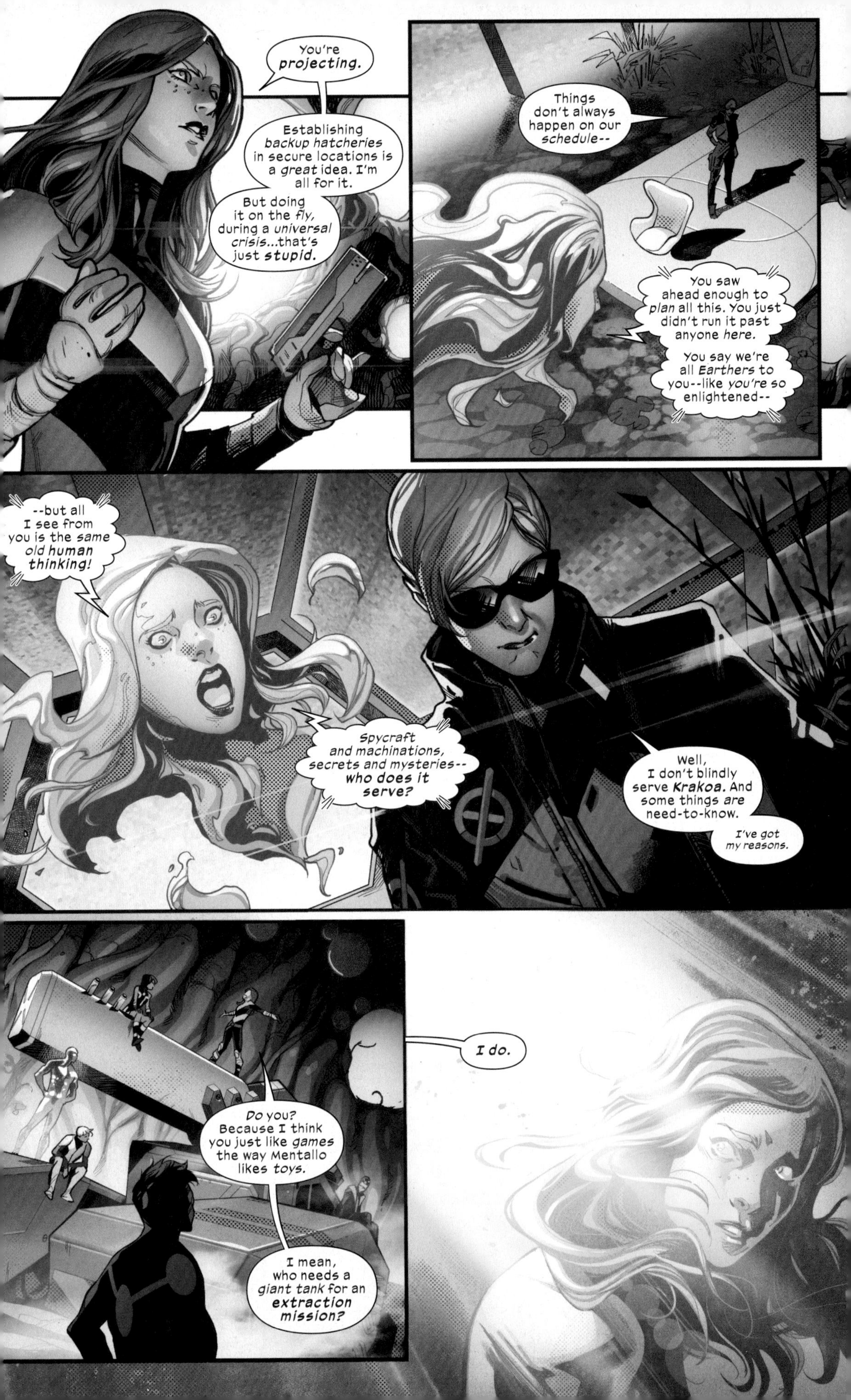

You're *projecting.*
Establishing *backup hatcheries* in secure locations is a *great* idea. I'm all for it.
But doing it on the *fly,* during a *universal crisis*...that's just **stupid.**
Things don't always happen on our *schedule*--
You saw ahead enough to *plan* all this. You just didn't run it past anyone *here.*
You say we're all *Earthers* to you--like *you're* so enlightened--
--but all I see from you is the *same old* **human thinking!**
Spycraft and machinations, secrets and mysteries-- ***who does it serve?***
Well, I don't blindly serve ***Krakoa.*** And some things *are* need-to-know.
I've got my reasons.
I do.
Do you? Because I think you just like *games* the way Mentallo likes *toys.*
I mean, who needs a *giant tank* for an ***extraction mission?***

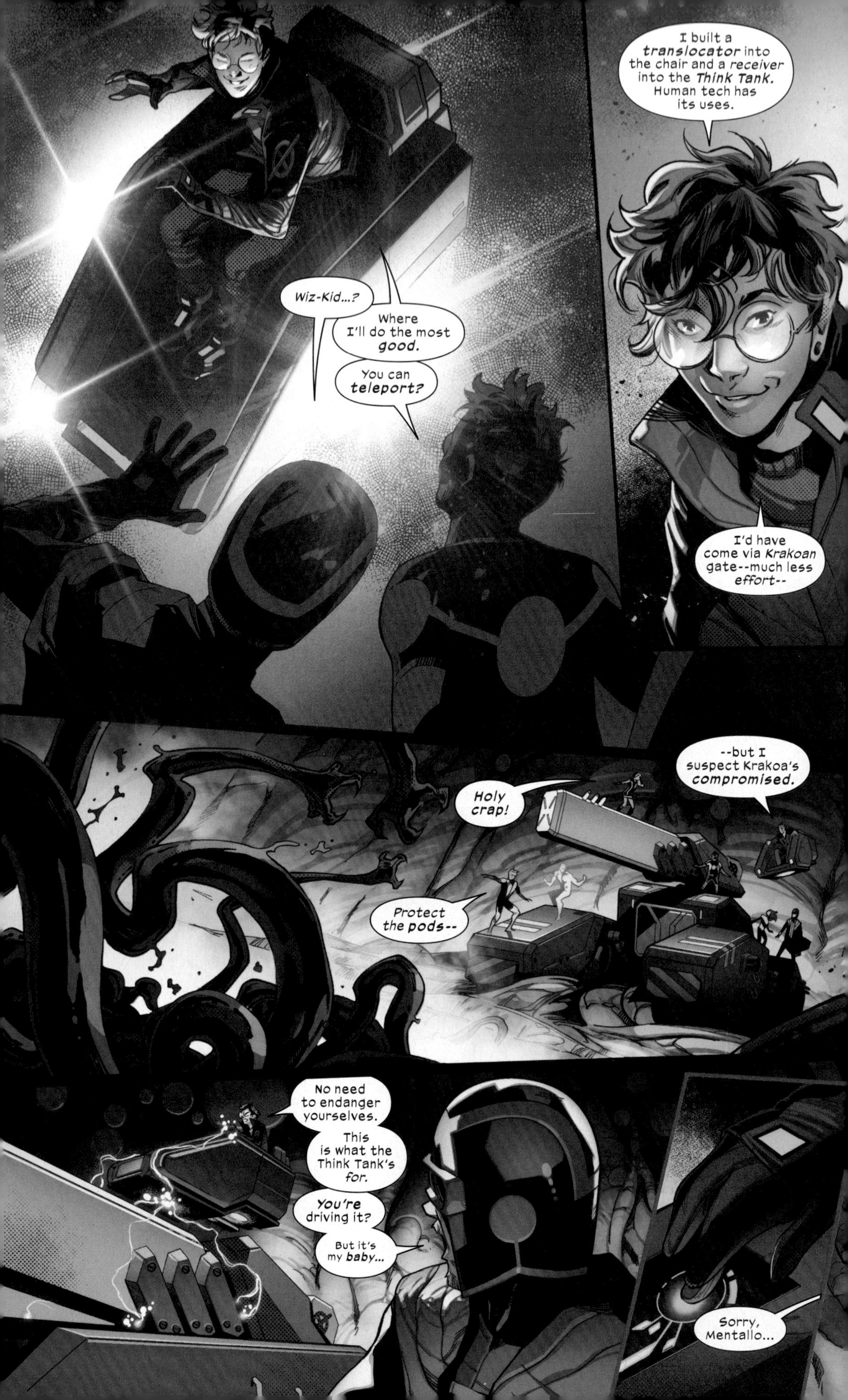
I built a translocator into the chair and a receiver into the Think Tank. Human tech has its uses.
Wiz-Kid...?
Where I'll do the most good.
You can teleport?
I'd have come via Krakoan gate--much less effort--
--but I suspect Krakoa's compromised.
Holy crap!
Protect the pods--
No need to endanger yourselves.
This is what the Think Tank's for.
You're driving it?
But it's my baby...
Sorry, Mentallo...

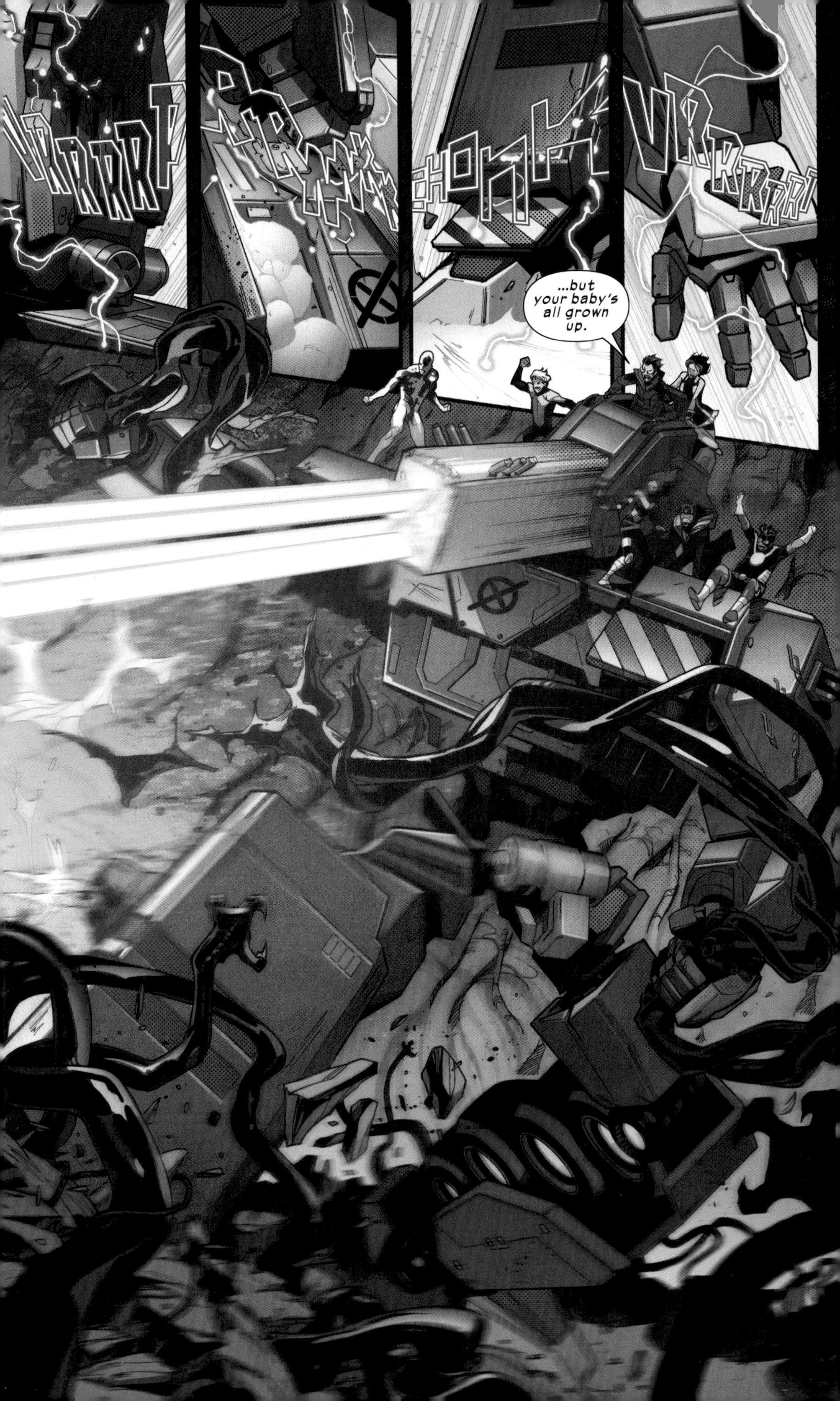
VRRRRRT
...but your baby's all grown up.

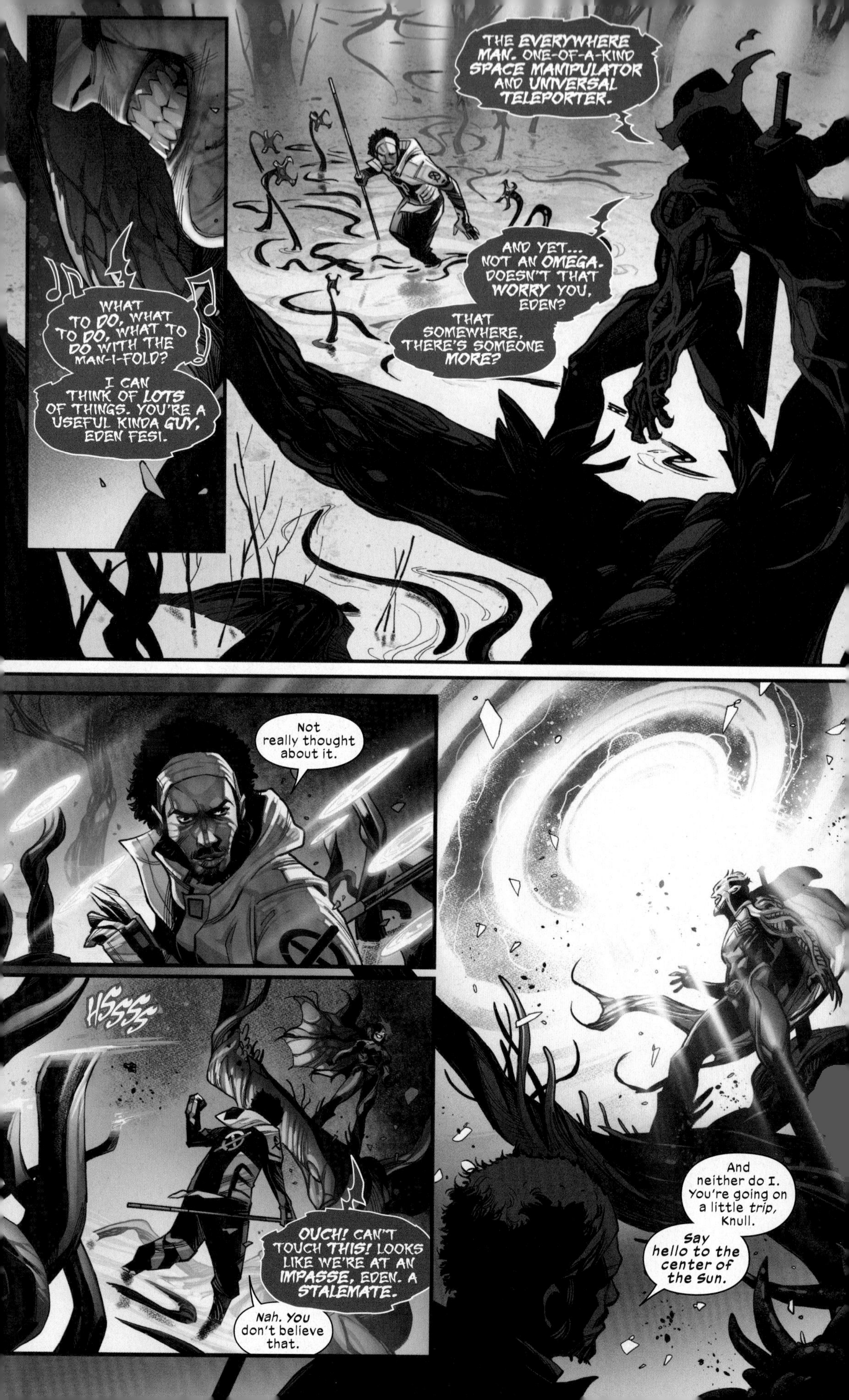
THE EVERYWHERE MAN. ONE-OF-A-KIND SPACE MANIPULATOR AND UNIVERSAL TELEPORTER.
WHAT TO DO, WHAT TO DO, WHAT TO DO WITH THE MAN-I-FOLD?
I CAN THINK OF LOTS OF THINGS. YOU'RE A USEFUL KINDA GUY, EDEN FESI.
AND YET... NOT AN OMEGA. DOESN'T THAT WORRY YOU, EDEN?
THAT SOMEWHERE, THERE'S SOMEONE MORE?
Not really thought about it.
HSSSS
OUCH! CAN'T TOUCH THIS! LOOKS LIKE WE'RE AT AN IMPASSE, EDEN. A STALEMATE.
Nah. You don't believe that.
And neither do I. You're going on a little trip, Knull.
Say hello to the center of the Sun.

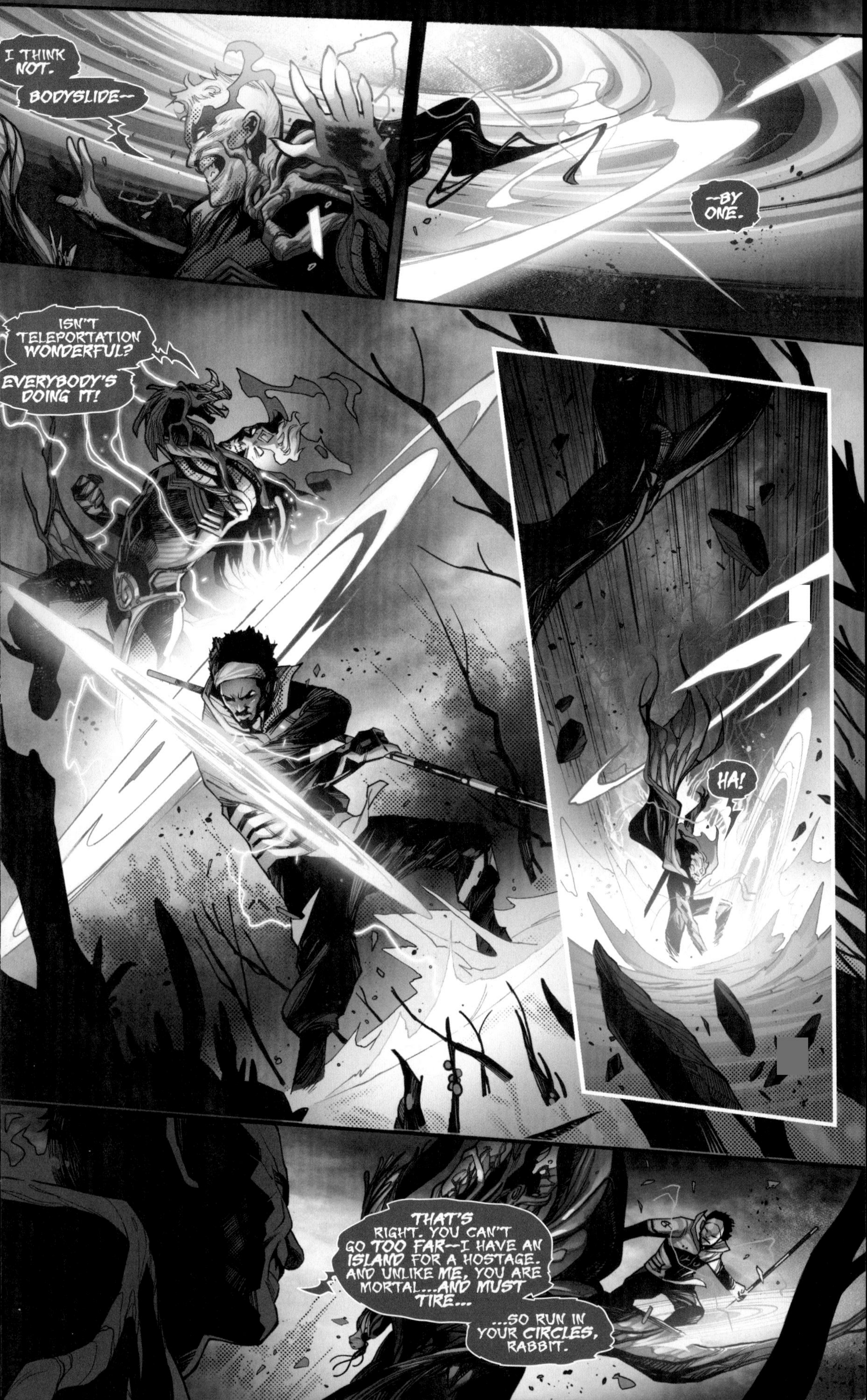
I THINK NOT.
BODYSLIDE--
--BY ONE.
ISN'T TELEPORTATION WONDERFUL?
EVERYBODY'S DOING IT!
HA!
THAT'S RIGHT. YOU CAN'T GO TOO FAR--I HAVE AN ISLAND FOR A HOSTAGE. AND UNLIKE ME, YOU ARE MORTAL...AND MUST TIRE...
...SO RUN IN YOUR CIRCLES, RABBIT.

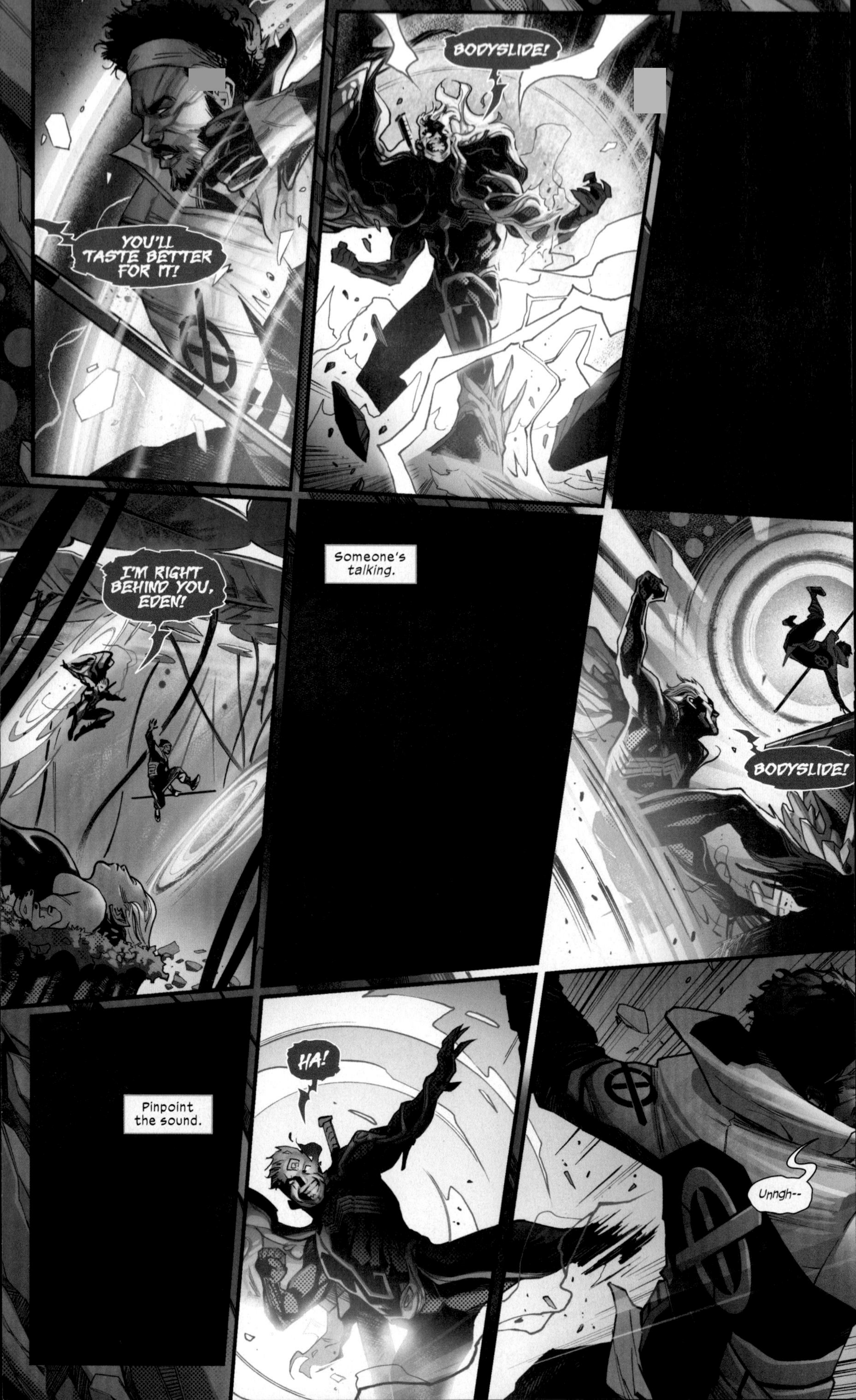

YOU'LL TASTE BETTER FOR IT!
BODYSLIDE!
I'M RIGHT BEHIND YOU, EDEN!
Someone's talking.
BODYSLIDE!
Pinpoint the sound.
HA!
Unngh--

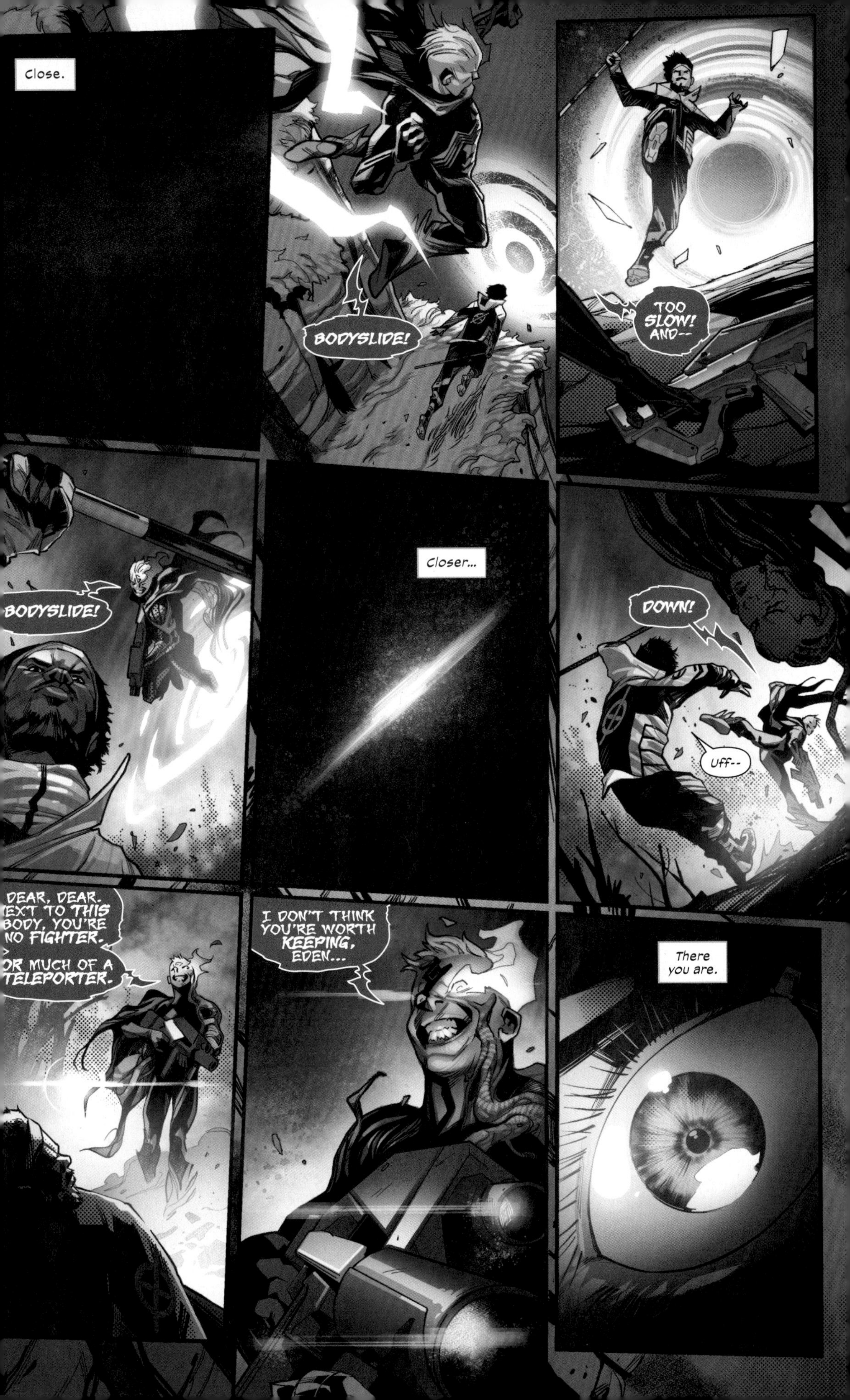

Close.
BODYSLIDE!
TOO SLOW! AND--
BODYSLIDE!
Closer...
DOWN!
Uff--
DEAR, DEAR. NEXT TO THIS BODY, YOU'RE NO FIGHTER.
OR MUCH OF A TELEPORTER.
I DON'T THINK YOU'RE WORTH KEEPING, EDEN...
There you are.

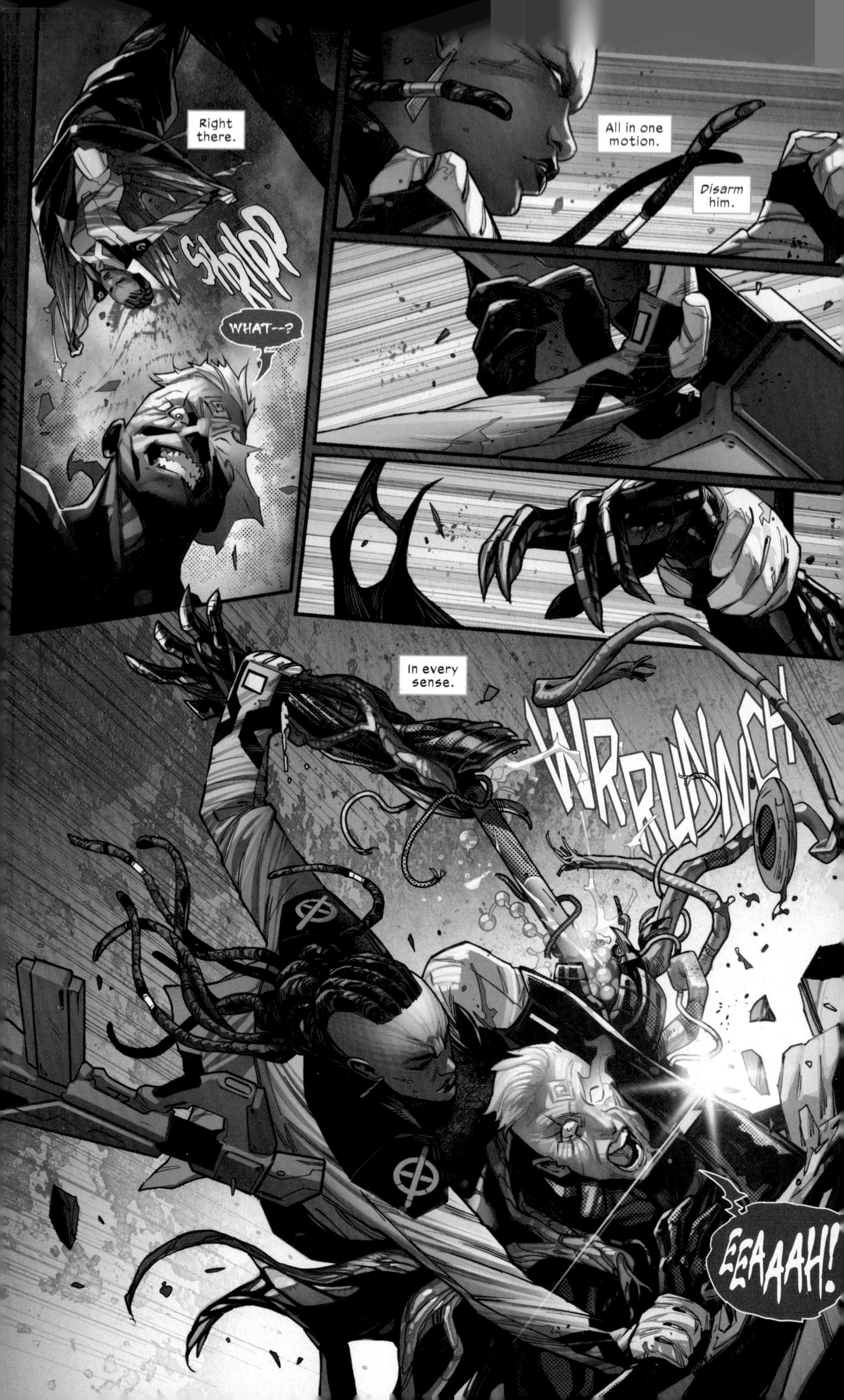
Right there.
SHLIP
WHAT--?
All in one motion.
Disarm him.
In every sense.
WRRUNNCH
EEAAAH!

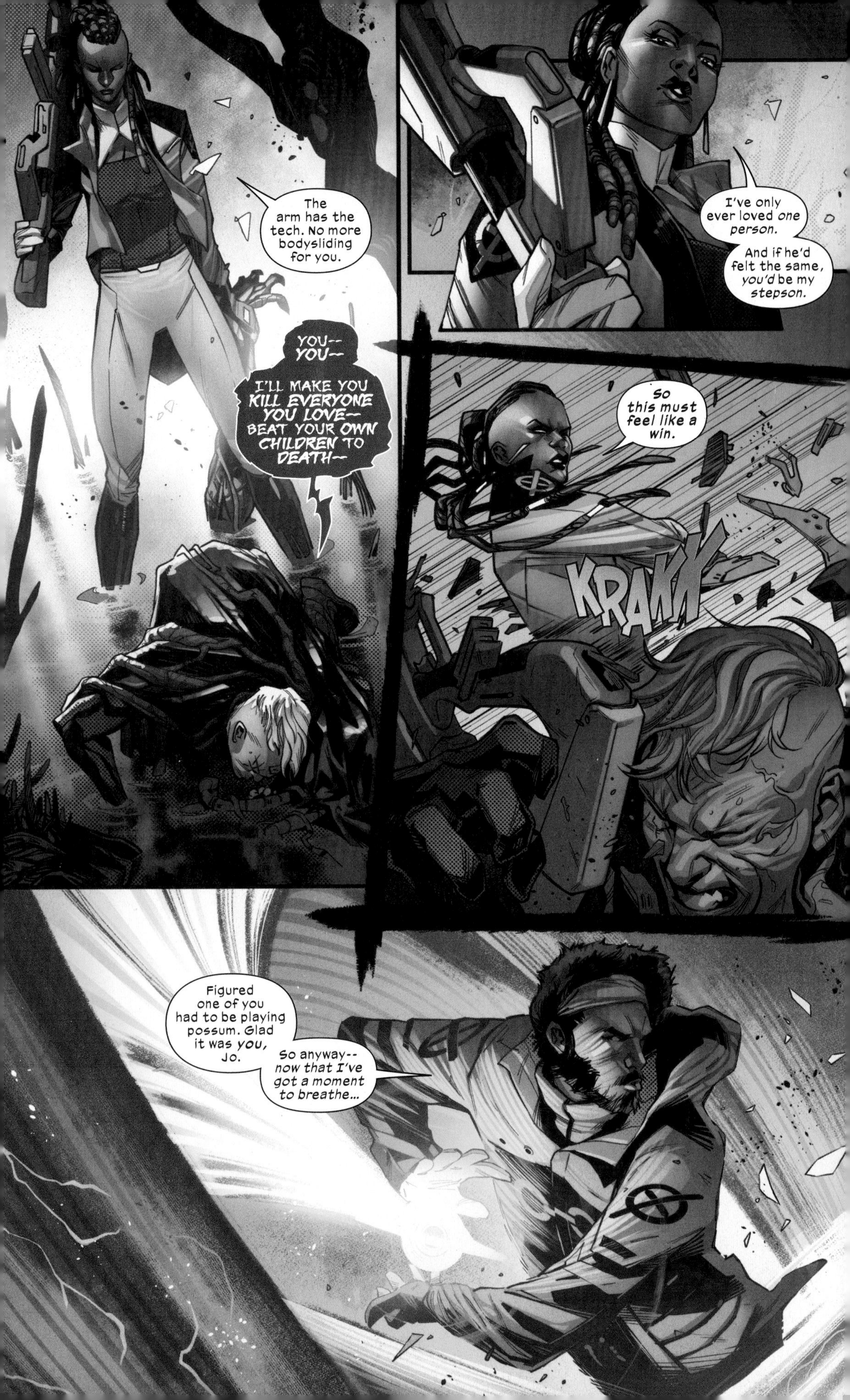
The arm has the tech. No more bodysliding for you.
I've only ever loved *one* person.
And if he'd felt the same, *you'd* be my stepson.
YOU-- *YOU*--
I'LL MAKE YOU *KILL EVERYONE YOU LOVE*-- BEAT YOUR *OWN CHILDREN* TO *DEATH*--
So this must feel like a win.
KRAKK
Figured one of you had to be playing possum. Glad it was *you*, Jo.
So anyway-- now that I've got a moment to breathe...

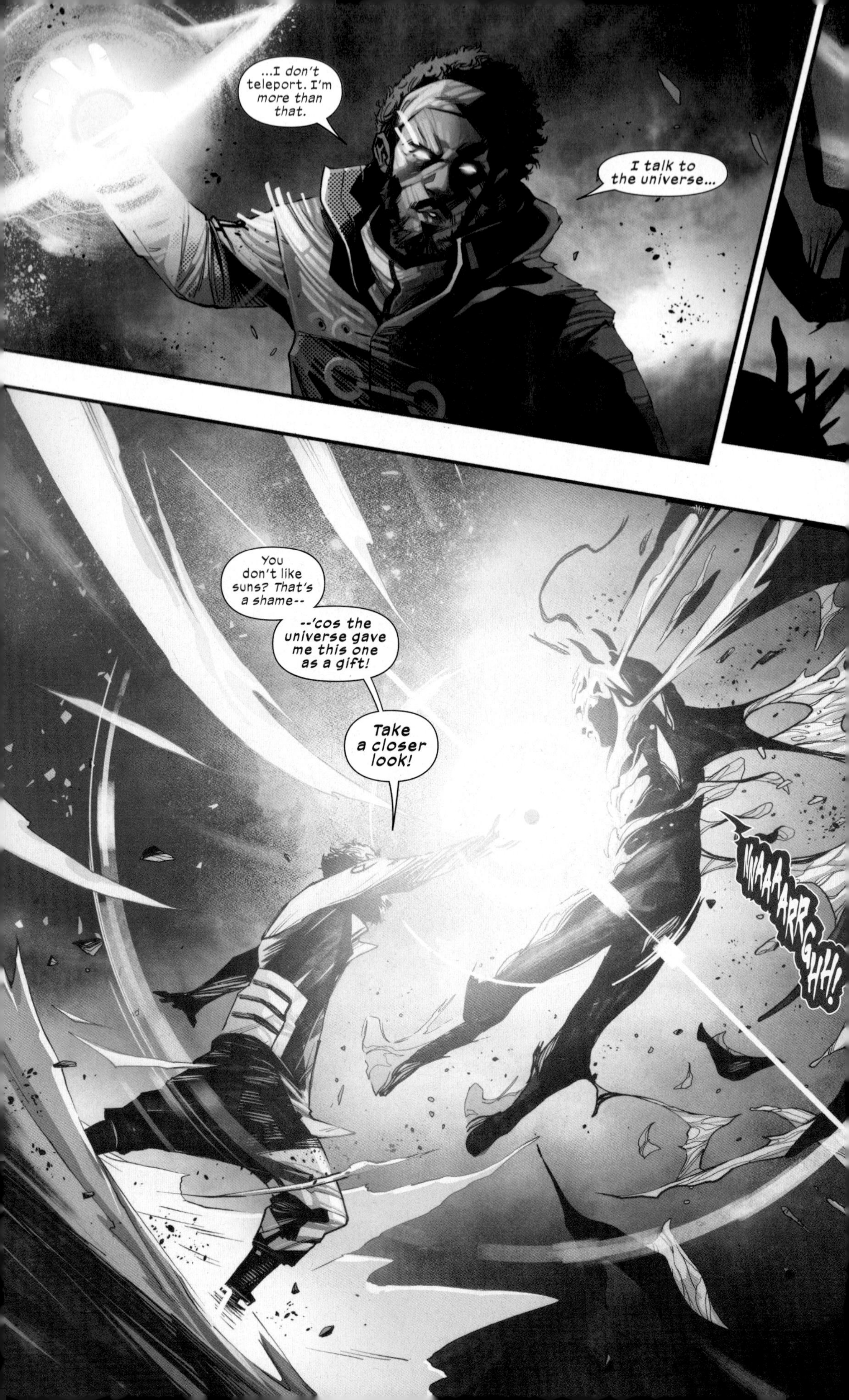
...I don't teleport. I'm more than that.
I talk to the universe...
You don't like suns? That's a shame--
--'cos the universe gave me this one as a gift!
Take a closer look!
NNAAAARRGHH!

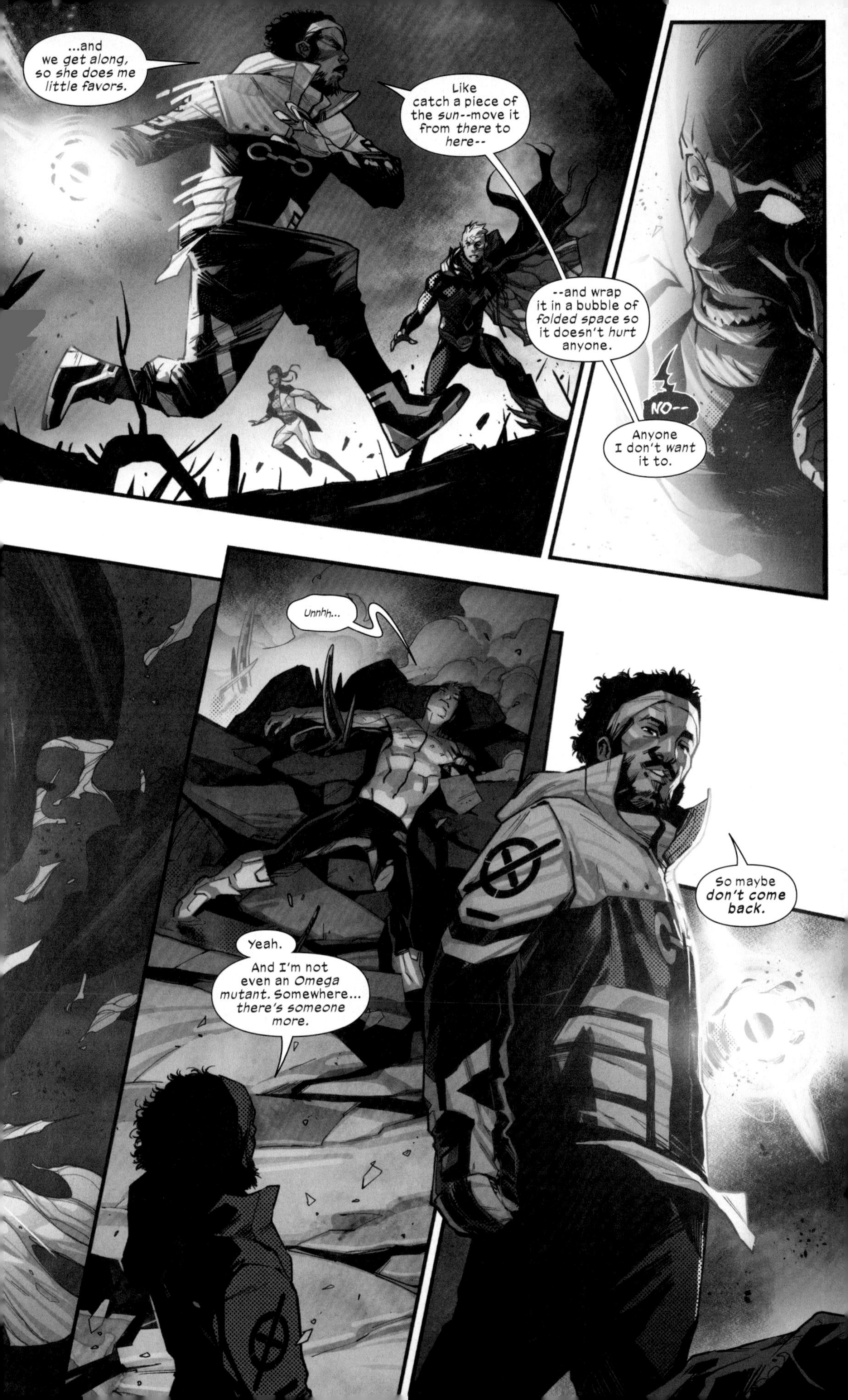
...and we get along, so she does me little favors.
Like catch a piece of the sun--move it from there to here--
--and wrap it in a bubble of folded space so it doesn't hurt anyone.
NO--
Anyone I don't want it to.
Unnhh...
So maybe don't come back.
Yeah.
And I'm not even an Omega mutant. Somewhere... there's someone more.

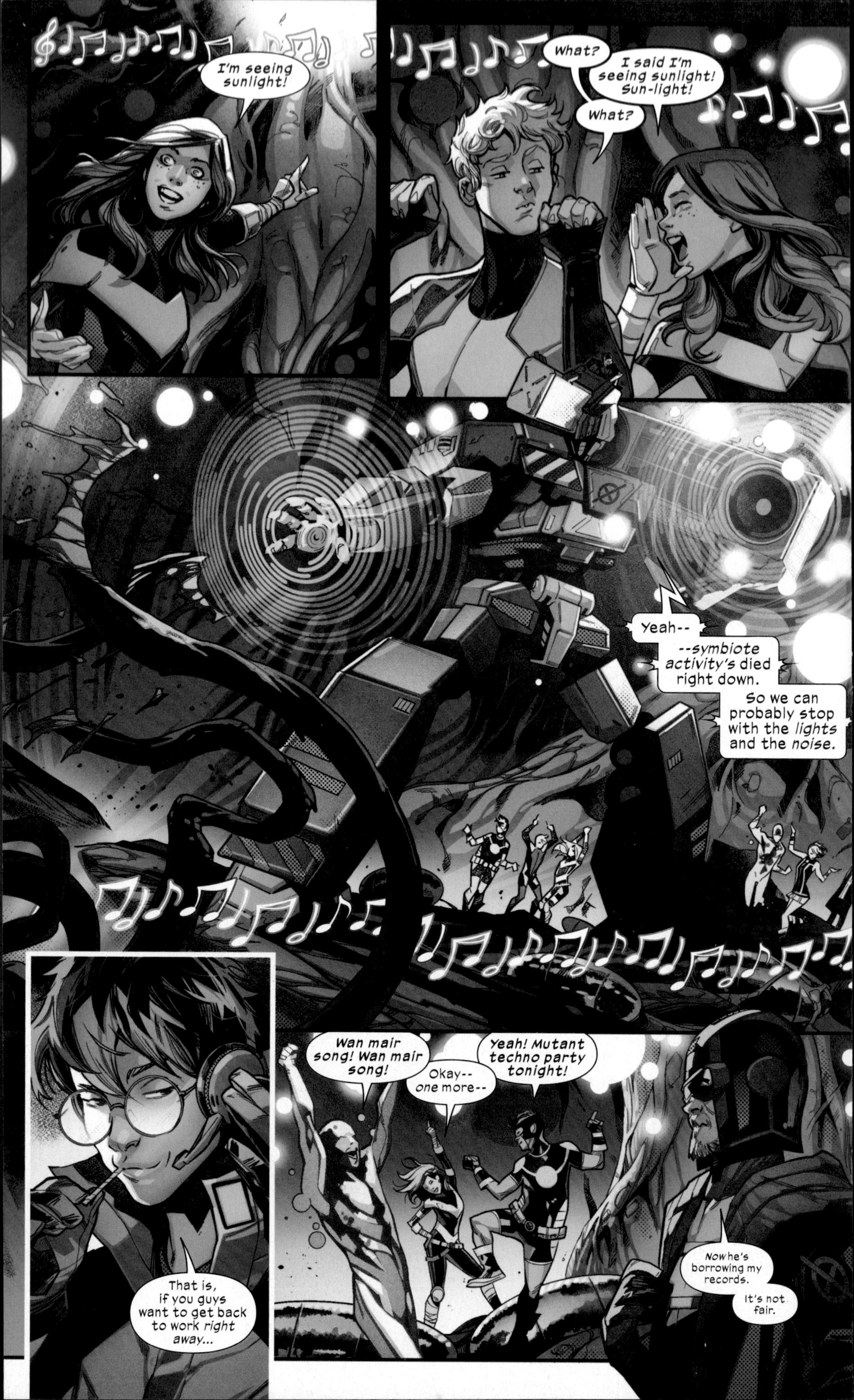
I'm seeing sunlight!
What?
I said I'm seeing sunlight! Sun-light!
What?
Yeah--
--symbiote activity's died right down.
So we can probably stop with the *lights* and the *noise*.
That is, if you guys want to get back to work *right* away...
Wan mair song! Wan mair song!
Okay-- one more--
Yeah! Mutant techno party tonight!
Now he's borrowing my records.
It's not fair.

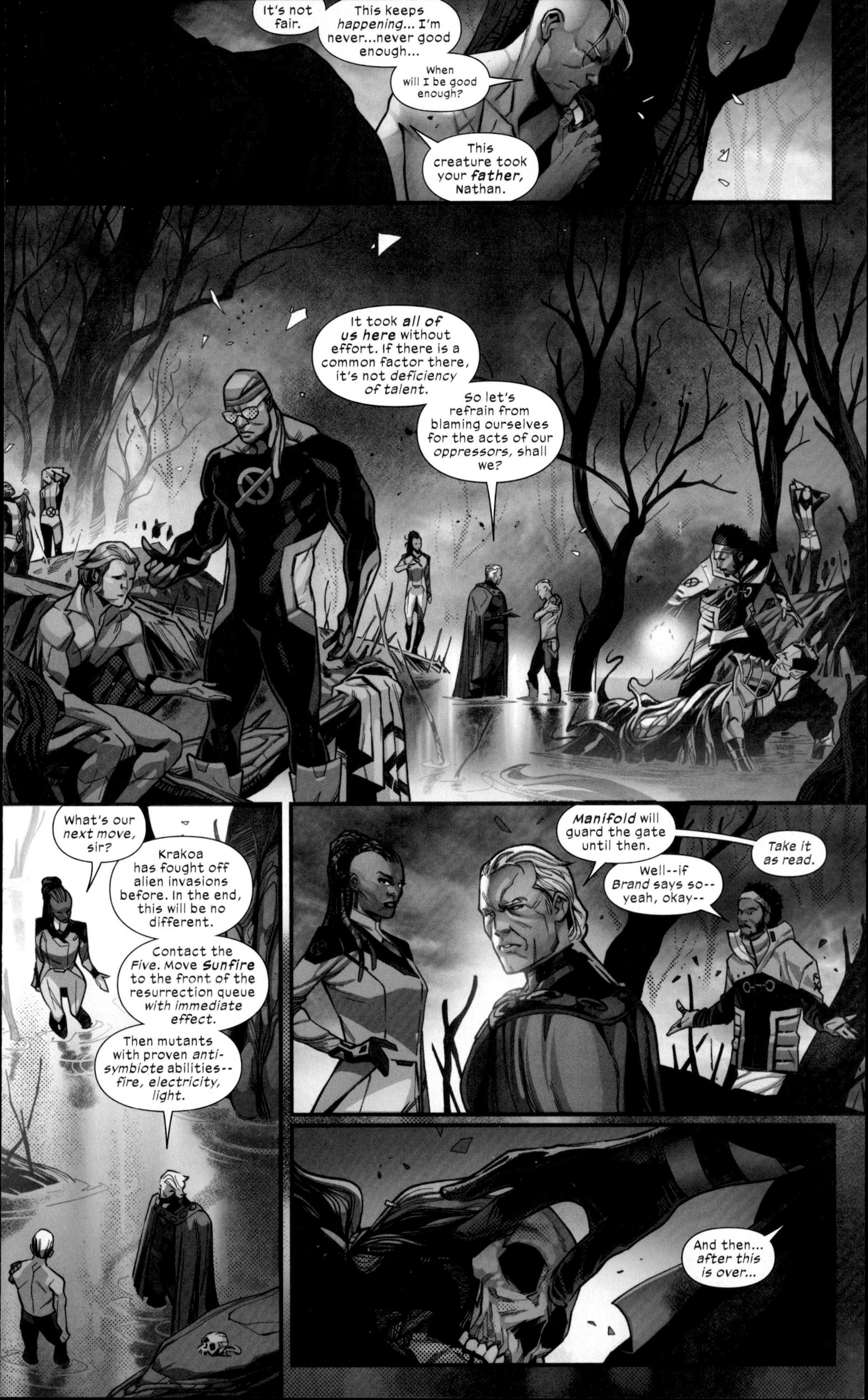

It's not fair.
This keeps happening... I'm never...never good enough...
When will I be good enough?
This creature took your father, Nathan.
It took all of us here without effort. If there is a common factor there, it's not deficiency of talent.
So let's refrain from blaming ourselves for the acts of our oppressors, shall we?
What's our next move, sir?
Krakoa has fought off alien invasions before. In the end, this will be no different.
Contact the Five. Move Sunfire to the front of the resurrection queue with immediate effect.
Then mutants with proven anti-symbiote abilities--fire, electricity, light.
Manifold will guard the gate until then.
Take it as read.
Well--if Brand says so--yeah, okay--
And then... after this is over...

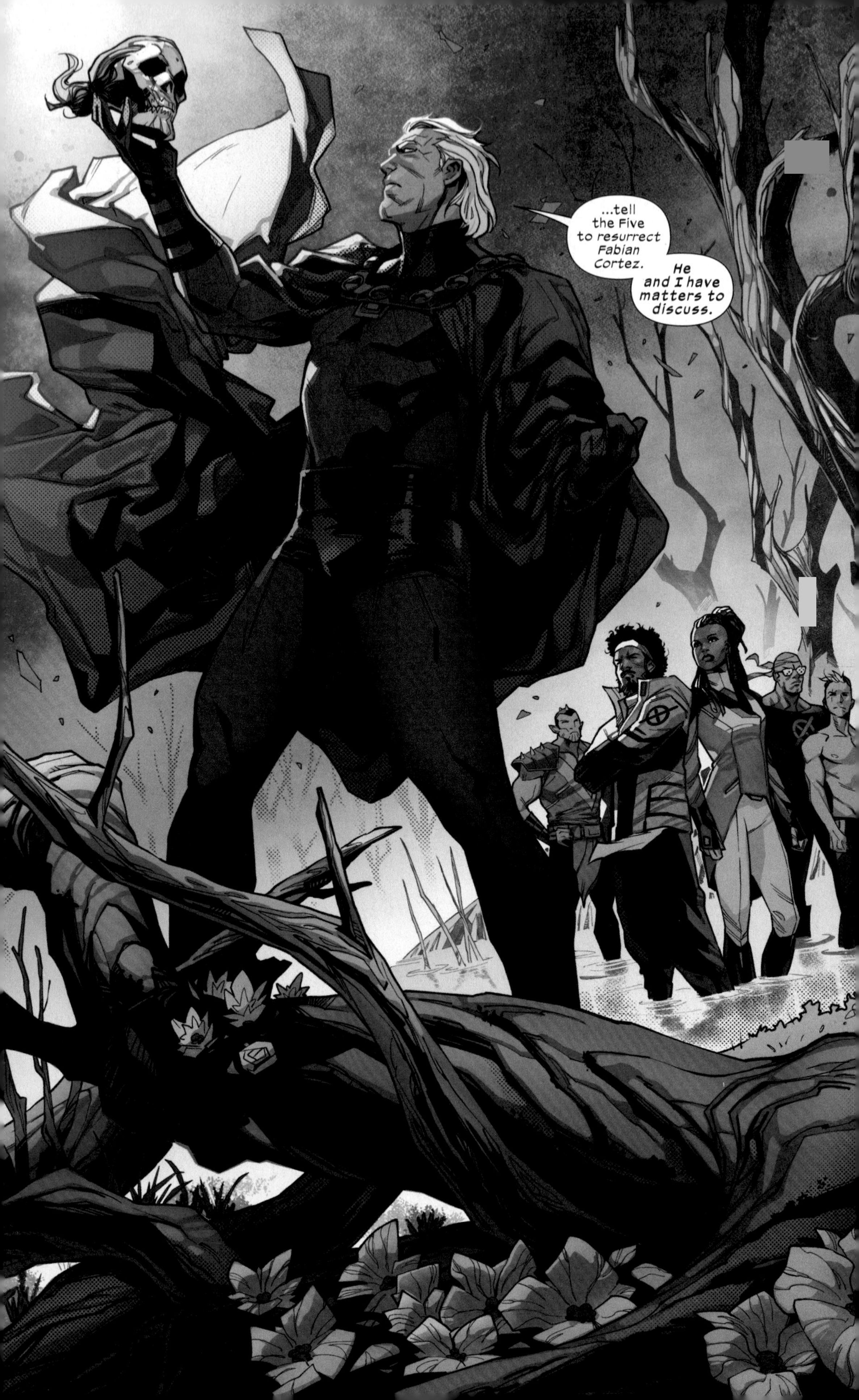
...tell the Five to *resurrect* Fabian Cortez.
He and I have matters to discuss.

THE QUIET COUNCIL OF KRAKOA

RE: MEETING REQUEST :: EARLIEST CONVENIENCE :: MAGNETO

As requested, there will be a Council meeting at [redacted] on the [redacted]th of [redacted] for the purposes of discussing the second law of mutantdom and potential amendments thereto.

As certain members of the Quiet Council are unable to attend, the matter will be debated by a quorum of eight, with any binding resolutions to be brought before the full Council at such time as all twelve are in attendance.

In addition, there will be three guests in attendance [Fabian Cortez, [redacted] and [redacted]] -- and, as always, *Krakoa will be listening.*

—

Erik -

While there's no technical reason not to grant your request for this meeting, I strongly urge you to reconsider.

It's playing with fire, old friend.

Charles

++ [redacted]
++ [redacted]
++ [redacted] *VOGHT*

++ [redacted]
++ [redacted]
++ [redacted] / [redacted]
++ [redacted] / [redacted]
++ [redacted] / [redacted]
++ [redacted] / [redacted]
++ [redacted]
++ [redacted] / [redacted]

++ [redacted]
++ [redacted] SNARKWAR [redacted]
++ [redacted] +
++ [redacted] SOL [redacted] +

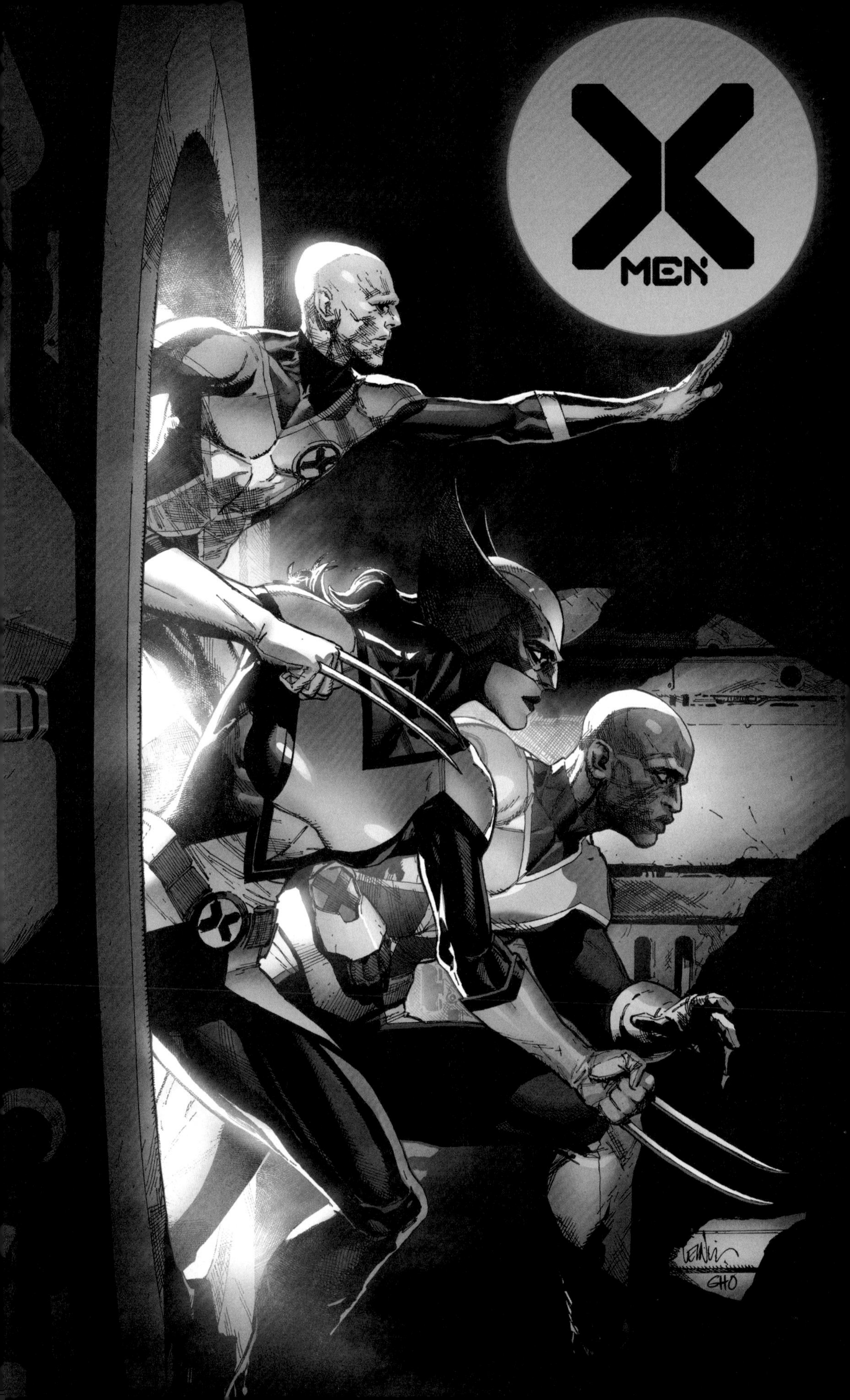
MEN

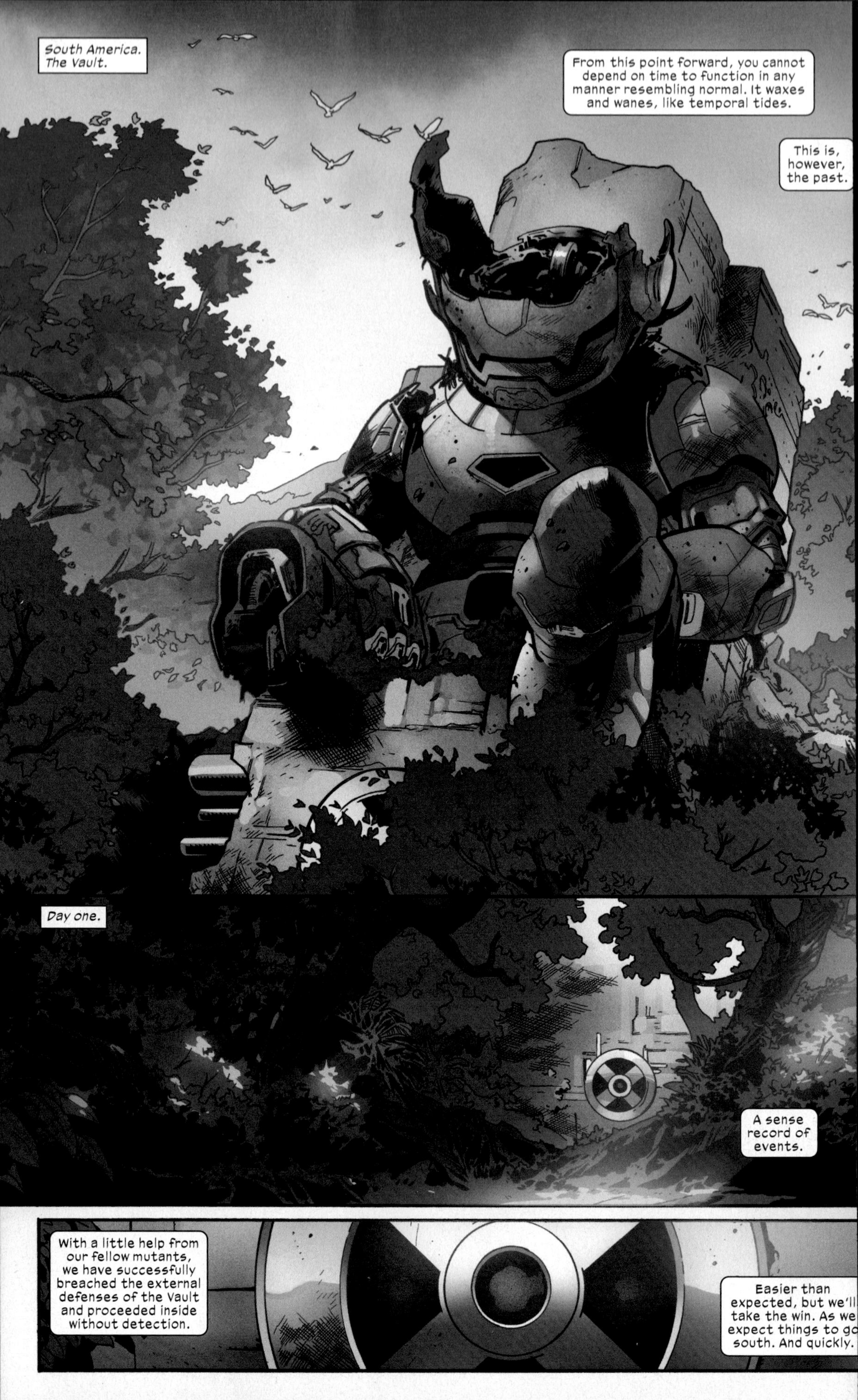
South America. The Vault.
From this point forward, you cannot depend on time to function in any manner resembling normal. It waxes and wanes, like temporal tides.
This is, however, the past.
Day one.
A sense record of events.
With a little help from our fellow mutants, we have successfully breached the external defenses of the Vault and proceeded inside without detection.
Easier than expected, but we'll take the win. As we expect things to go south. And quickly.

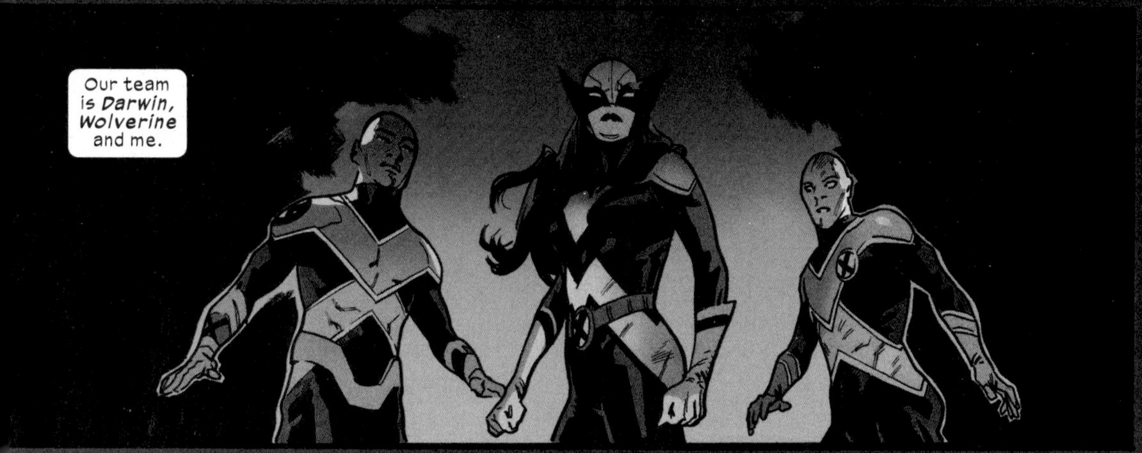
Our team is *Darwin*, *Wolverine* and me.

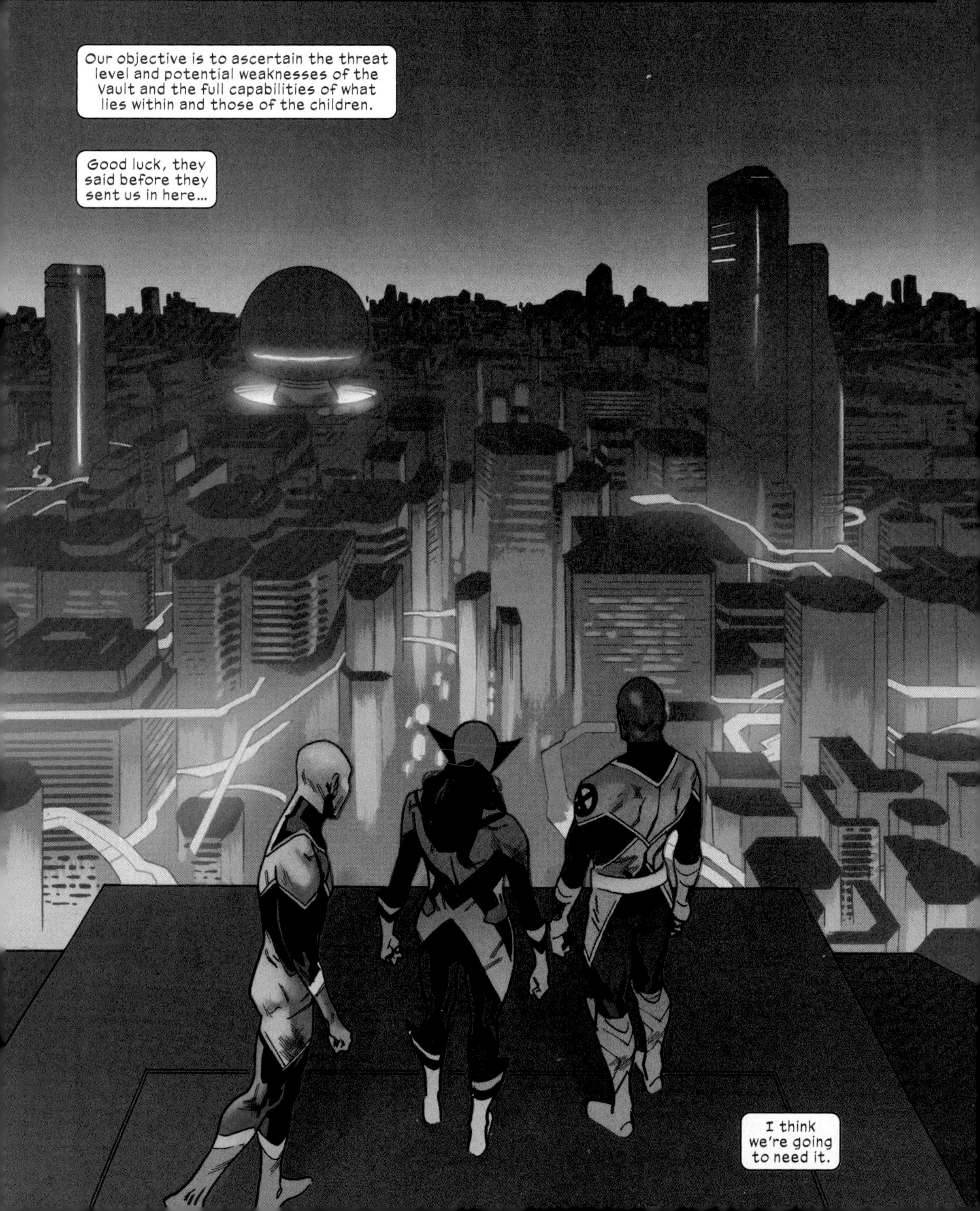
Our objective is to ascertain the threat level and potential weaknesses of the Vault and the full capabilities of what lies within and those of the children.
Good luck, they said before they sent us in here...
I think we're going to need it.

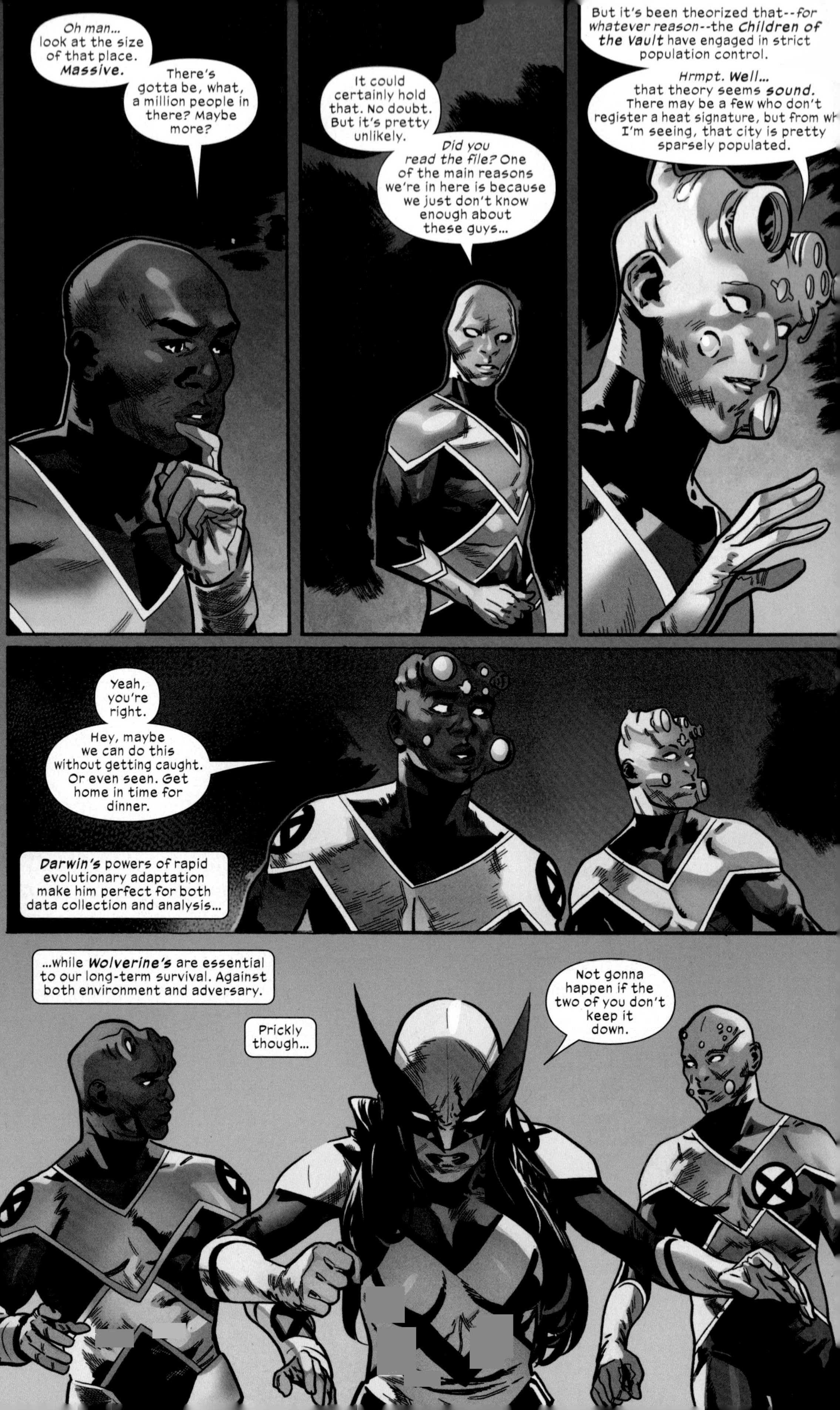
Oh man... look at the size of that place. Massive.
There's gotta be, what, a million people in there? Maybe more?
It could certainly hold that. No doubt. But it's pretty unlikely.
Did you read the file? One of the main reasons we're in here is because we just don't know enough about these guys...
But it's been theorized that--for whatever reason--the Children of the Vault have engaged in strict population control.
Hrmpt. Well... that theory seems sound. There may be a few who don't register a heat signature, but from wh
I'm seeing, that city is pretty sparsely populated.
Yeah, you're right.
Hey, maybe we can do this without getting caught. Or even seen. Get home in time for dinner.
Darwin's powers of rapid evolutionary adaptation make him perfect for both data collection and analysis...
...while Wolverine's are essential to our long-term survival. Against both environment and adversary.
Prickly though...
Not gonna happen if the two of you don't keep it down.

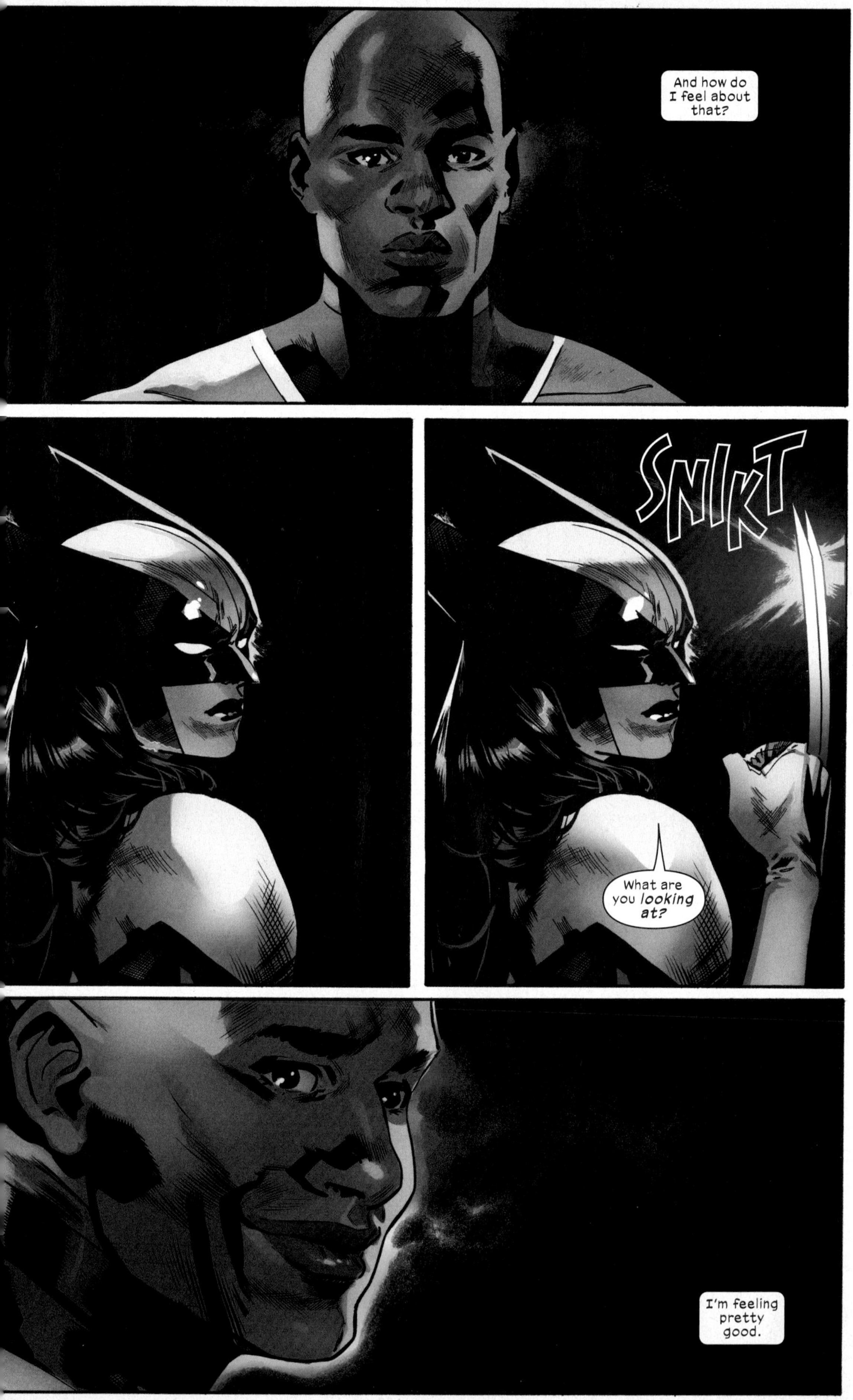
And how do I feel about that?
SNIKT
What are you *looking* at?
I'm feeling pretty good.

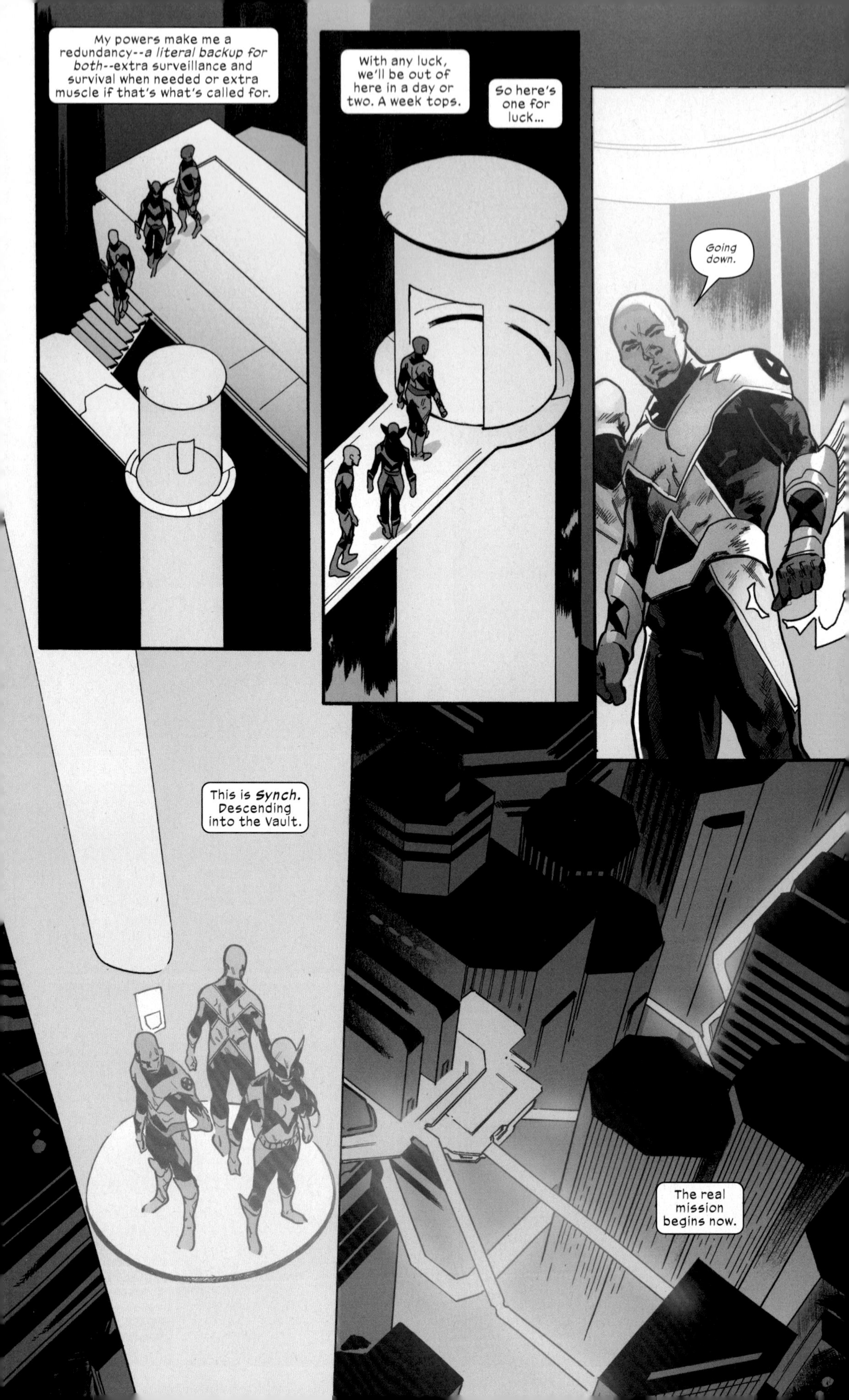
My powers make me a redundancy--*a literal backup for both*--extra surveillance and survival when needed or extra muscle if that's what's called for.
With any luck, we'll be out of here in a day or two. A week tops.
So here's one for luck...
Going down.
This is *Synch.* Descending into the Vault.
The real mission begins now.

MEDICAL REPORT

PATIENT FILE: #14
RE: Post-resurrection analysis of Synch [Everett Thomas]

ADDENDUM: MANIFESTATION

As stated in earlier notes: Synch clearly demonstrated a four percent increase in power post-resurrection than what he displayed while undergoing testing at the Massachusetts Academy during his previous life. There were other slight anomalies to his baseline scans, but they were so minuscule compared to his power increase that I wrote them off as fluctuations and focused primarily on the more dominant measurables.

Now, after a series of follow-up scans, it has become obvious that Synch's power no longer has a dormant and active state. Instead, it is clear that while he may not be acquiring powers he is in proximity to, his Synchronistic field is constantly seeking out a live connection to other power sets.

This seemed, at first, to be a potential secondary mutation, but now I think it is going to be a potential reoccurring phenomenon among all resurrected mutants. A mutant husk grown from mutant's DNA is a tabula rasa of mutant powers -- a body that has never been "mutant active." However, the backup that is then placed in the husk is one that has been "mutant active" before, often times for years.

So when that experienced mutant mind activates their powers inside a never-before, powered husk, I believe this "breakthrough" experience -- a first breach of a mutant womb -- enables a mutant to surpass their original power levels and possible native parameters.

In Synch's case, I believe that his adaptability is no longer confined to previous operational limits. This merits further observation.

- Dr. Cecelia Reyes

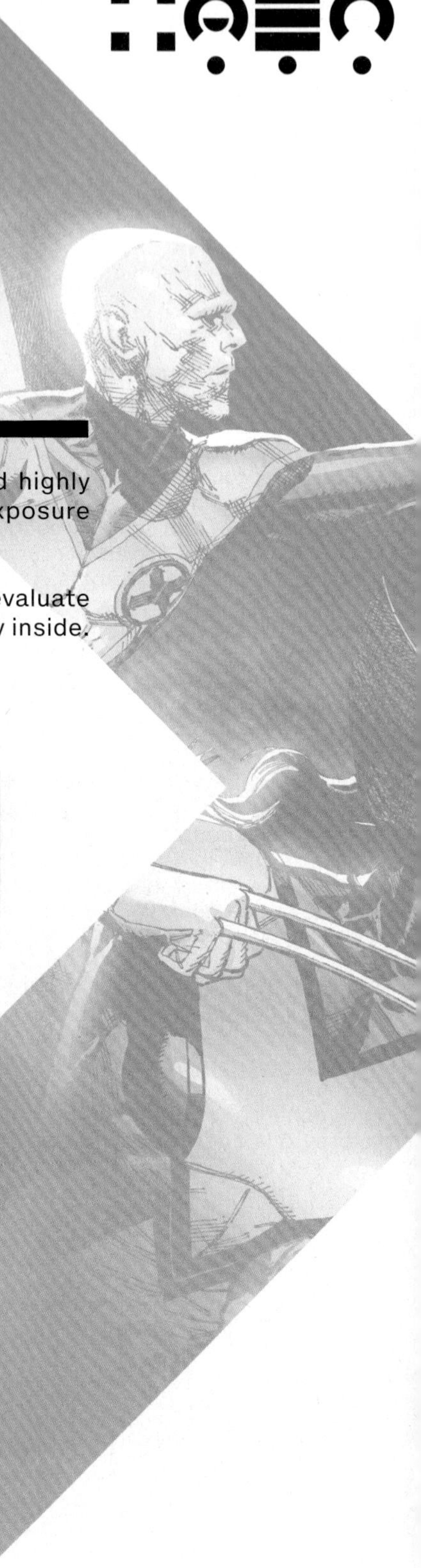

AND STEP BACK IN

The Children of the Vault -- a highly evolved and highly dangerous super-powered group developed via exposure to temporal acceleration -- have re-appeared.

Wolverine, Synch and Darwin entered the Vault to evaluate this threat, knowing only that time flows differently inside.

Everything else remains to be discovered.

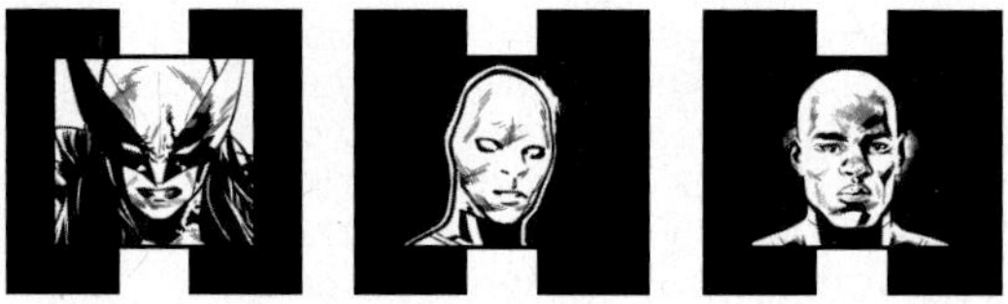

Wolverine Darwin Synch

X-MEN
[X_18]

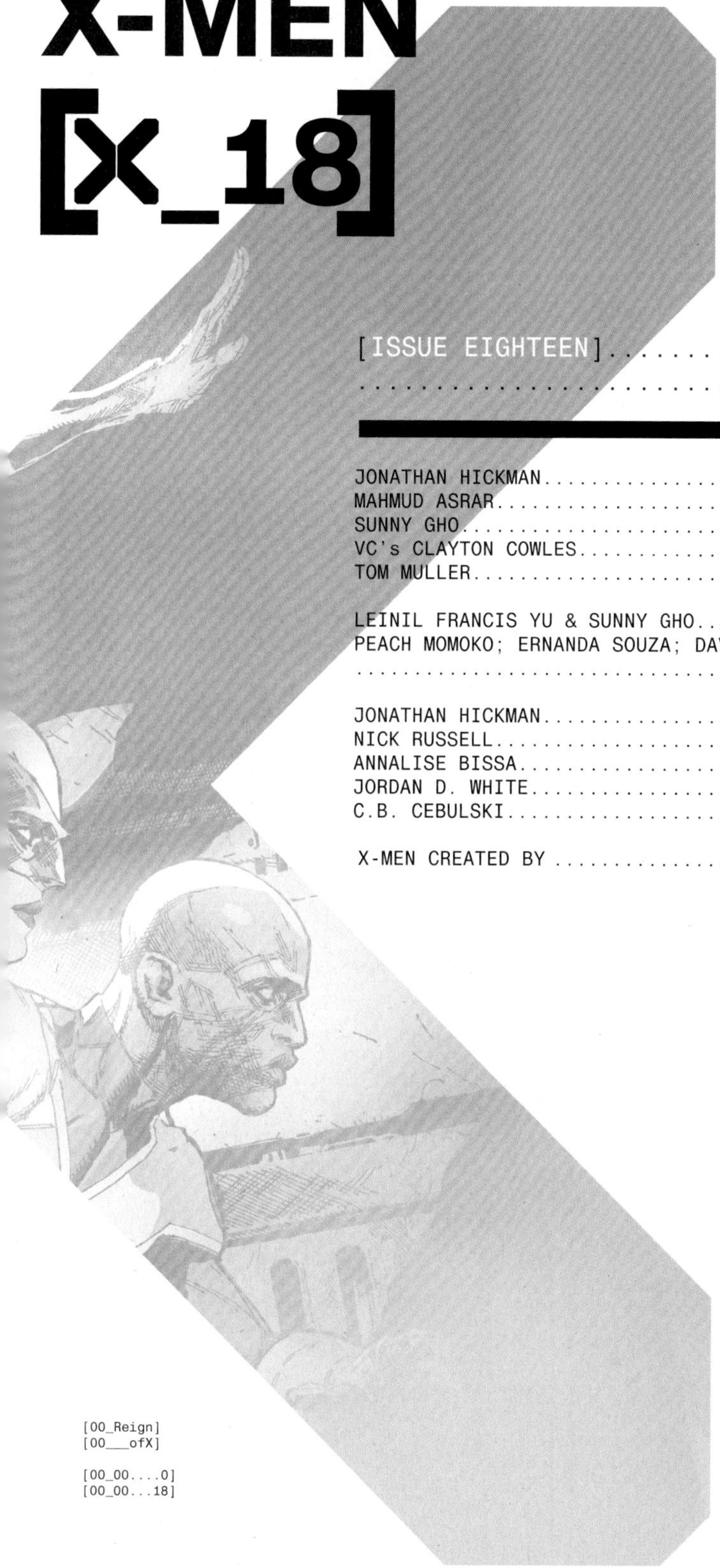

[ISSUE EIGHTEEN]............................
................................INSIDE THE VAULT

JONATHAN HICKMAN..................................[WRITER]
MAHMUD ASRAR......................................[ARTIST]
SUNNY GHO...................................[COLOR ARTIST]
VC's CLAYTON COWLES...........................[LETTERER]
TOM MULLER..[DESIGN]

LEINIL FRANCIS YU & SUNNY GHO..............[COVER ARTISTS]
PEACH MOMOKO; ERNANDA SOUZA; DAVID FINCH & FRANK D'ARMATA..
..................................[VARIANT COVER ARTISTS]

JONATHAN HICKMAN...............................[HEAD OF X]
NICK RUSSELL..................................[PRODUCTION]
ANNALISE BISSA.........................[ASSOCIATE EDITOR]
JORDAN D. WHITE...................................[EDITOR]
C.B. CEBULSKI............................[EDITOR IN CHIEF]

X-MEN CREATED BY ....STAN LEE & JACK KIRBY

[00_Reign]
[00___ofX]

[00_00....0]
[00_00...18]

[00_Reign_]
[00______]

[00___of__]

[00______X]

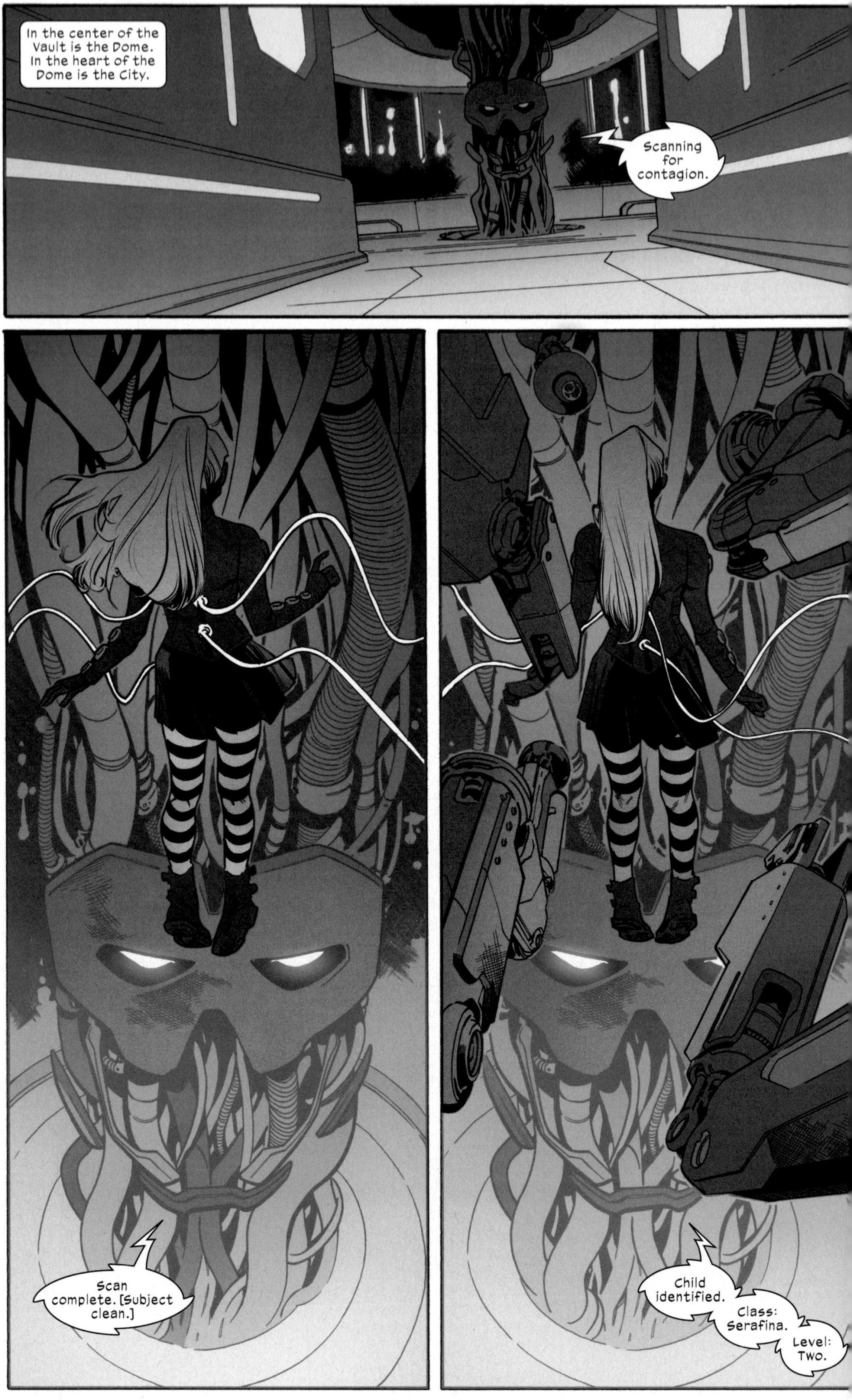
In the center of the Vault is the Dome. In the heart of the Dome is the City.
Scanning for contagion.
Scan complete. [Subject clean.]
Child identified.
Class: Serafina.
Level: Two.

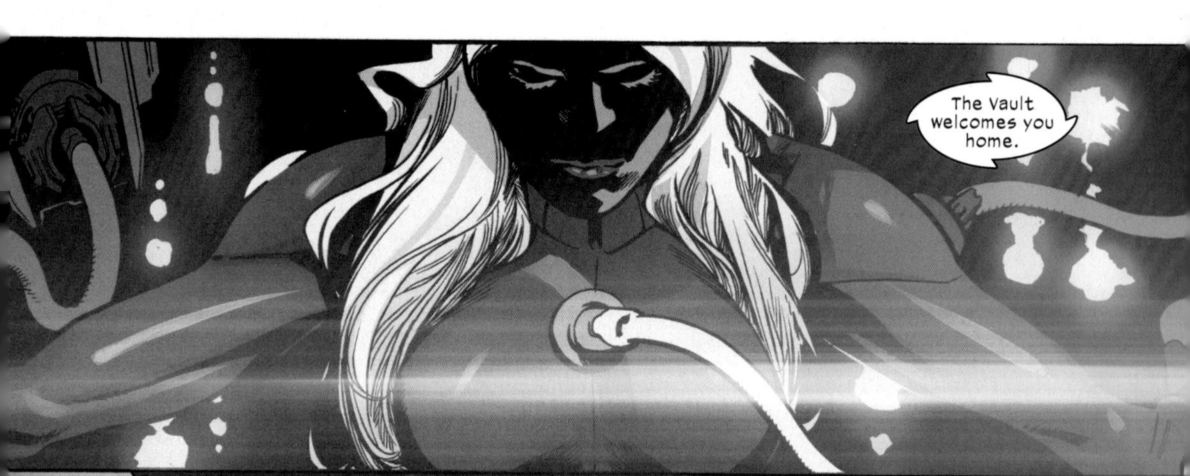
The Vault welcomes you home.

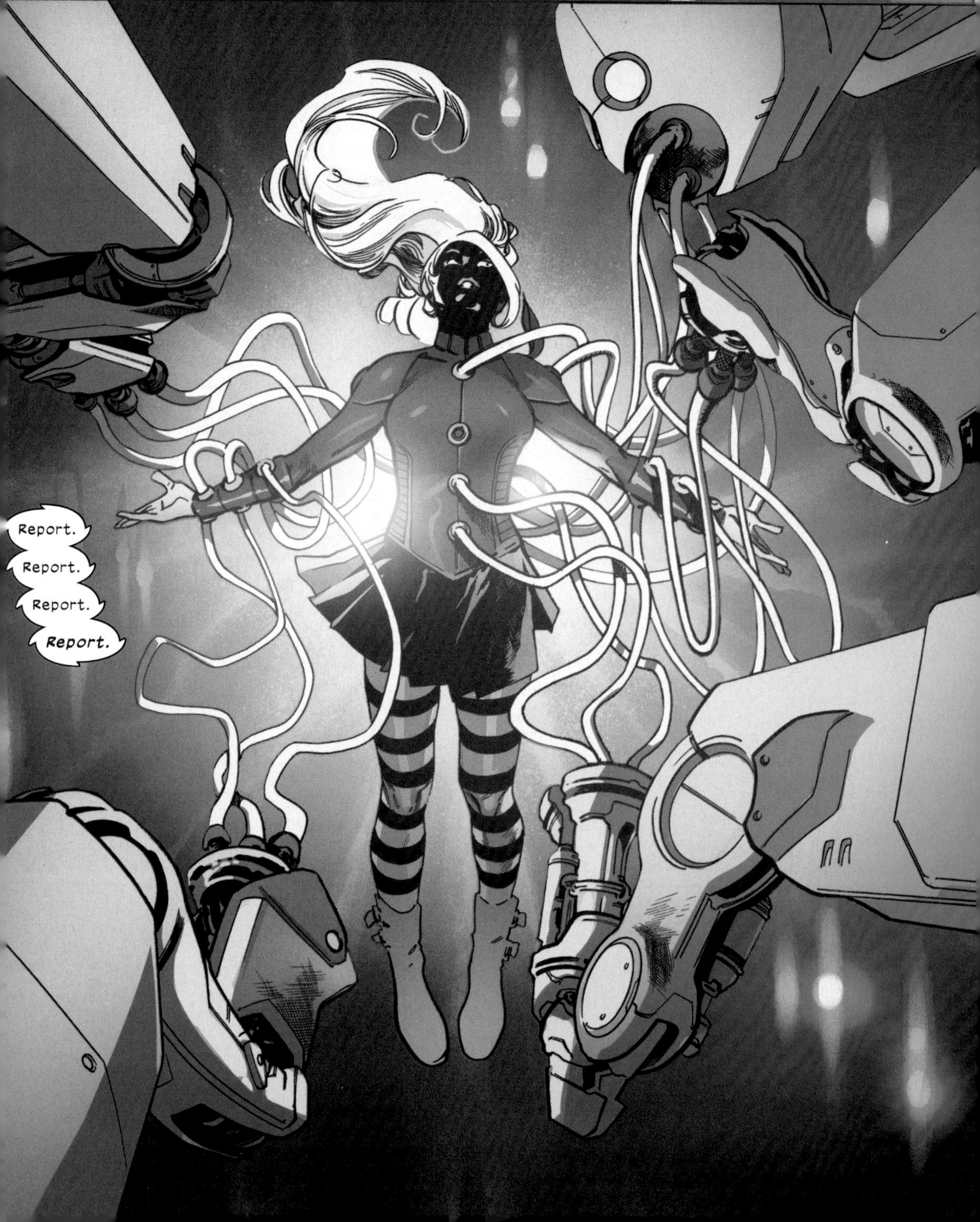
Report.
Report.
Report.
Report.

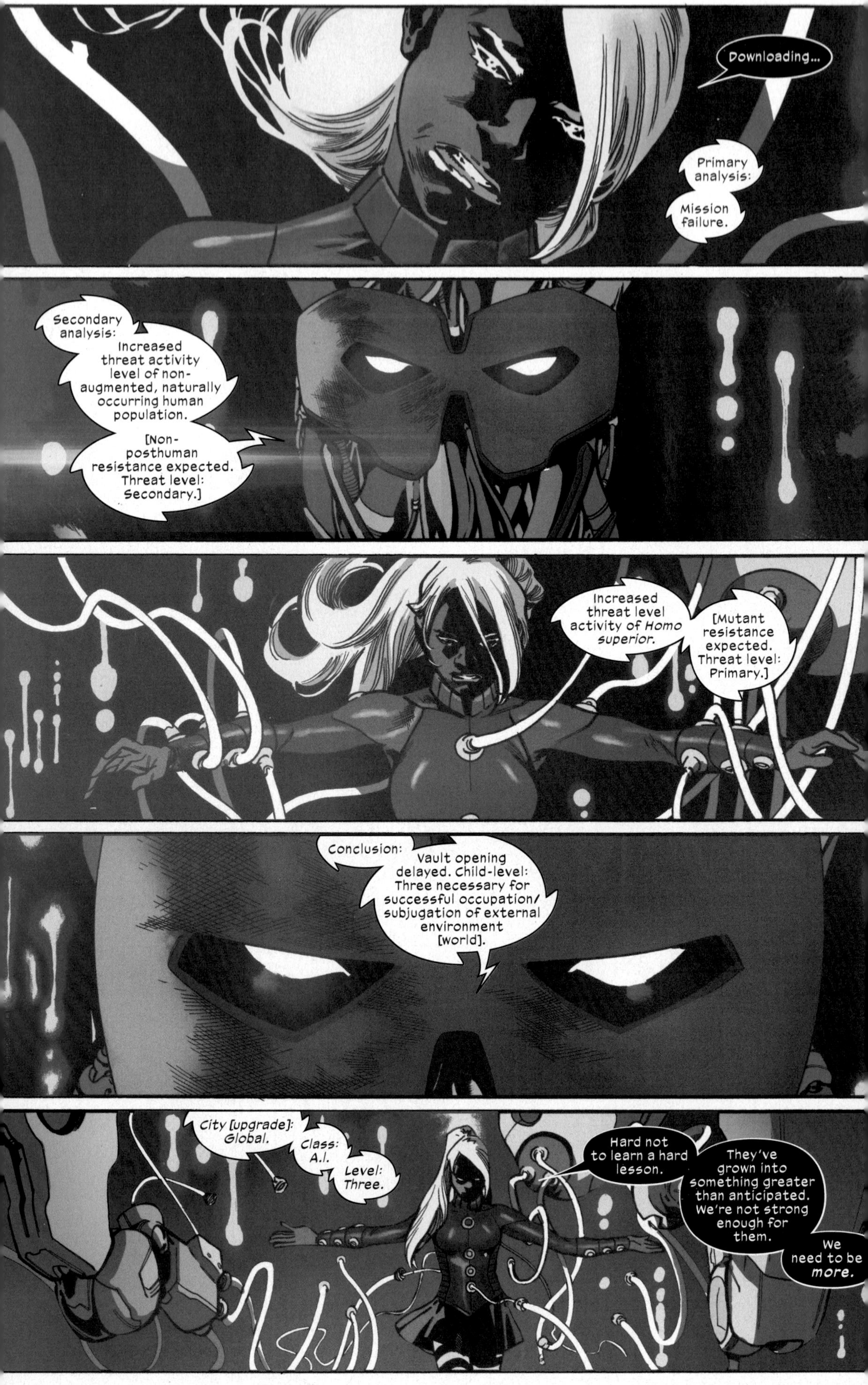

Downloading...
Primary analysis:
Mission failure.
Secondary analysis:
Increased threat activity level of non-augmented, naturally occurring human population.
[Non-posthuman resistance expected. Threat level: Secondary.]
Increased threat level activity of *Homo superior.*
[Mutant resistance expected. Threat level: Primary.]
Conclusion:
Vault opening delayed. Child-level: Three necessary for successful occupation/ subjugation of external environment [world].
City [upgrade]: Global.
Class: A.I.
Level: Three.
Hard not to learn a hard lesson.
They've grown into something greater than anticipated. We're not strong enough for them.
We need to be *more.*

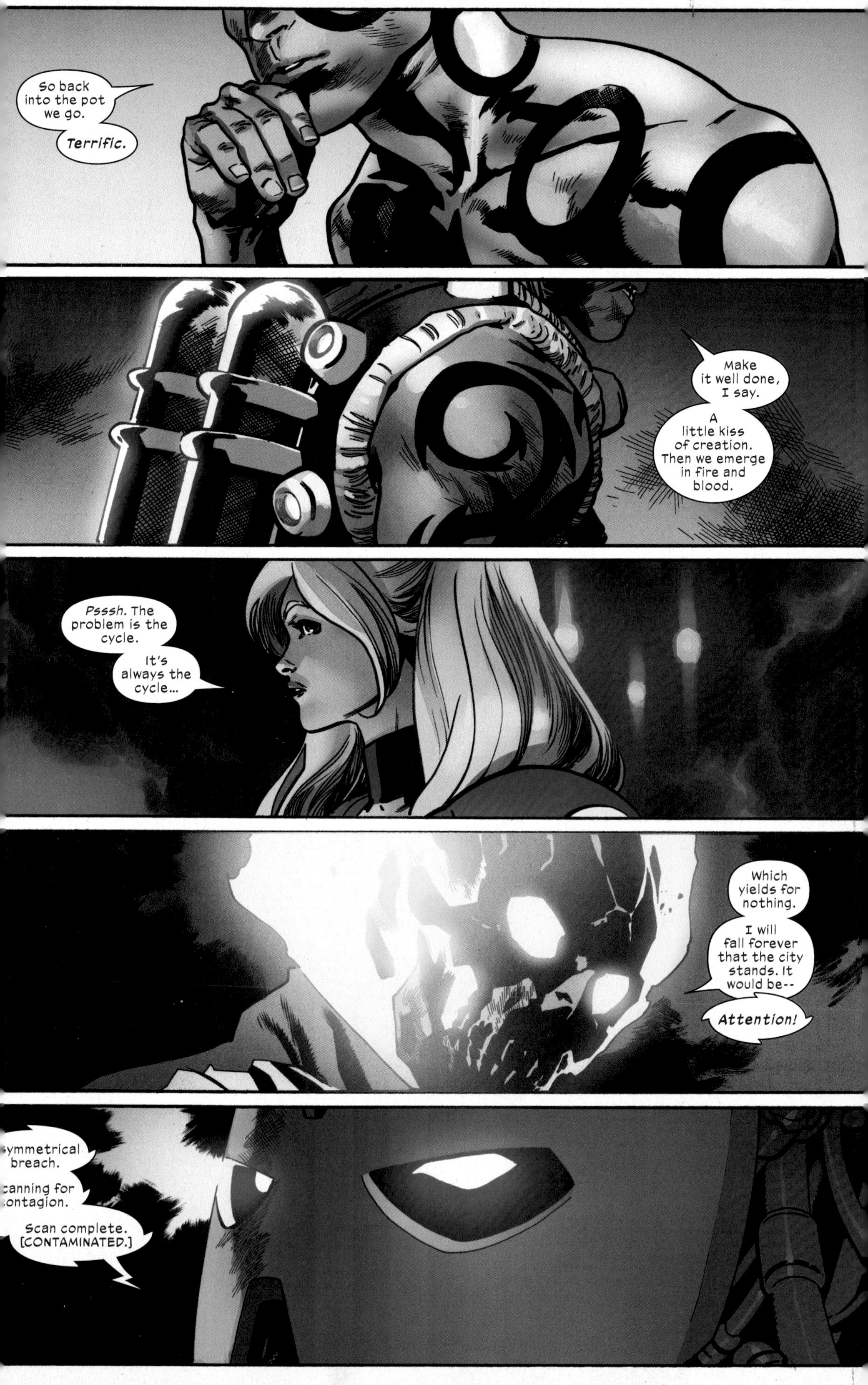

So back into the pot we go.
Terrific.
Make it well done, I say.
A little kiss of creation. Then we emerge in fire and blood.
Psssh. The problem is the cycle.
It's always the cycle...
Which yields for nothing.
I will fall forever that the city stands. It would be--
Attention!
ymmetrical breach.
canning for ontagion.
Scan complete. [CONTAMINATED.]

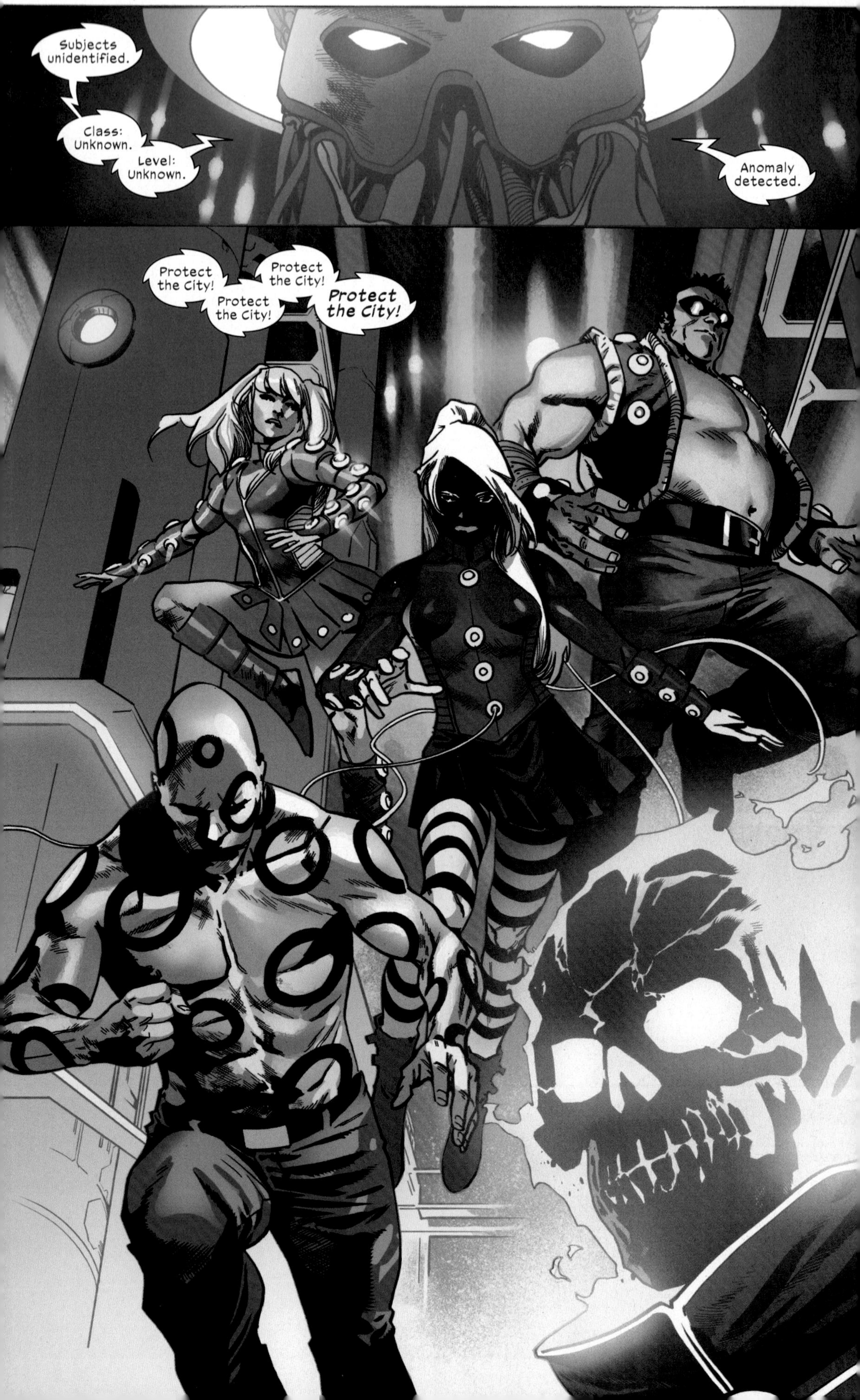
Subjects unidentified.
Class: Unknown.
Level: Unknown.
Anomaly detected.
Protect the City!
Protect the City!
Protect the City!
Protect the City!

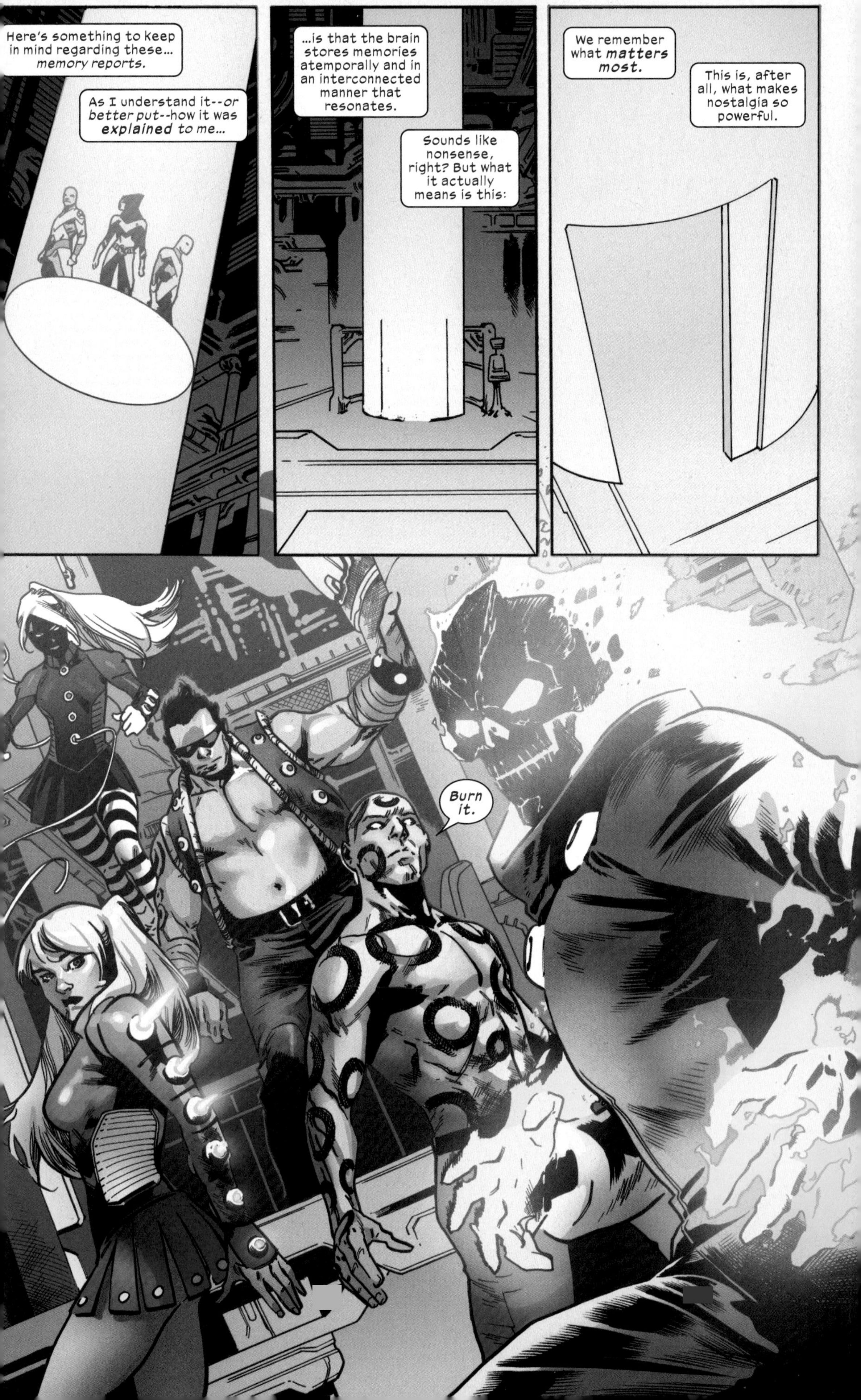
Here's something to keep in mind regarding these... *memory reports.*
As I understand it--*or better put*--how it was ***explained*** *to me...*
...is that the brain stores memories atemporally and in an interconnected manner that resonates.
Sounds like nonsense, right? But what it actually means is this:
We remember what ***matters most.***
This is, after all, what makes nostalgia so powerful.
Burn it.

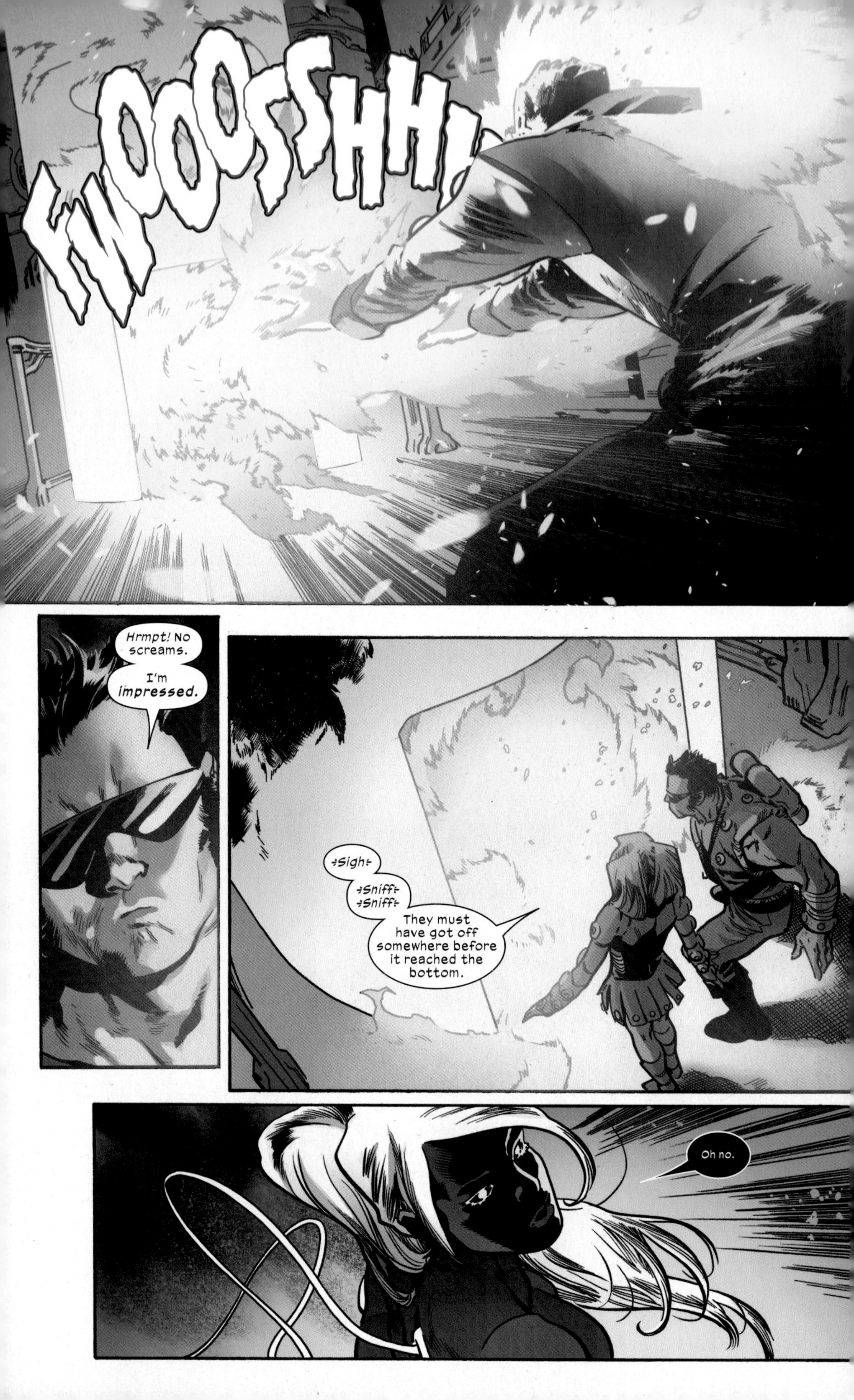
FWOOOSSHH
Hrmpt! No screams.
I'm impressed.
-Sigh-
-Sniff- -Sniff-
They must have got off somewhere before it reached the bottom.
Oh no.

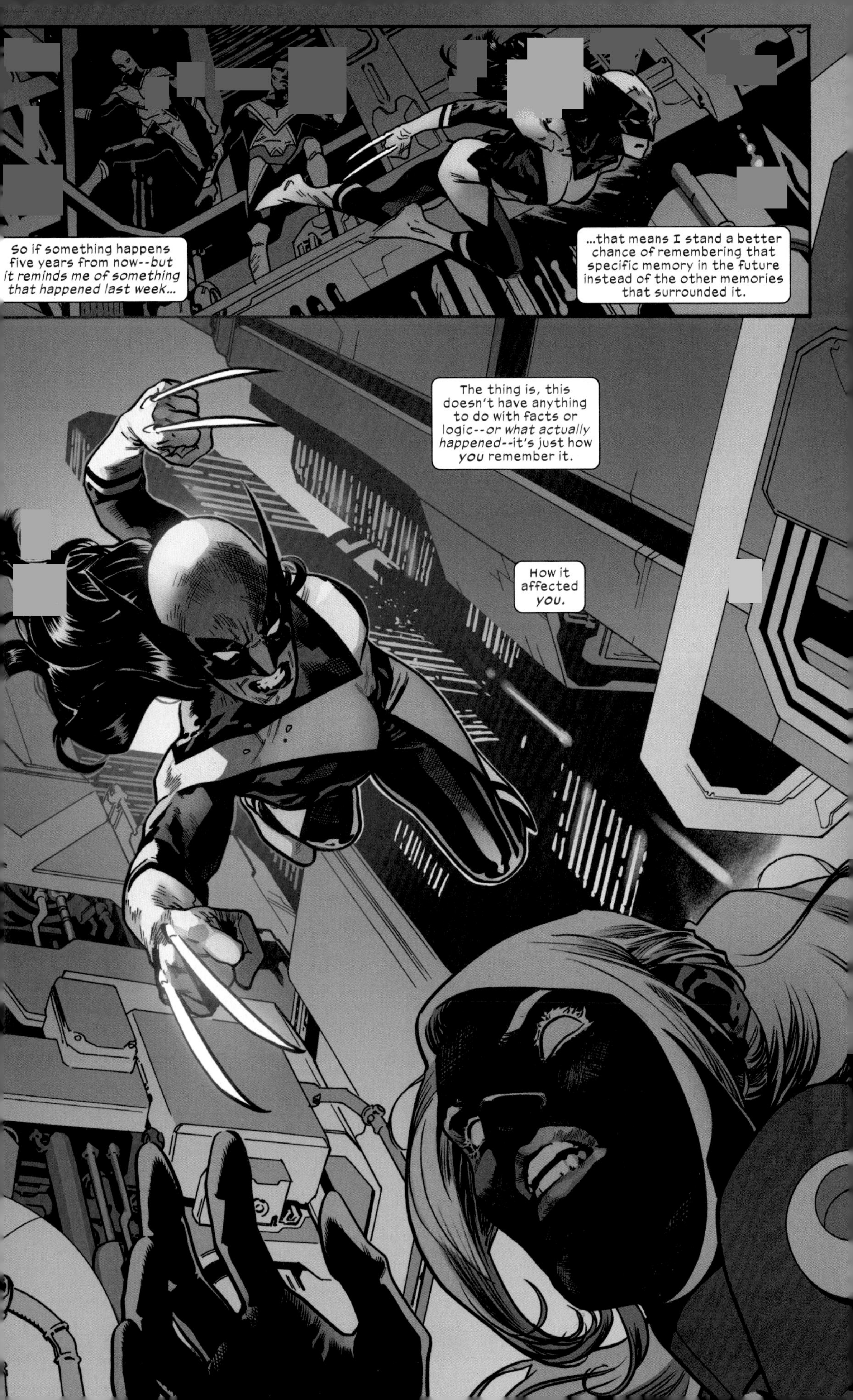
So if something happens five years from now--*but it reminds me of something that happened last week...*
...that means I stand a better chance of remembering that specific memory in the future instead of the other memories that surrounded it.
The thing is, this doesn't have anything to do with facts or logic--*or what actually happened*--it's just how *you* remember it.
How it affected *you.*

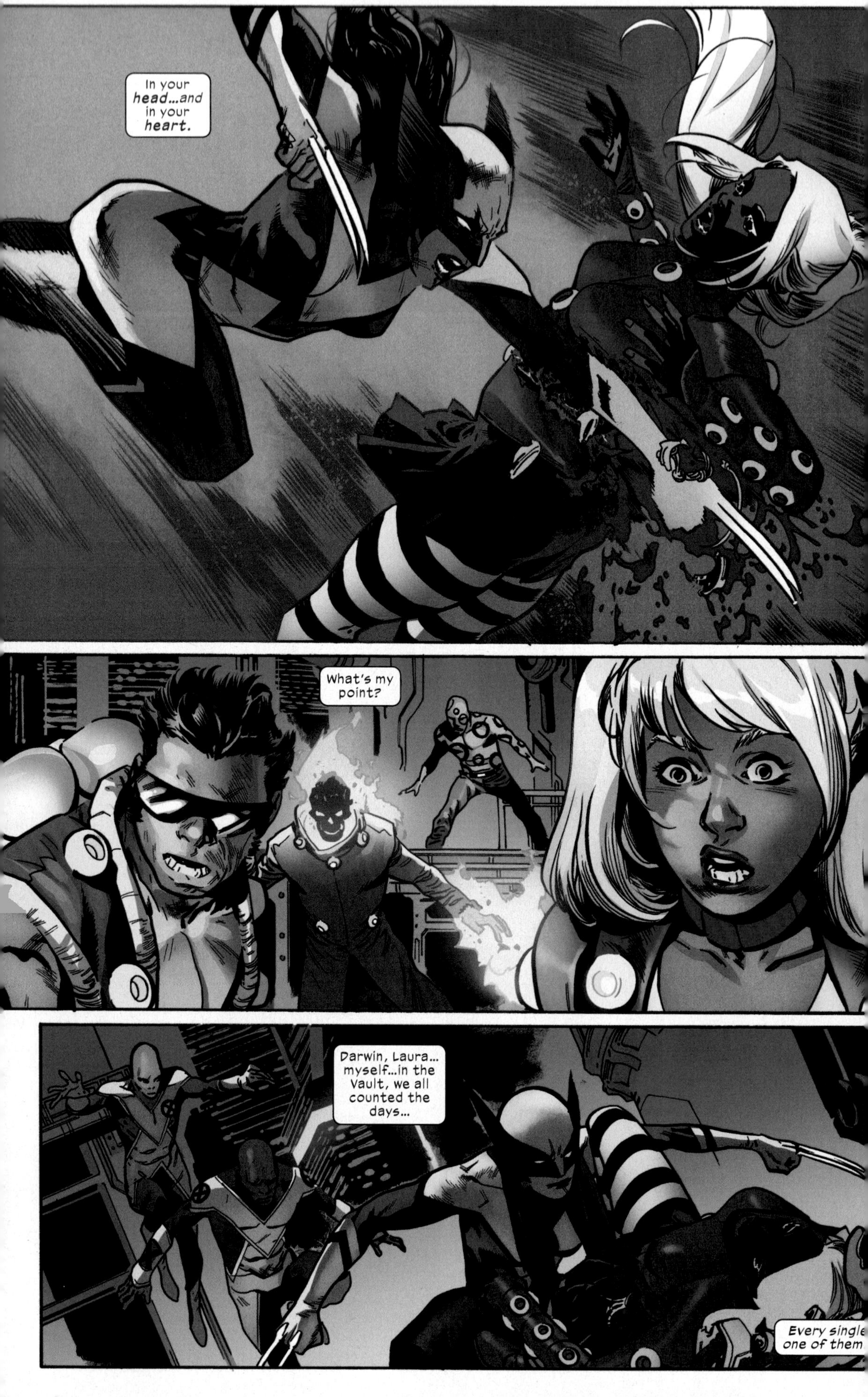
In your head...and in your heart.
What's my point?
Darwin, Laura... myself...in the Vault, we all counted the days...
Every single one of them

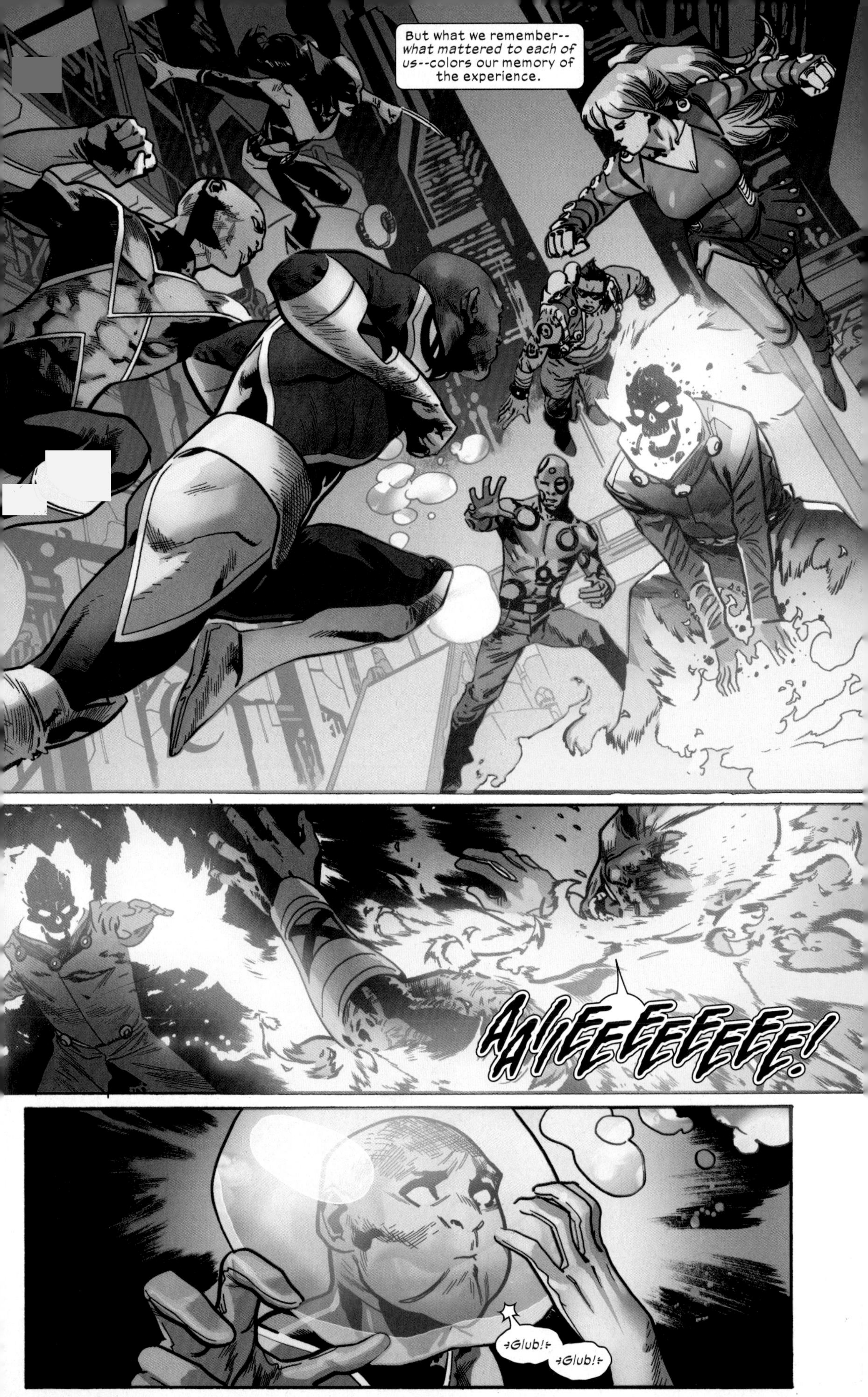
But what we remember-- what mattered to each of us--colors our memory of the experience.
AAIIEEEEEEEEE!
Glub!
Glub!

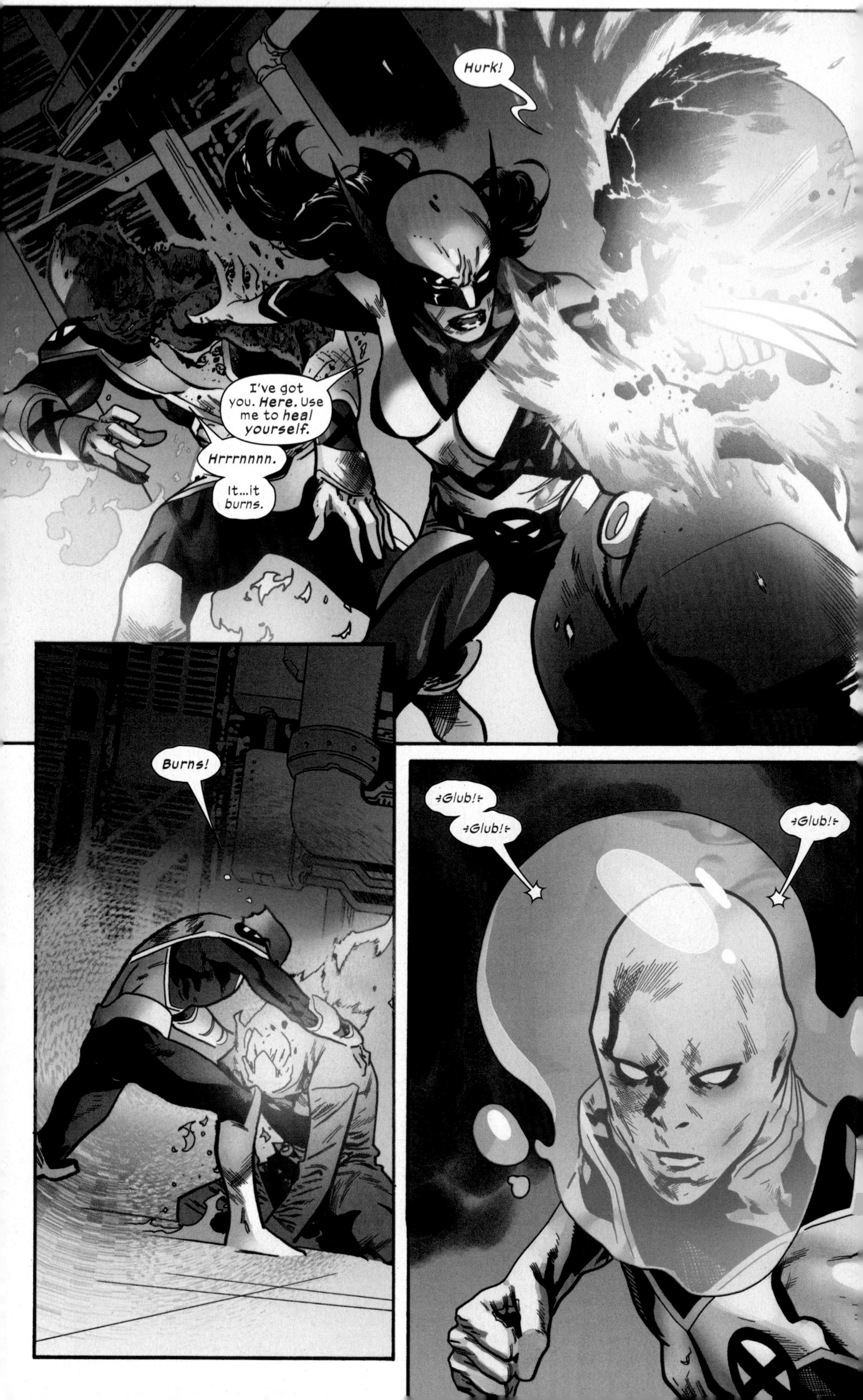
Hurk!
I've got you. Here. Use me to heal yourself.
Hrrrnnnn.
It...it burns.
Burns!
Glub!
Glub!
Glub!

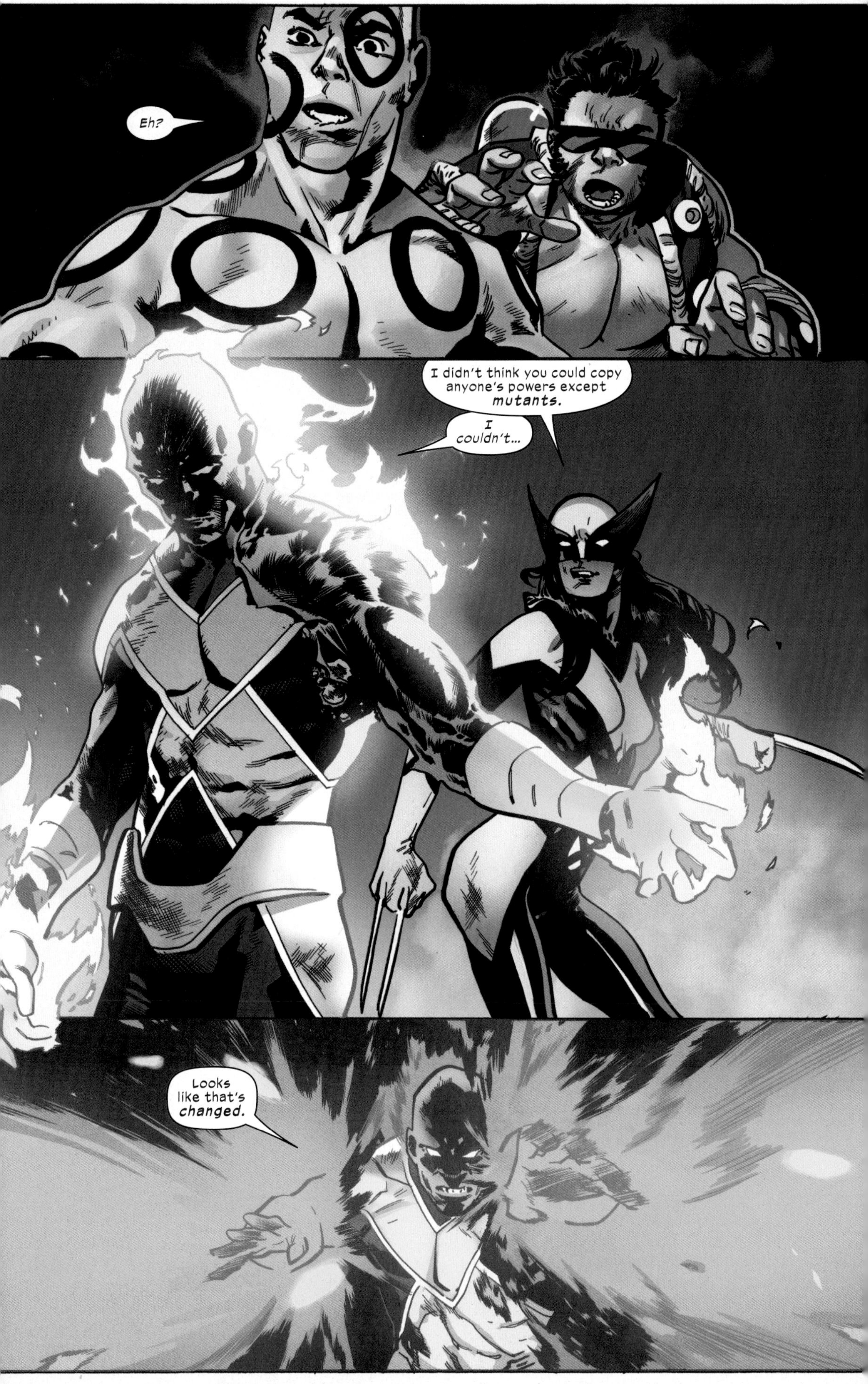
Eh?
I didn't think you could copy anyone's powers except mutants.
I couldn't...
Looks like that's changed.

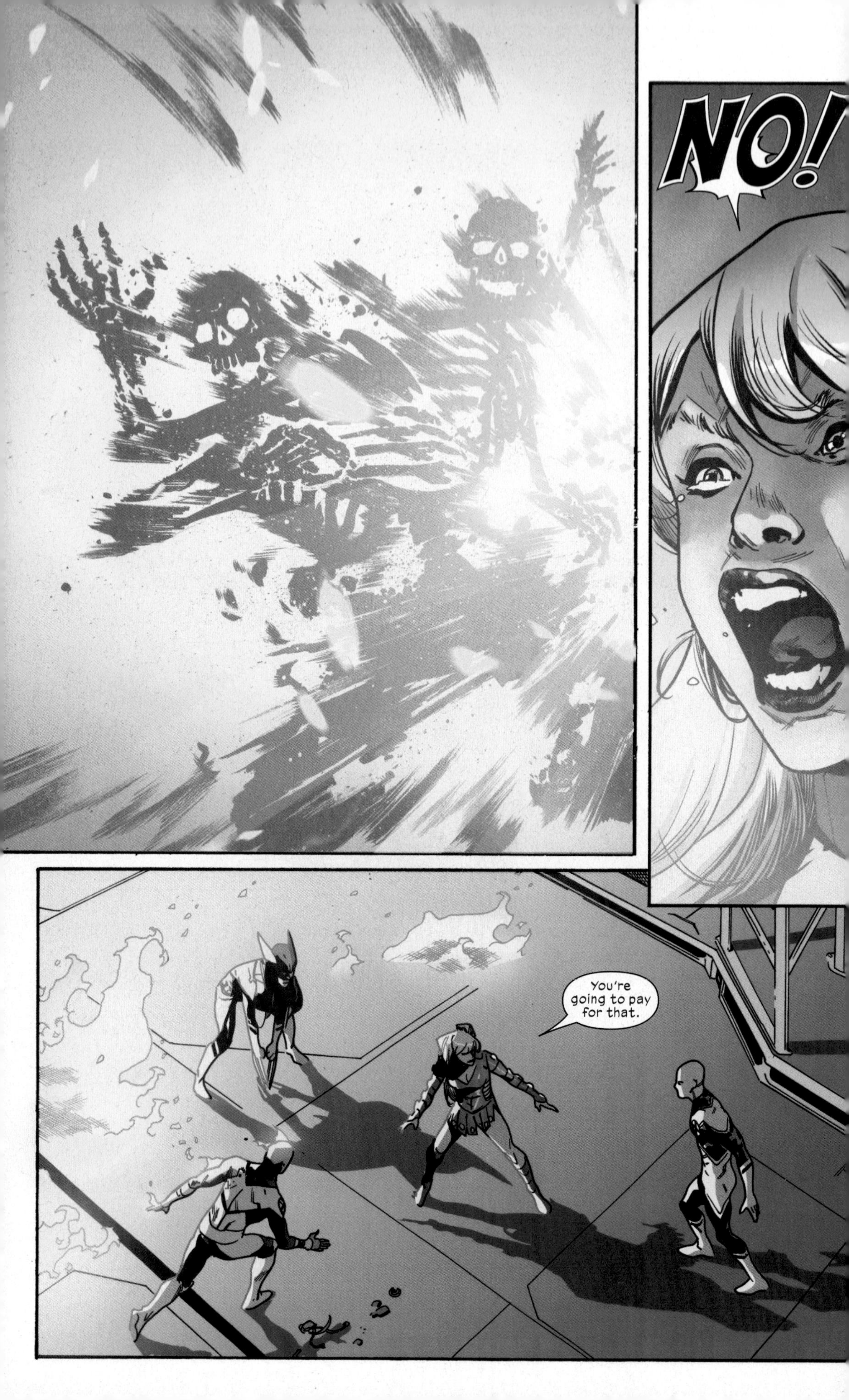
NO!
You're going to pay for that.

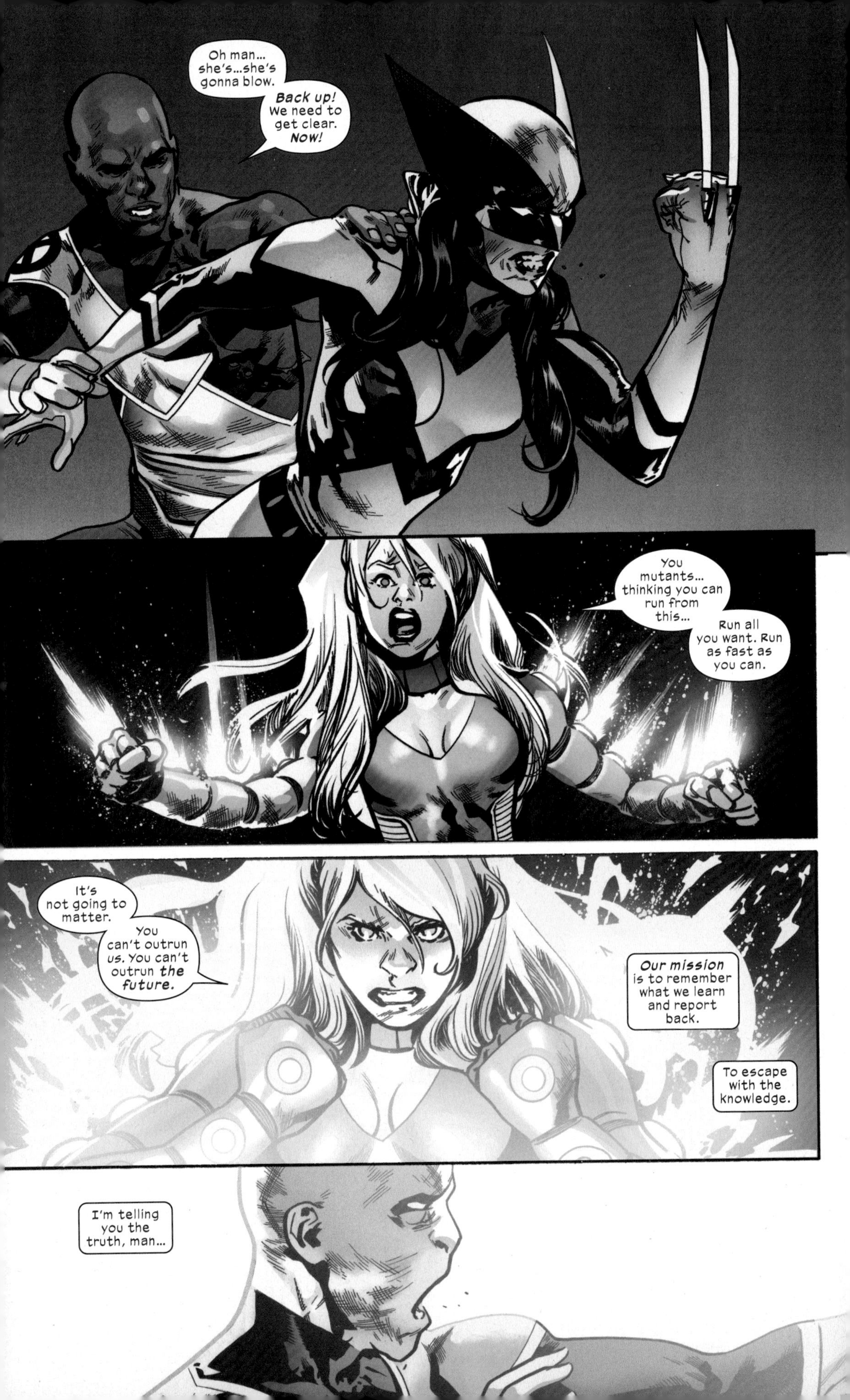
Oh man... she's...she's gonna blow.
Back up! We need to get clear. NOW!
You mutants... thinking you can run from this...
Run all you want. Run as fast as you can.
It's not going to matter.
You can't outrun us. You can't outrun the future.
Our mission is to remember what we learn and report back.
To escape with the knowledge.
I'm telling you the truth, man...

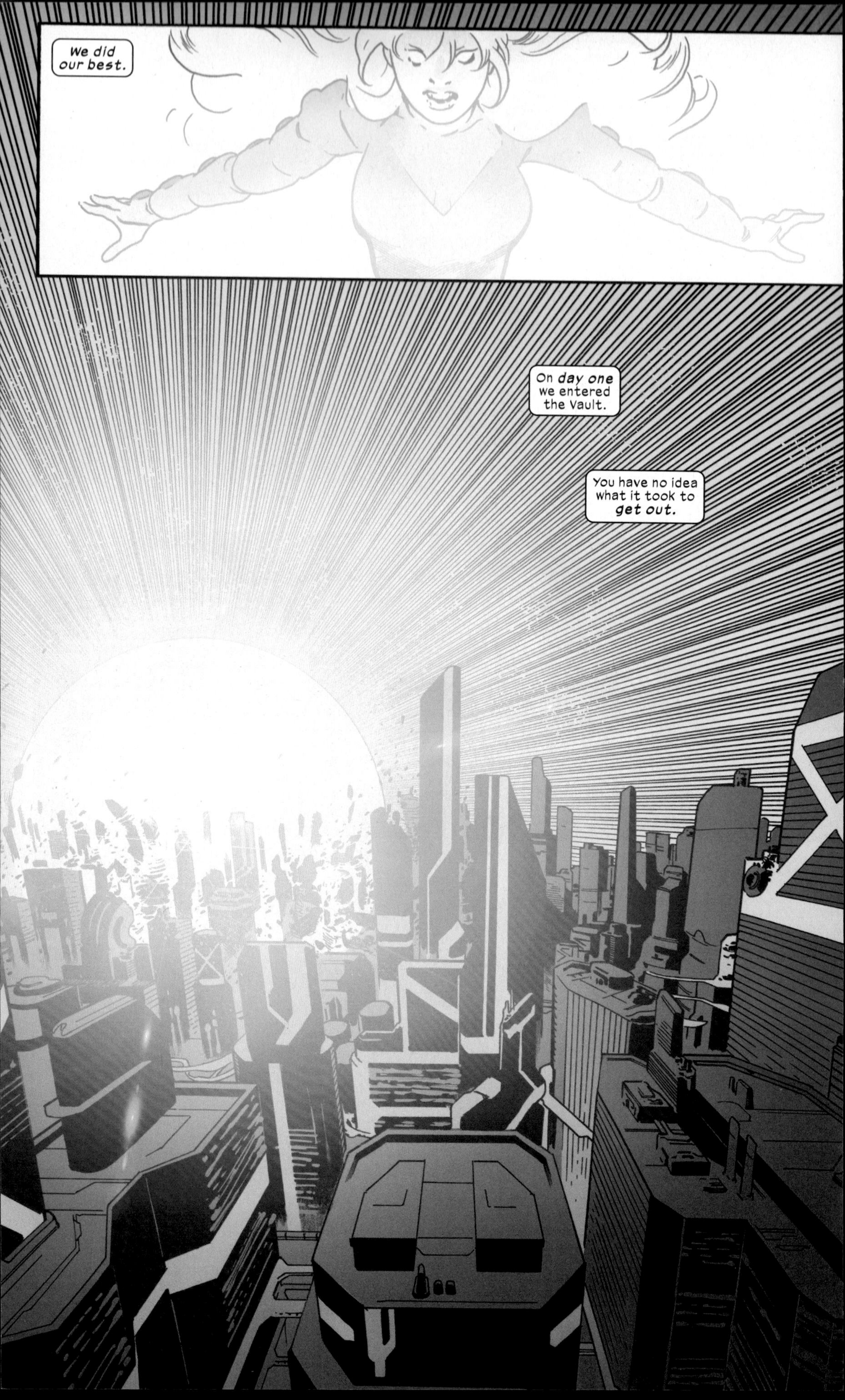
We did our best.
On day one we entered the Vault.
You have no idea what it took to get out.

[the__2nd_law]
[of_mutantdom]

+

MURDER NO MAN

+

-- Confidential --

As this Council is completely aware, only FORCE protocols allow the suspension of the three laws of Krakoa. "Murder No Man" is the predictable primary concern of this body at this time.

Our approved reconnoissance operation into the Vault to ascertain the threat level of the Children of the Vault is expected to face stiff, and probably lethal, opposition during the mission. To compound this, it is the Council's expectation that said opposition will be progressively post-human in nature.

As the Children fall outside of the normal definition of "human," and the risk of data recovery seems improbable using current legal methods, FORCE protocol is initiated for this mission.

-- X --

[............]
[is_suspended]

[..............X]
[..............X]

[Krakoa_1]
[Vault__0]

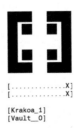

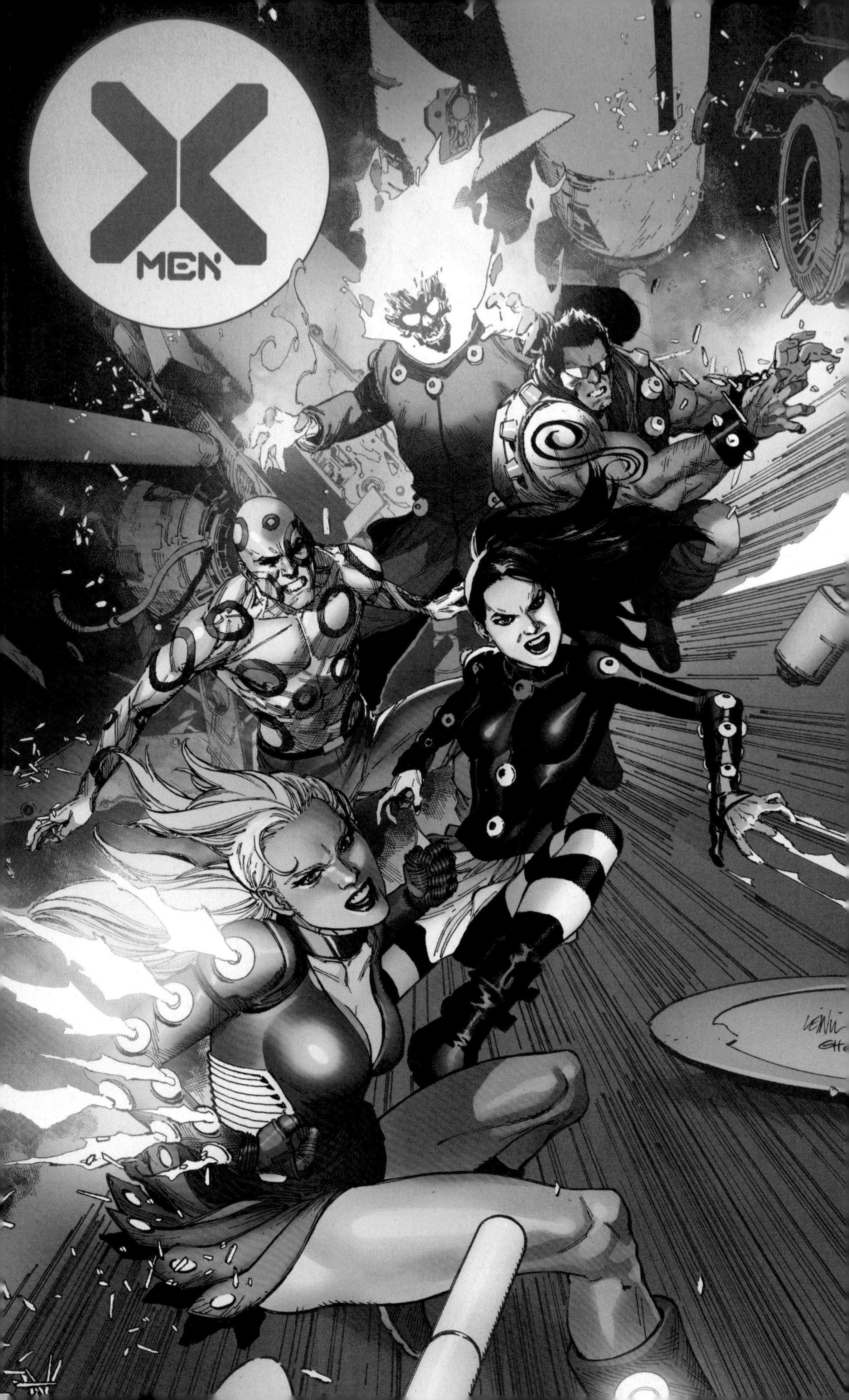
X
MEN

[........WOLVERINE]

[...........SYNCH]

[..........DARWIN]

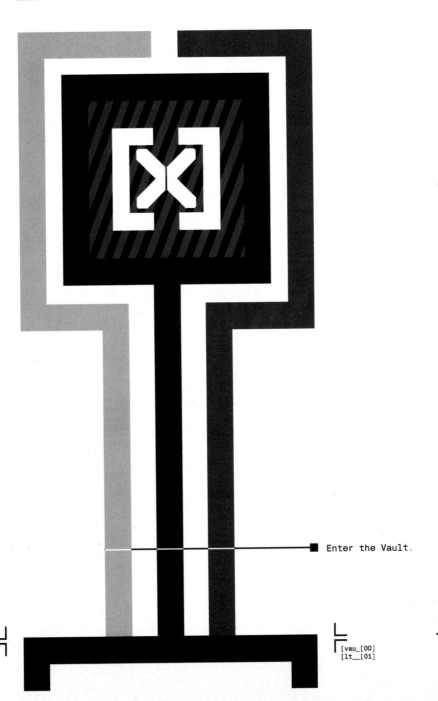

Enter the Vault.

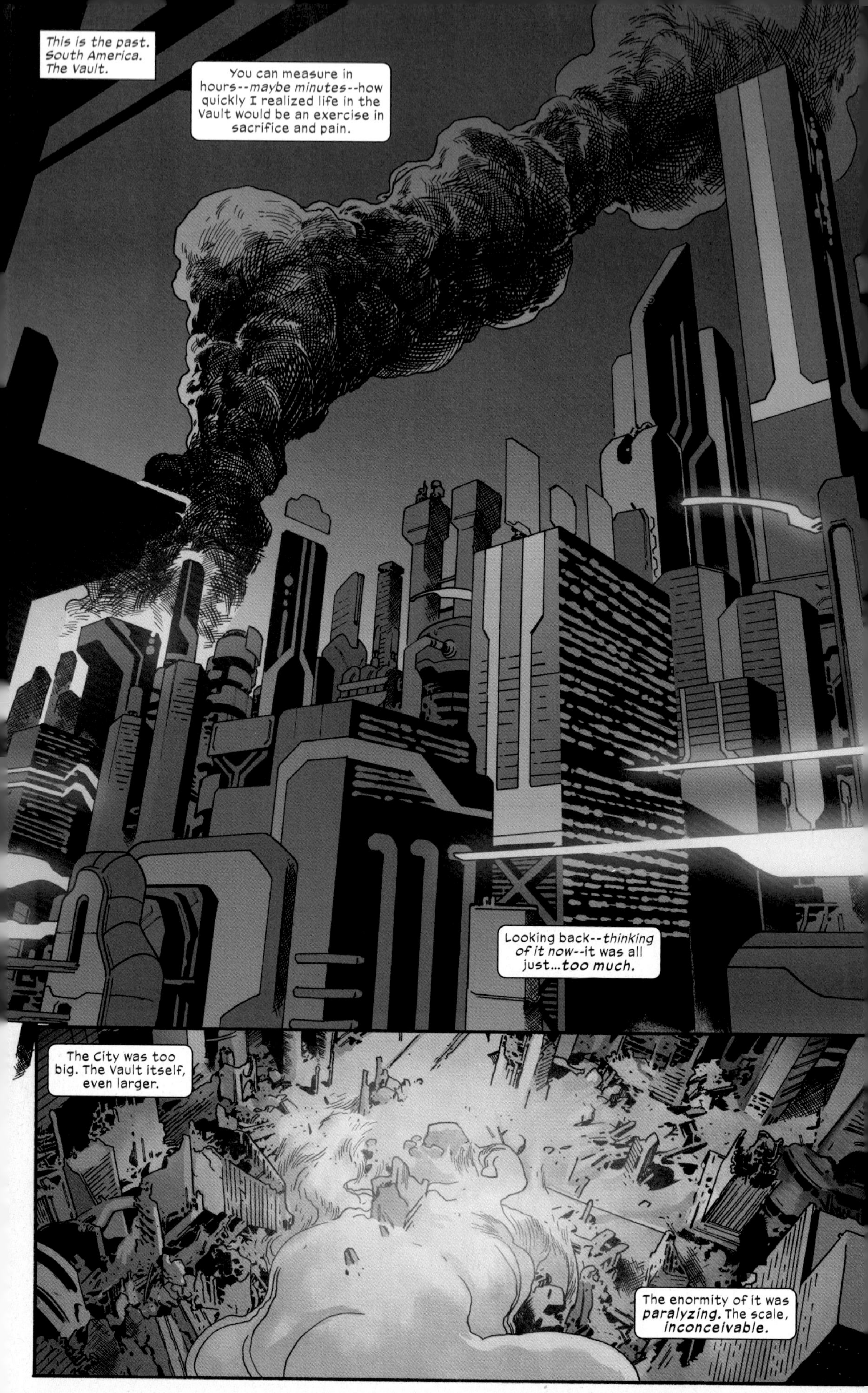
This is the past. South America. The Vault.
You can measure in hours--*maybe minutes*--how quickly I realized life in the Vault would be an exercise in sacrifice and pain.
Looking back--*thinking of it now*--it was all just...*too much.*
The City was too big. The Vault itself, even larger.
The enormity of it was *paralyzing.* The scale, *inconceivable.*

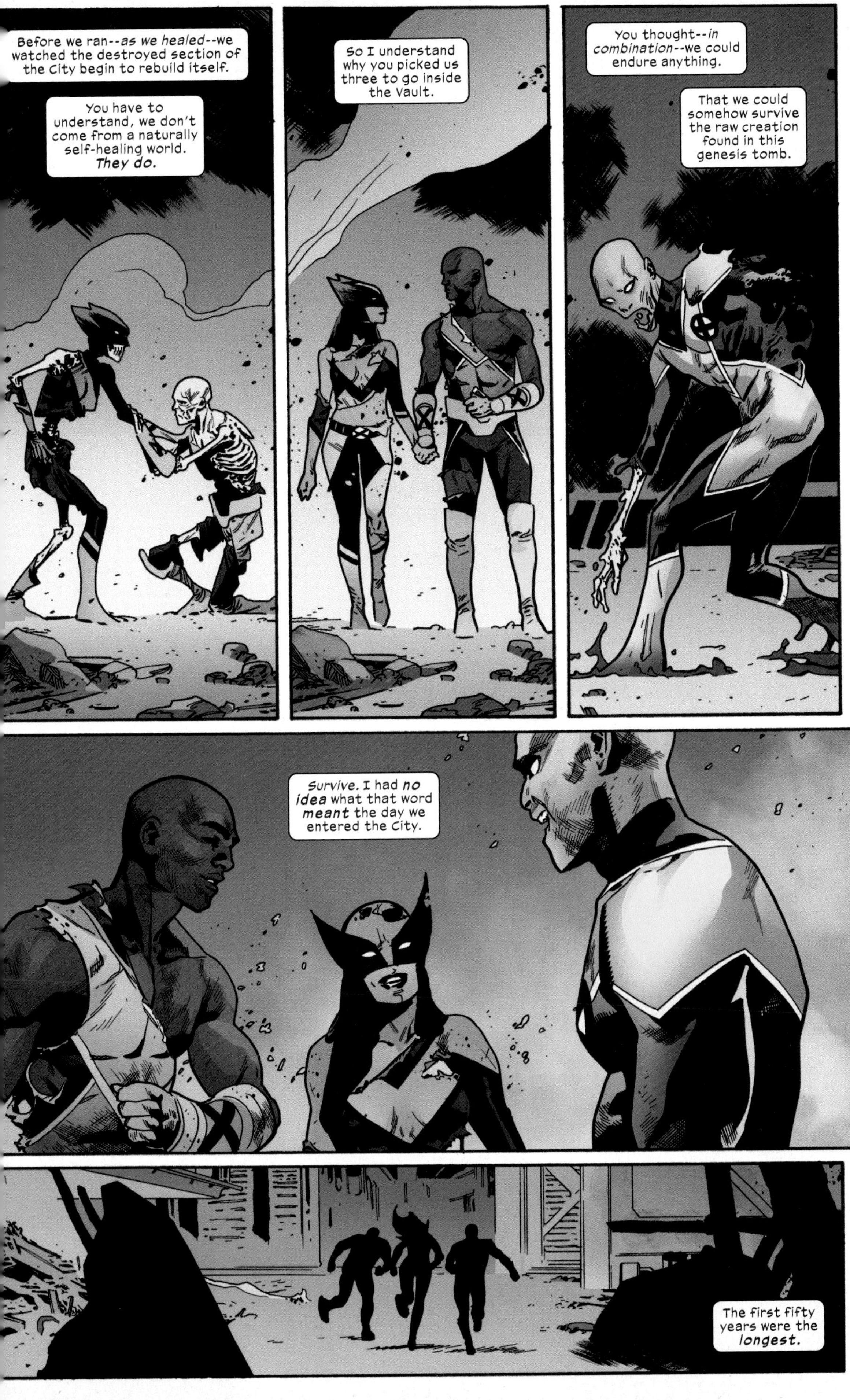
Before we ran--as we healed--we watched the destroyed section of the City begin to rebuild itself.
You have to understand, we don't come from a naturally self-healing world. They do.
So I understand why you picked us three to go inside the Vault.
You thought--in combination--we could endure anything.
That we could somehow survive the raw creation found in this genesis tomb.
Survive. I had no idea what that word meant the day we entered the City.
The first fifty years were the longest.

IN THE FIRE OF EACH OTHER

The Children of the Vault -- a highly evolved and highly dangerous super-powered group developed via exposure to temporal acceleration -- have re-appeared.

X-23, Synch and Darwin entered the Vault to evaluate this threat, knowing only that time flows differently inside. In their first encounter, one of the Children self-immolated, catching our team in the blast. But this is far from the end...

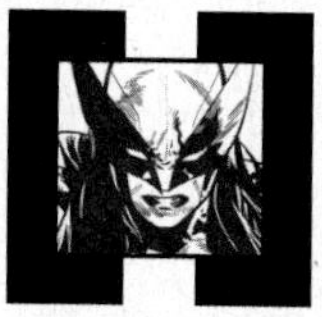
X-23

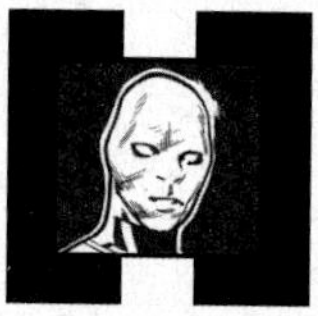
Darwin

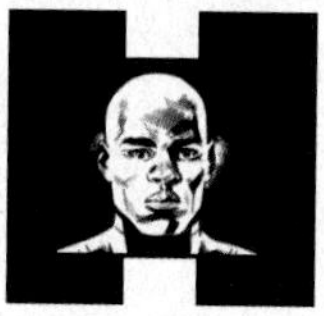
Synch

X-MEN [X_19]

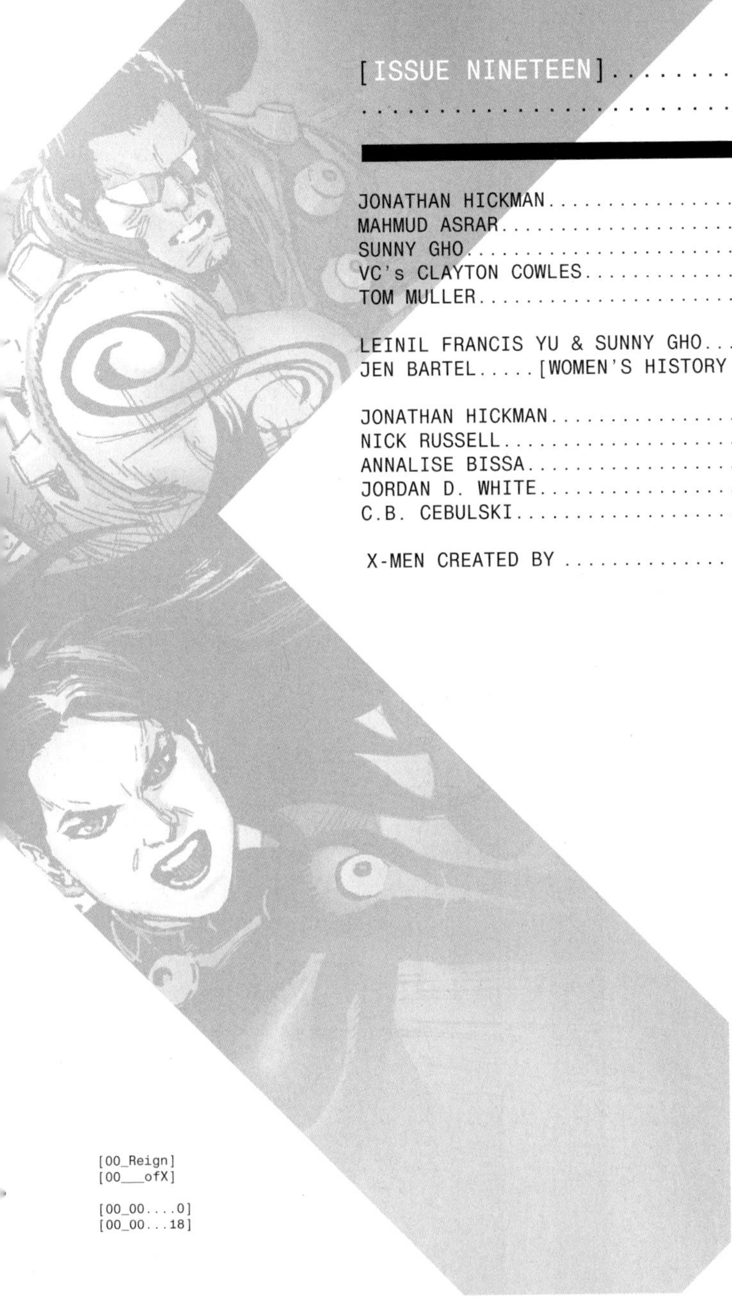

[ISSUE NINETEEN]..................................OUT OF THE VAULT

JONATHAN HICKMAN..........................[WRITER]
MAHMUD ASRAR..........................[ARTIST]
SUNNY GHO..........................[COLOR ARTIST]
VC's CLAYTON COWLES..........................[LETTERER]
TOM MULLER..........................[DESIGN]

LEINIL FRANCIS YU & SUNNY GHO...............[COVER ARTISTS]
JEN BARTEL.....[WOMEN'S HISTORY MONTH VARIANT COVER ARTIST]

JONATHAN HICKMAN..........................[HEAD OF X]
NICK RUSSELL..........................[PRODUCTION]
ANNALISE BISSA..........................[ASSOCIATE EDITOR]
JORDAN D. WHITE..........................[EDITOR]
C.B. CEBULSKI..........................[EDITOR IN CHIEF]

X-MEN CREATED BY ....STAN LEE & JACK KIRBY

[00_Reign]
[00___ofX]

[00_00....0]
[00_00...18]

[00_Reign_]
[00______]

[00___of__]

[00______X]

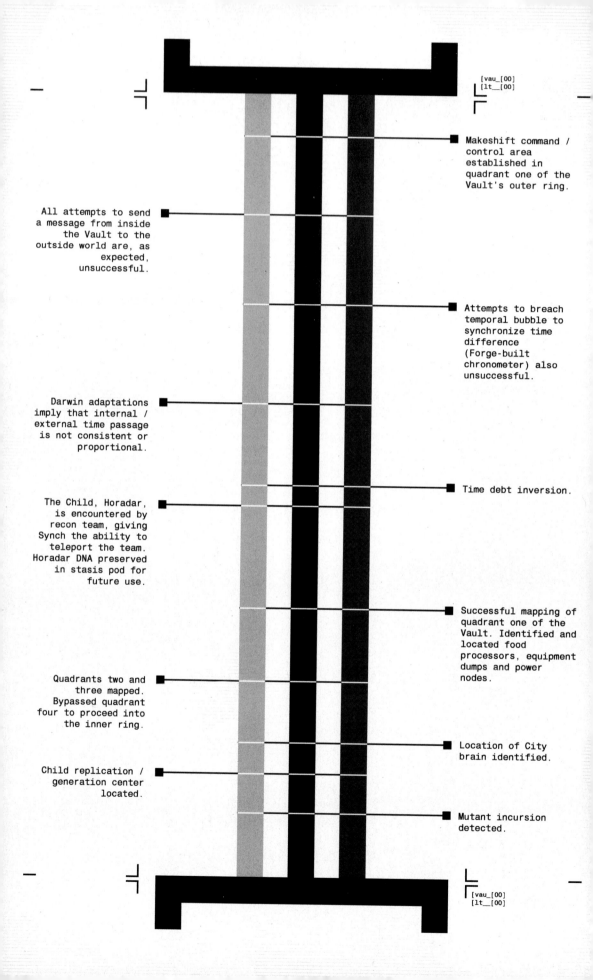

Makeshift command /
control area
established in
quadrant one of the
Vault's outer ring.

All attempts to send
a message from inside
the Vault to the
outside world are, as
expected,
unsuccessful.

Attempts to breach
temporal bubble to
synchronize time
difference
(Forge-built
chronometer) also
unsuccessful.

Darwin adaptations
imply that internal /
external time passage
is not consistent or
proportional.

Time debt inversion.

The Child, Horadar,
is encountered by
recon team, giving
Synch the ability to
teleport the team.
Horadar DNA preserved
in stasis pod for
future use.

Successful mapping of
quadrant one of the
Vault. Identified and
located food
processors, equipment
dumps and power
nodes.

Quadrants two and
three mapped.
Bypassed quadrant
four to proceed into
the inner ring.

Location of City
brain identified.

Child replication /
generation center
located.

Mutant incursion
detected.

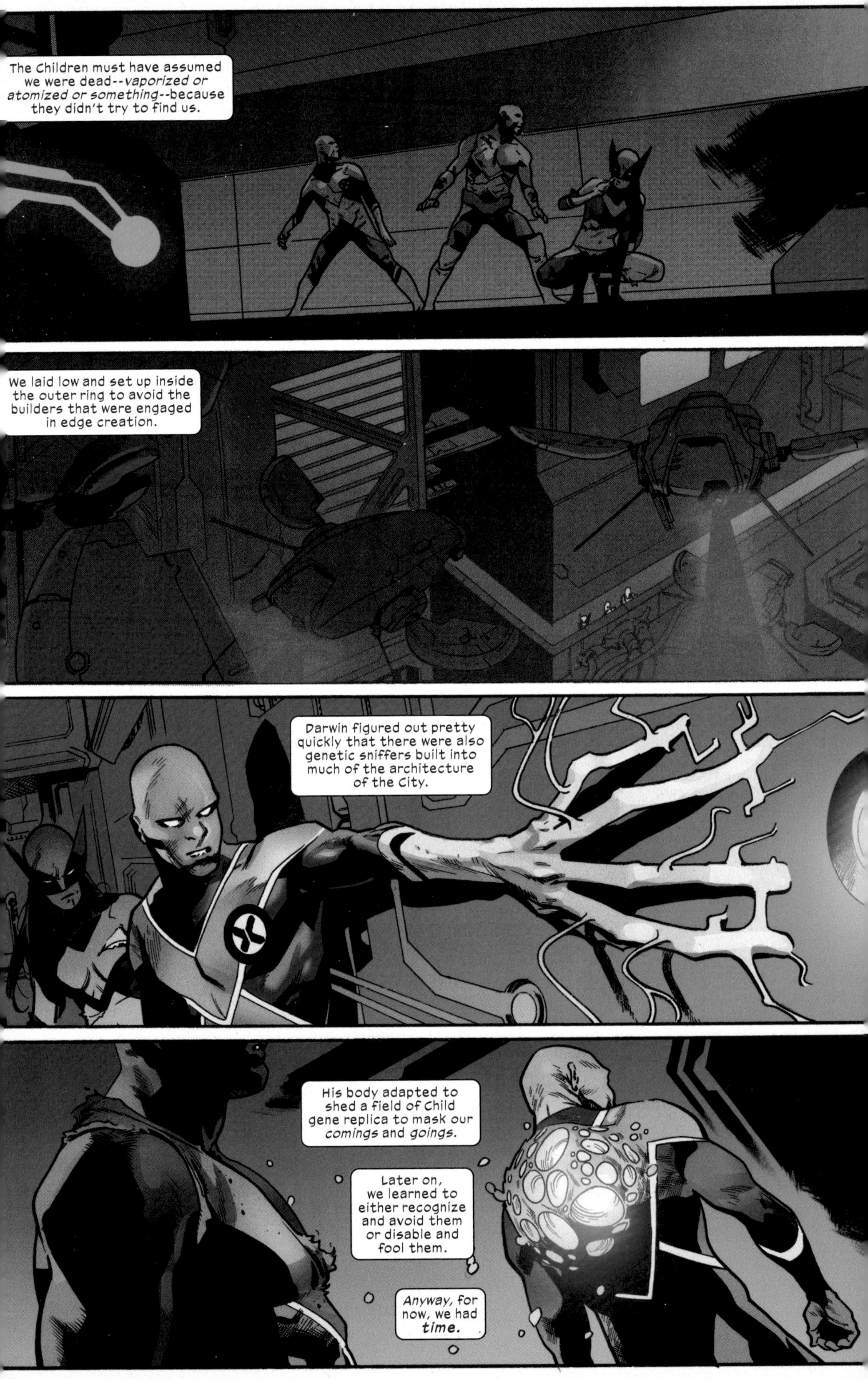

The Children must have assumed we were dead--*vaporized or atomized or something*--because they didn't try to find us.
We laid low and set up inside the outer ring to avoid the builders that were engaged in edge creation.
Darwin figured out pretty quickly that there were also genetic sniffers built into much of the architecture of the City.
His body adapted to shed a field of Child gene replica to mask our *comings* and *goings*.
Later on, we learned to either recognize and avoid them or disable and fool them.
Anyway, for now, we had ***time.***

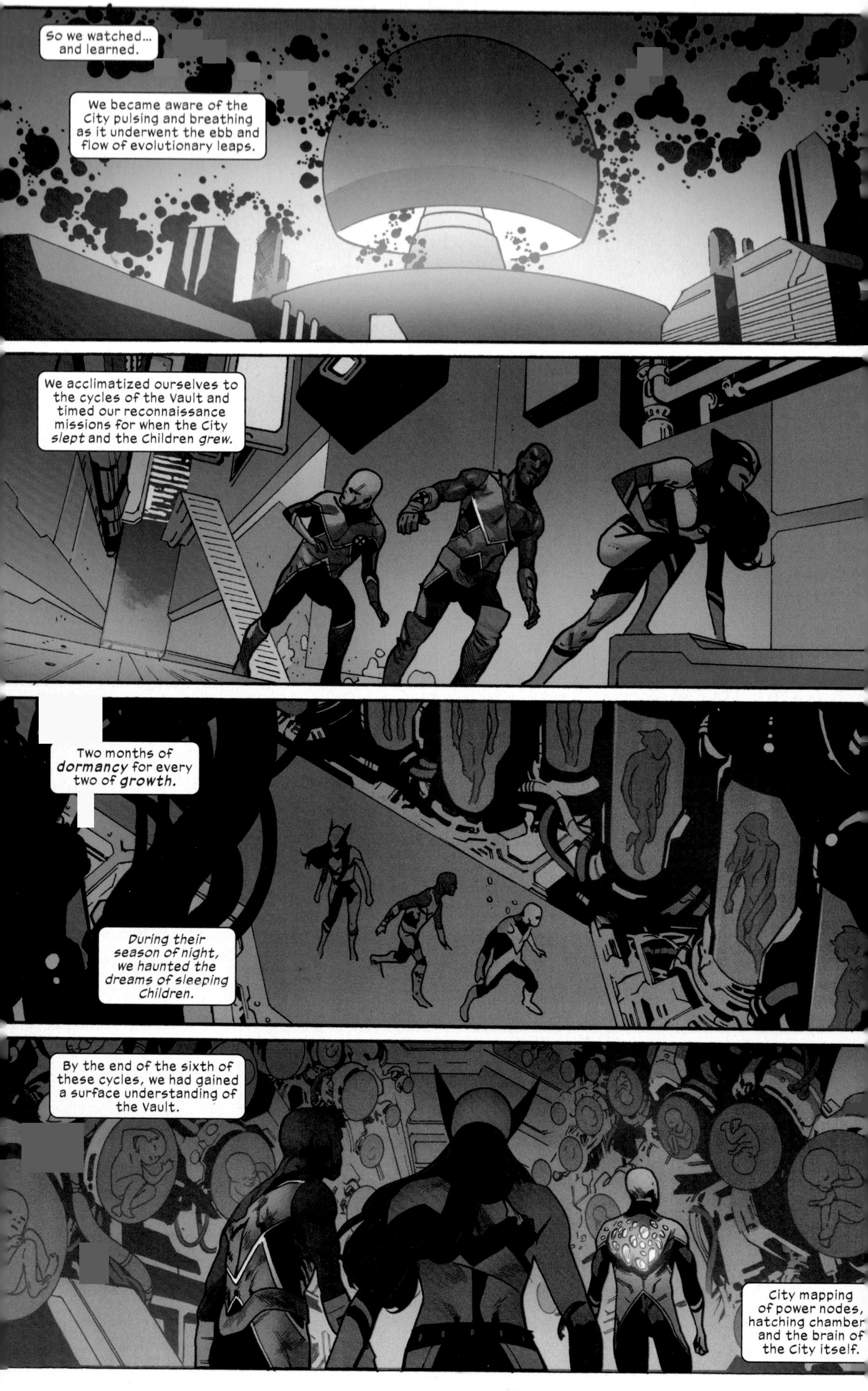
So we watched... and learned.
We became aware of the City pulsing and breathing as it underwent the ebb and flow of evolutionary leaps.
We acclimatized ourselves to the cycles of the Vault and timed our reconnaissance missions for when the City *slept* and the Children *grew.*
Two months of *dormancy* for every two of *growth.*
During their season of night, we haunted the dreams of sleeping Children.
By the end of the sixth of these cycles, we had gained a surface understanding of the Vault.
City mapping of power nodes, hatching chamber and the brain of the City itself.

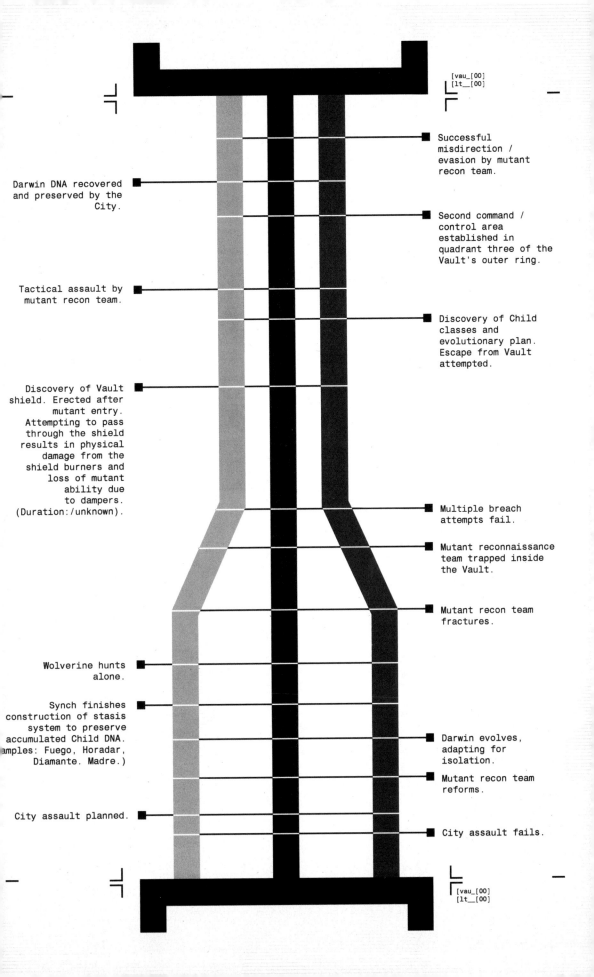

Successful misdirection / evasion by mutant recon team.

Darwin DNA recovered and preserved by the City.

Second command / control area established in quadrant three of the Vault's outer ring.

Tactical assault by mutant recon team.

Discovery of Child classes and evolutionary plan. Escape from Vault attempted.

Discovery of Vault shield. Erected after mutant entry. Attempting to pass through the shield results in physical damage from the shield burners and loss of mutant ability due to dampers. (Duration:/unknown).

Multiple breach attempts fail.

Mutant reconnaissance team trapped inside the Vault.

Mutant recon team fractures.

Wolverine hunts alone.

Synch finishes construction of stasis system to preserve accumulated Child DNA. amples: Fuego, Horadar, Diamante. Madre.)

Darwin evolves, adapting for isolation.

Mutant recon team reforms.

City assault planned.

City assault fails.

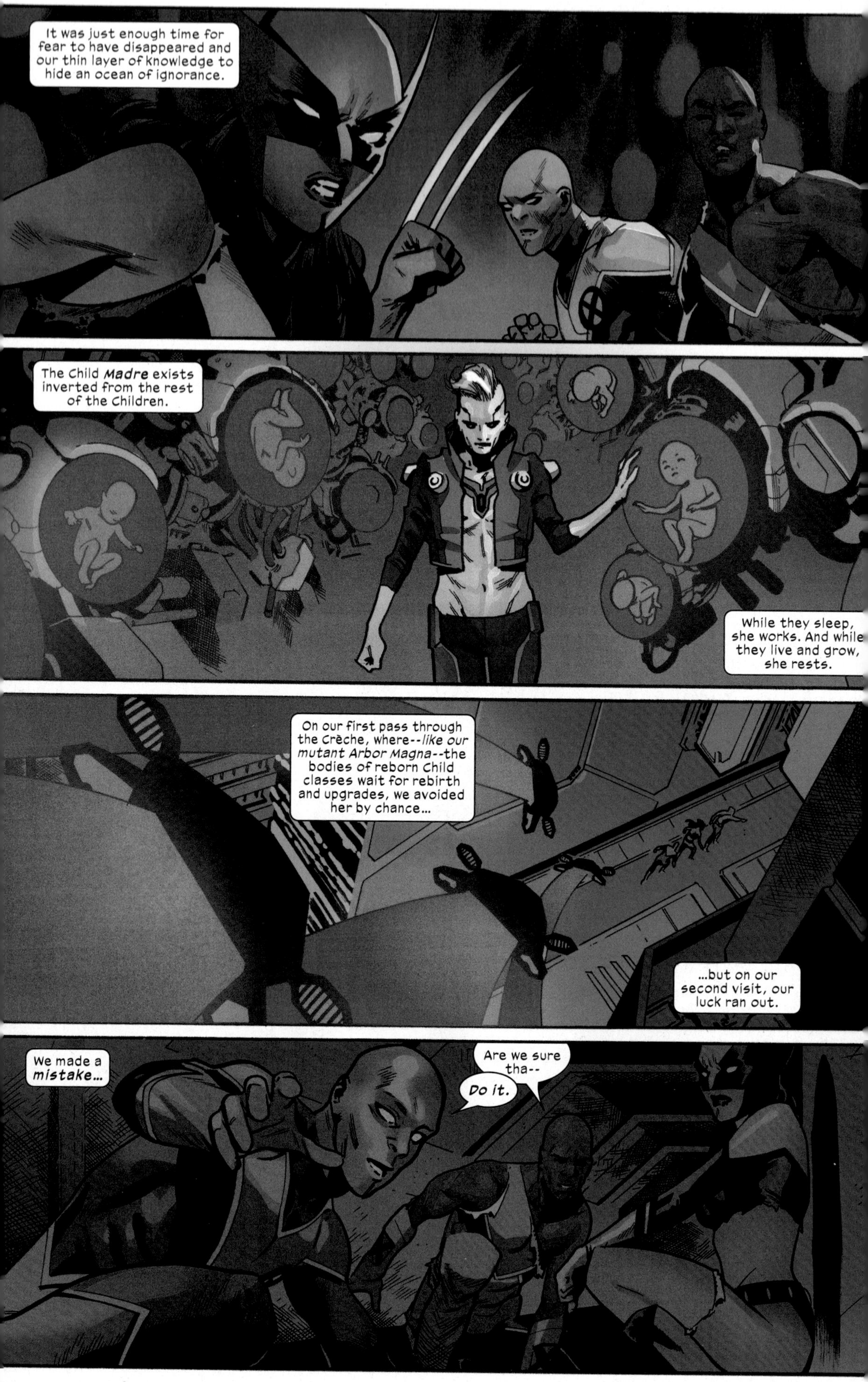

It was just enough time for fear to have disappeared and our thin layer of knowledge to hide an ocean of ignorance.
The Child *Madre* exists inverted from the rest of the Children.
While they sleep, she works. And while they live and grow, she rests.
On our first pass through the Crèche, where--*like our mutant Arbor Magna*--the bodies of reborn Child classes wait for rebirth and upgrades, we avoided her by chance...
...but on our second visit, our luck ran out.
We made a *mistake...*
Are we sure tha--
Do it.

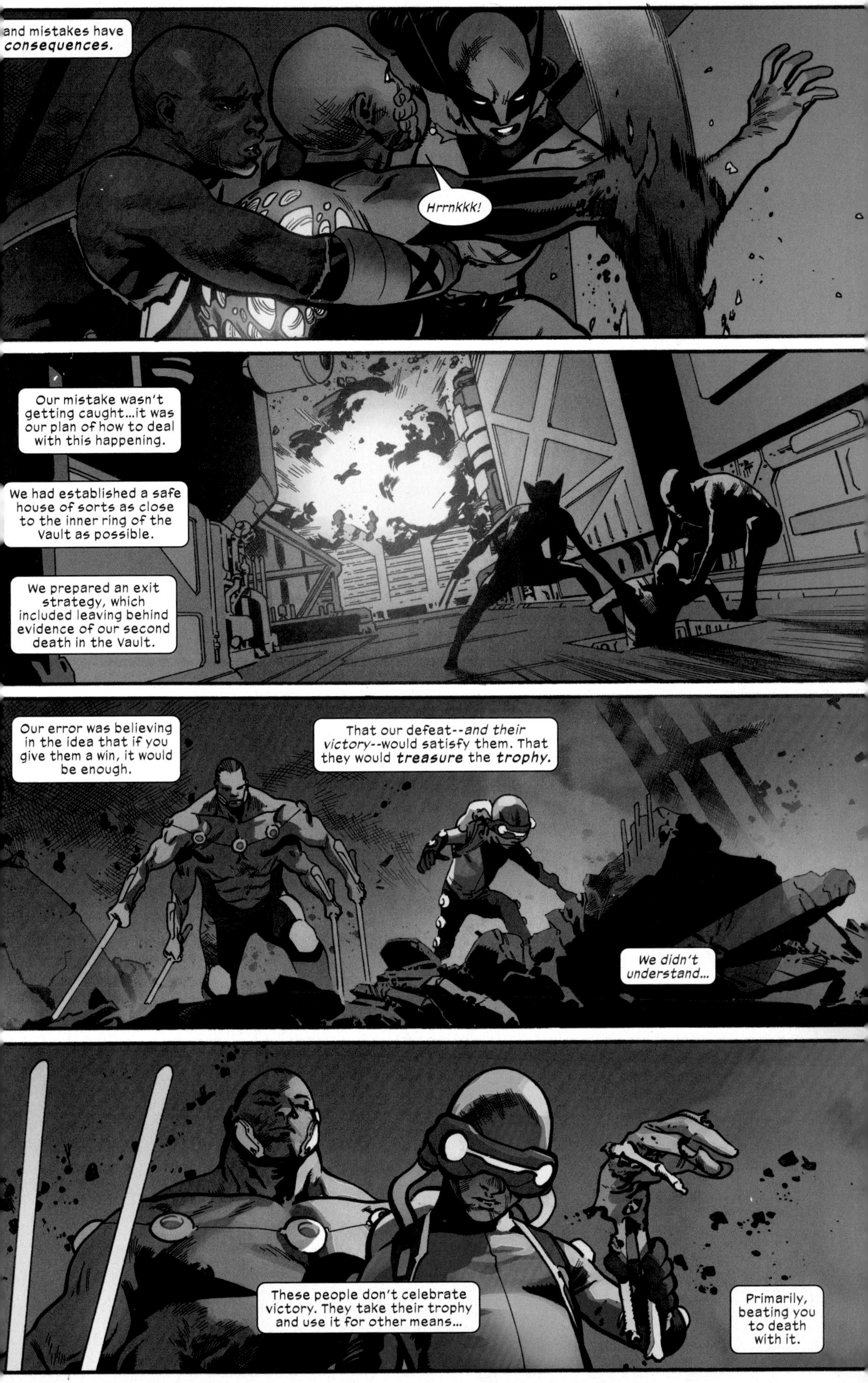
and mistakes have *consequences.*
Hrrnkkk!
Our mistake wasn't getting caught...it was our plan of how to deal with this happening.
We had established a safe house of sorts as close to the inner ring of the Vault as possible.
We prepared an exit strategy, which included leaving behind evidence of our second death in the Vault.
Our error was believing in the idea that if you give them a win, it would be enough.
That our defeat--*and their victory*--would satisfy them. That they would ***treasure*** the ***trophy.***
We didn't understand...
These people don't celebrate victory. They take their trophy and use it for other means...
Primarily, beating you to death with it.

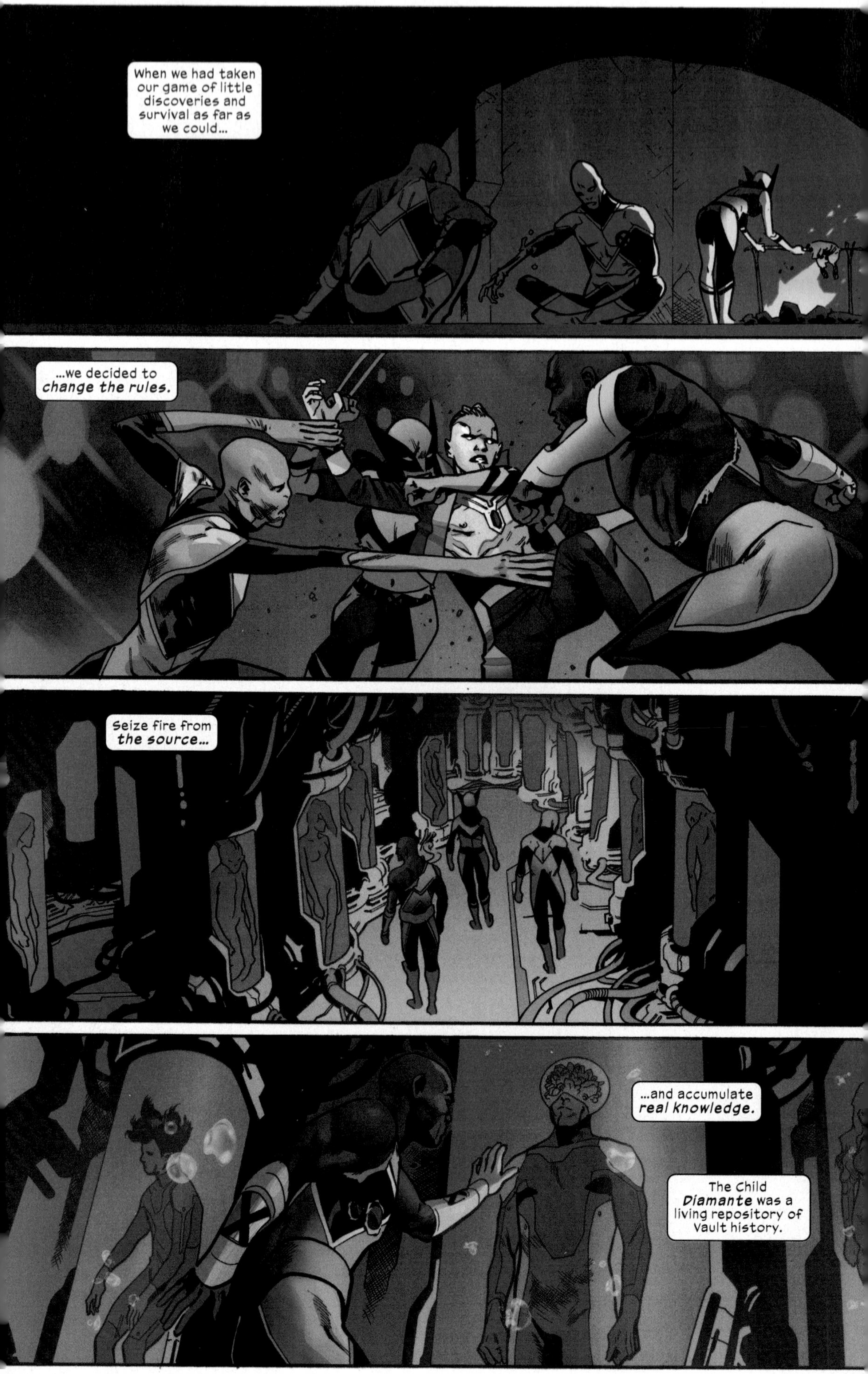
When we had taken our game of little discoveries and survival as far as we could...
...we decided to *change the rules.*
Seize fire from *the source...*
...and accumulate *real knowledge.*
The Child *Diamante* was a living repository of Vault history.

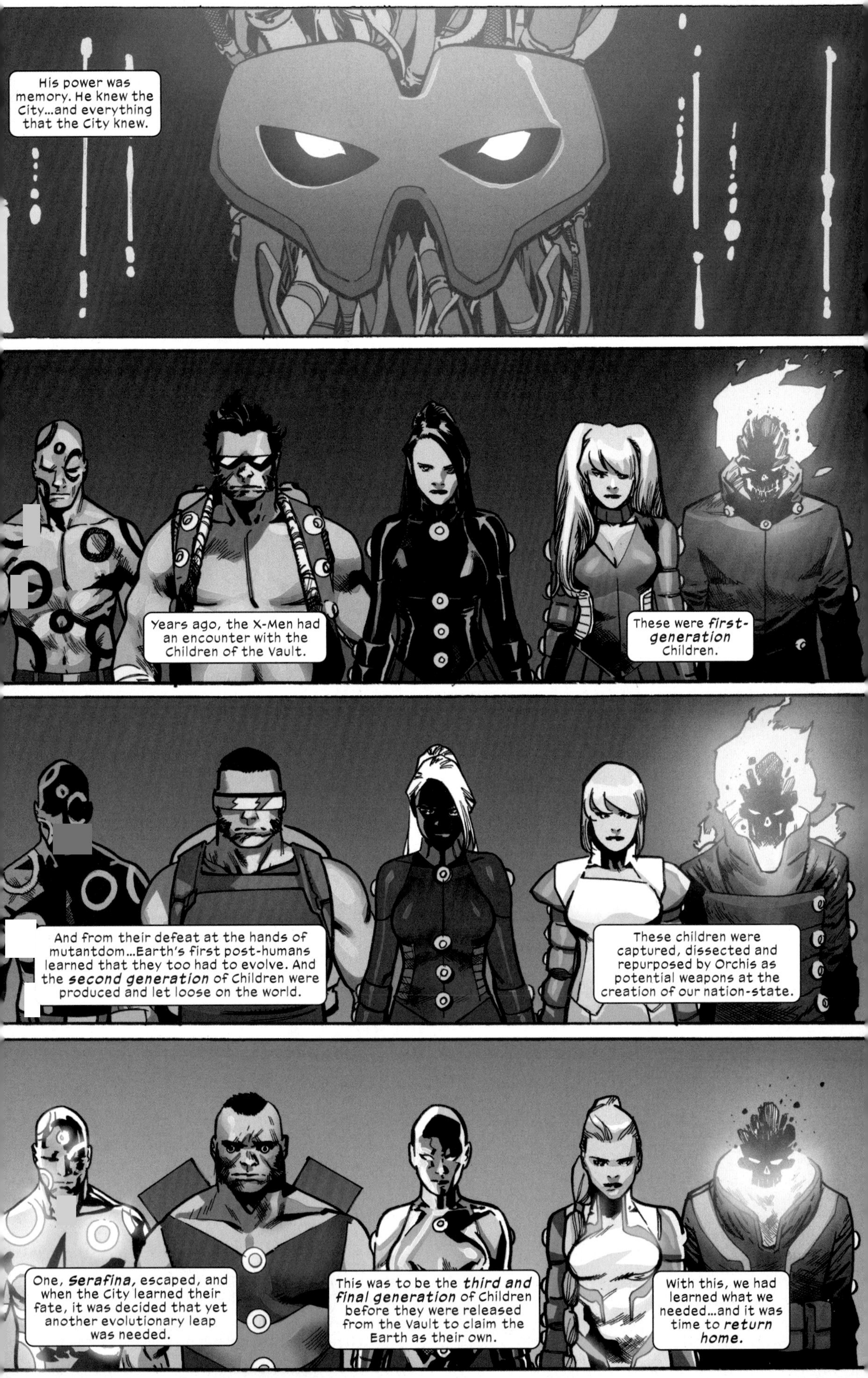
His power was memory. He knew the City...and everything that the City knew.
Years ago, the X-Men had an encounter with the Children of the Vault.
These were *first-generation* Children.
And from their defeat at the hands of mutantdom...Earth's first post-humans learned that they too had to evolve. And the *second generation* of Children were produced and let loose on the world.
These children were captured, dissected and repurposed by Orchis as potential weapons at the creation of our nation-state.
One, *Serafina,* escaped, and when the City learned their fate, it was decided that yet another evolutionary leap was needed.
This was to be the *third and final generation* of Children before they were released from the Vault to claim the Earth as their own.
With this, we had learned what we needed...and it was time to *return home.*

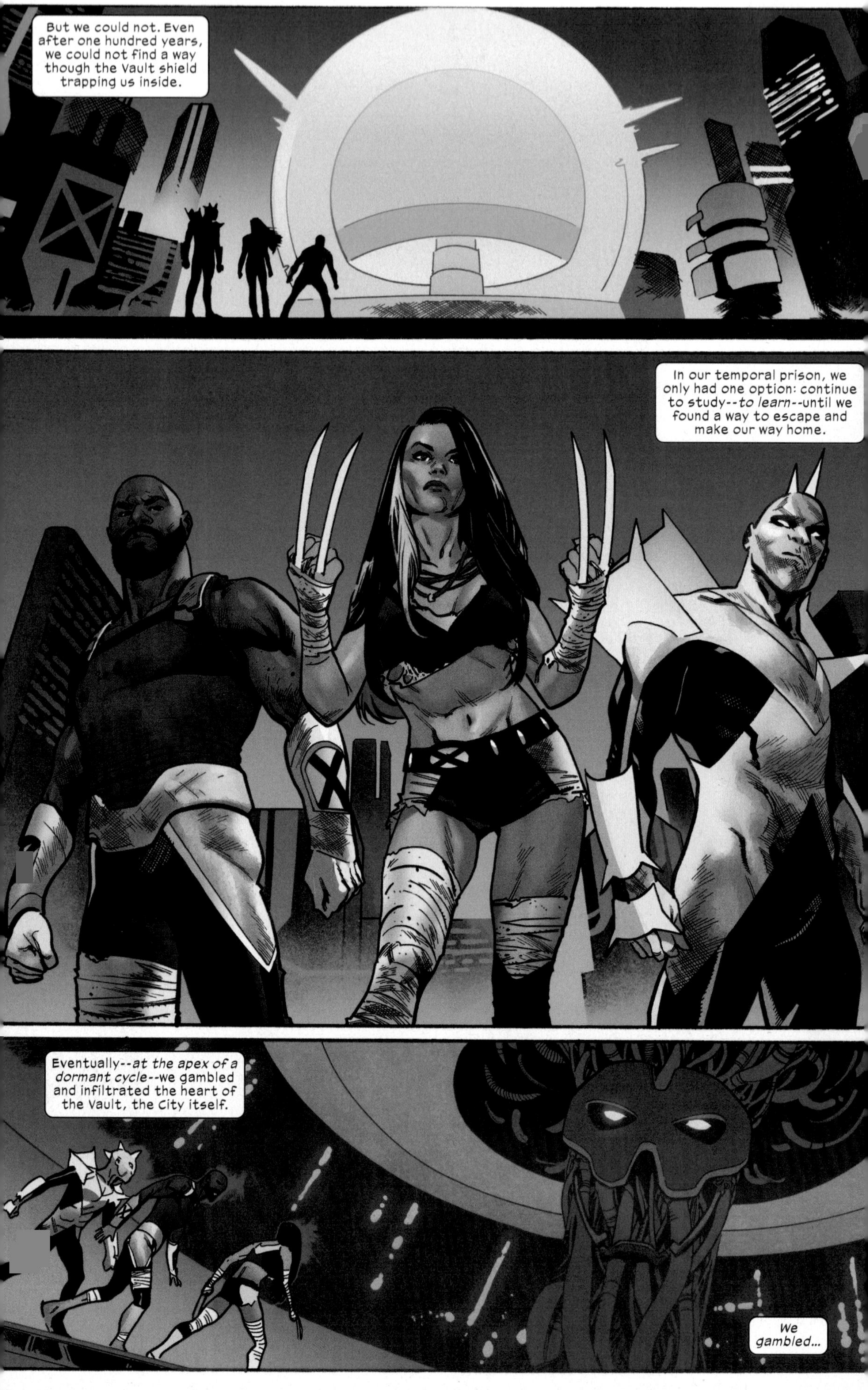
But we could not. Even after one hundred years, we could not find a way though the Vault shield trapping us inside.
In our temporal prison, we only had one option: continue to study--*to learn*--until we found a way to escape and make our way home.
Eventually--*at the apex of a dormant cycle*--we gambled and infiltrated the heart of the Vault, the City itself.
We gambled...

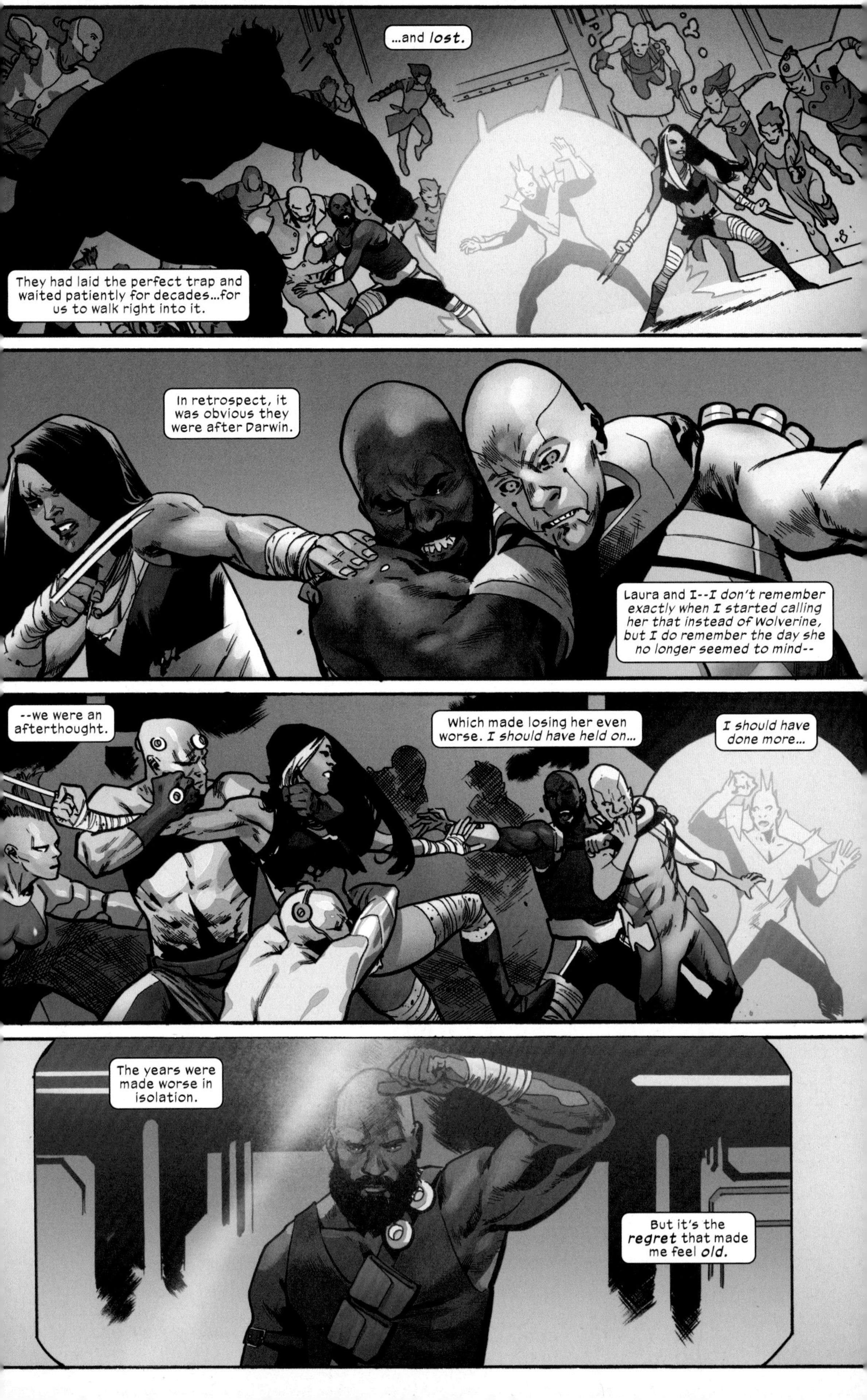
...and *lost.*
They had laid the perfect trap and waited patiently for decades...for us to walk right into it.
In retrospect, it was obvious they were after Darwin.
Laura and I--*I don't remember exactly when I started calling her that instead of Wolverine, but I do remember the day she no longer seemed to mind--*
--we were an afterthought.
Which made losing her even worse. *I should have held on...*
I should have done more...
The years were made worse in isolation.
But it's the ***regret*** that made me feel ***old.***

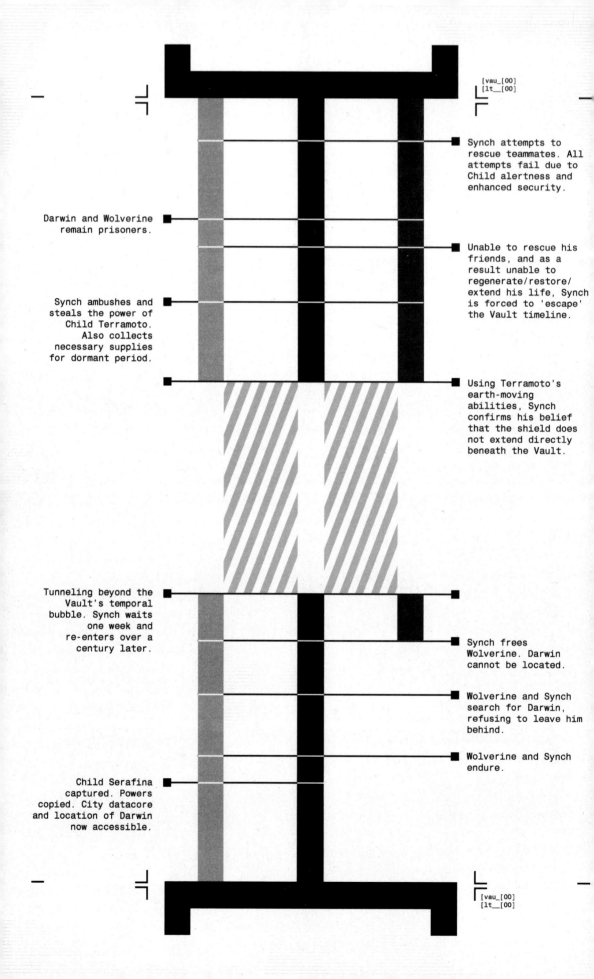

[vau_[00]
[1t__[00]

Synch attempts to
rescue teammates. All
attempts fail due to
Child alertness and
enhanced security.

Darwin and Wolverine
remain prisoners.

Unable to rescue his
friends, and as a
result unable to
regenerate/restore/
extend his life, Synch
is forced to 'escape'
the Vault timeline.

Synch ambushes and
steals the power of
Child Terramoto.
Also collects
necessary supplies
for dormant period.

Using Terramoto's
earth-moving
abilities, Synch
confirms his belief
that the shield does
not extend directly
beneath the Vault.

Tunneling beyond the
Vault's temporal
bubble. Synch waits
one week and
re-enters over a
century later.

Synch frees
Wolverine. Darwin
cannot be located.

Wolverine and Synch
search for Darwin,
refusing to leave him
behind.

Wolverine and Synch
endure.

Child Serafina
captured. Powers
copied. City datacore
and location of Darwin
now accessible.

[vau_[00]
[1t__[00]

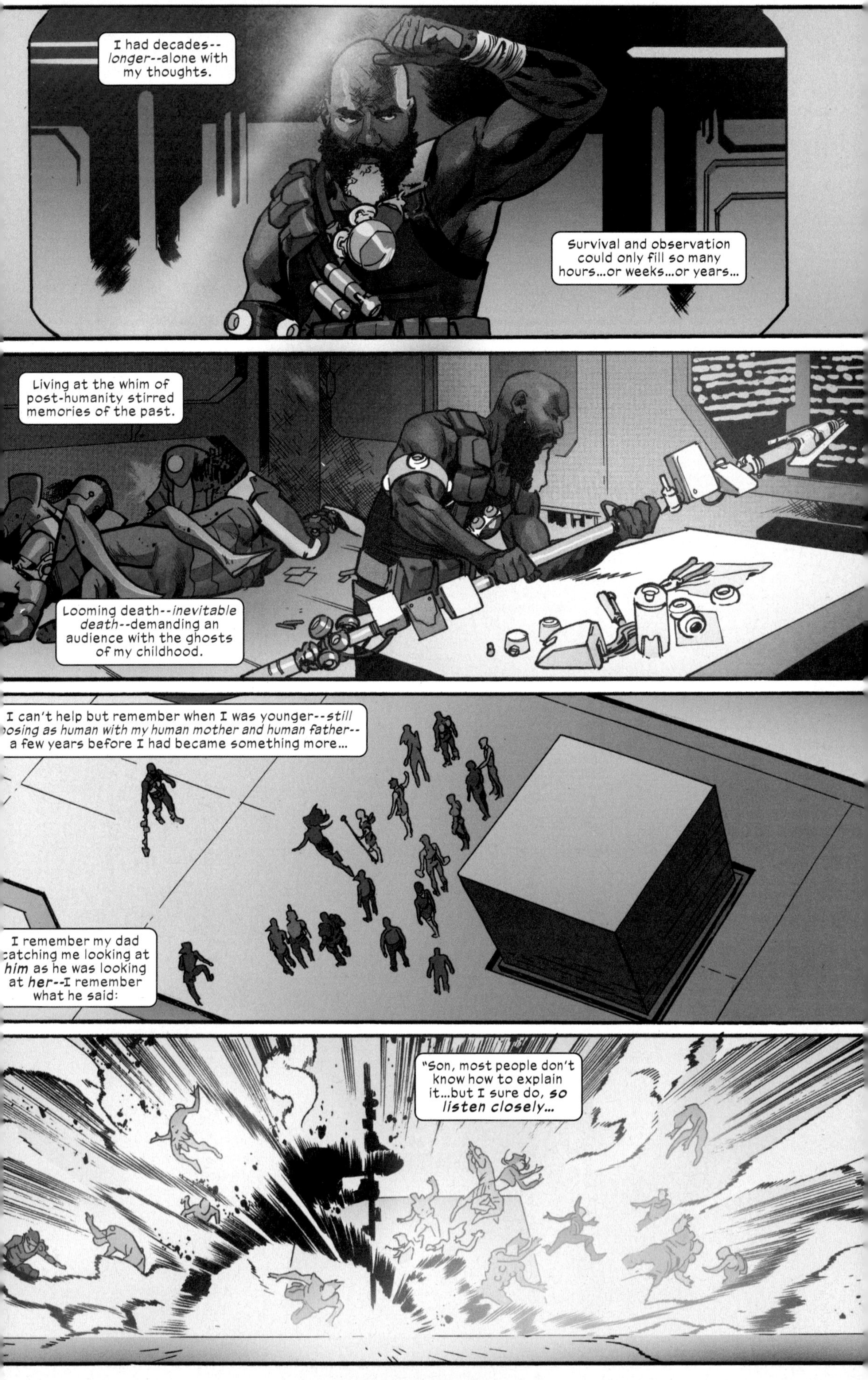

I had decades--*longer*--alone with my thoughts.
Survival and observation could only fill so many hours...or weeks...or years...
Living at the whim of post-humanity stirred memories of the past.
Looming death--*inevitable death*--demanding an audience with the ghosts of my childhood.
I can't help but remember when I was younger--*still* posing as human with my human mother and human father--a few years before I had became something more...
I remember my dad catching me looking at *him* as he was looking at *her*--I remember what he said:
"Son, most people don't know how to explain it...but I sure do, *so listen closely...*

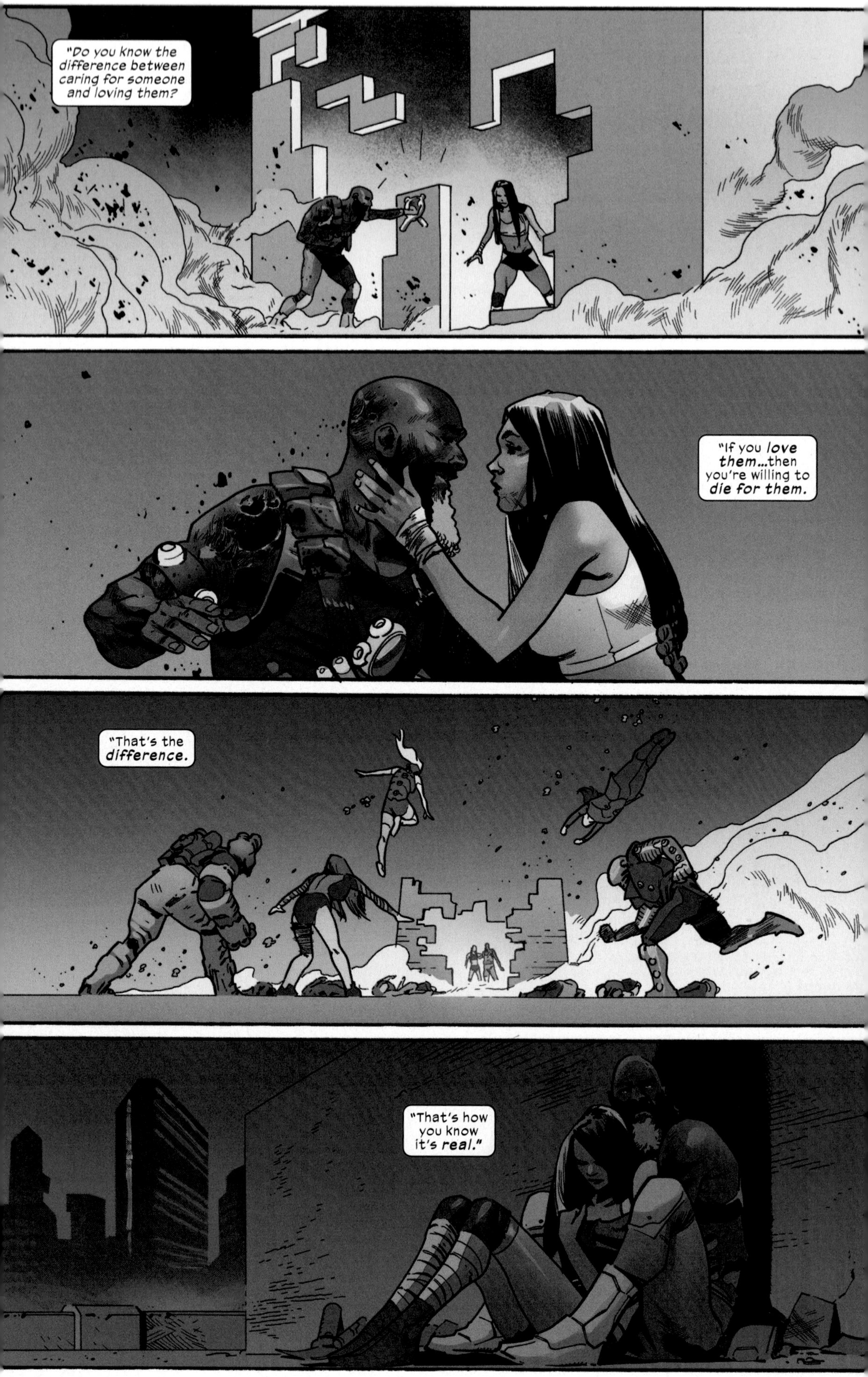
"Do you know the difference between caring for someone and loving them?
"If you love them...then you're willing to die for them.
"That's the difference.
"That's how you know it's real."

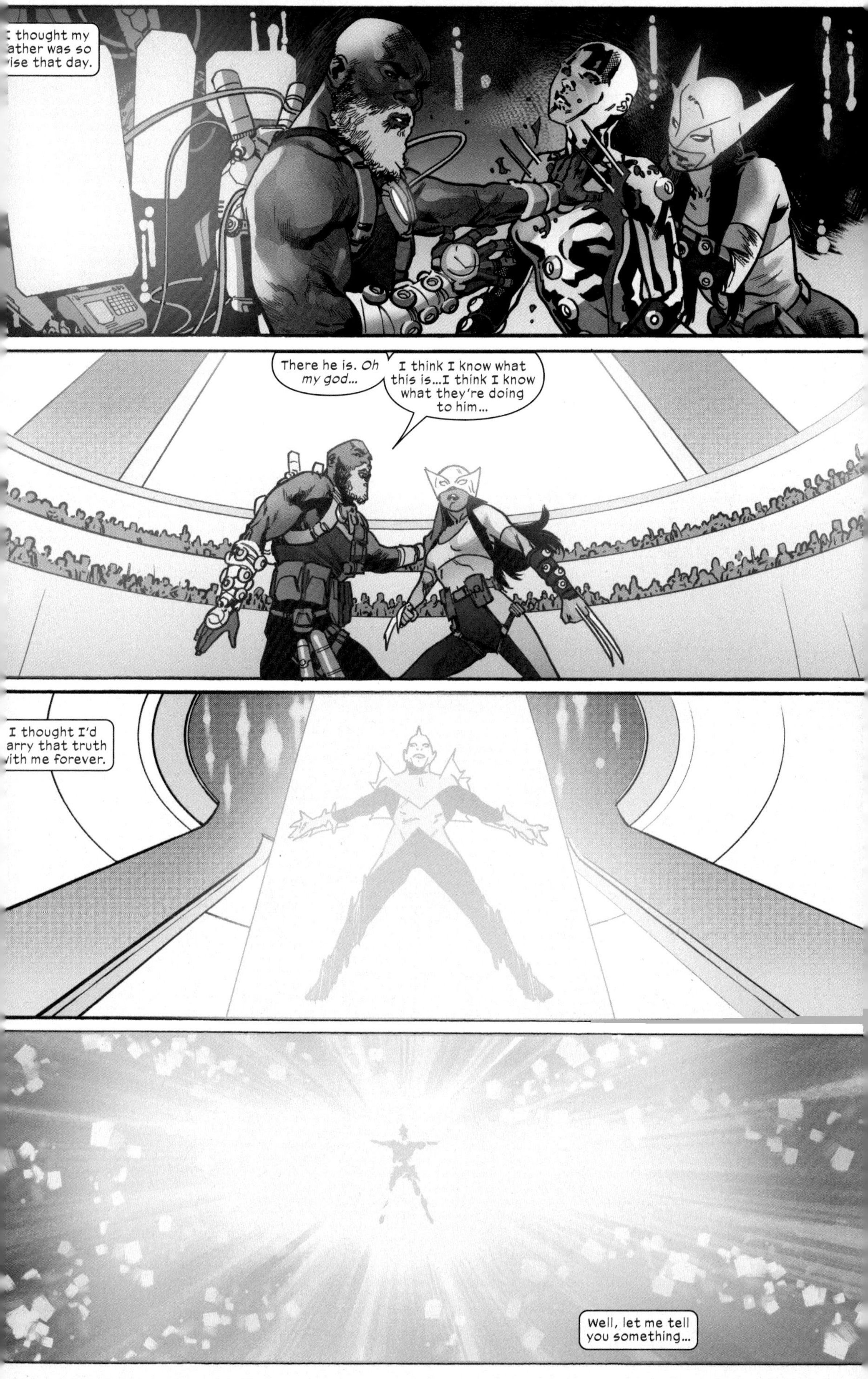
I thought my
ather was so
ise that day.
There he is. *Oh my god...*
I think I know what this is...I think I know what they're doing to him...
I thought I'd
arry that truth
ith me forever.
Well, let me tell you something...

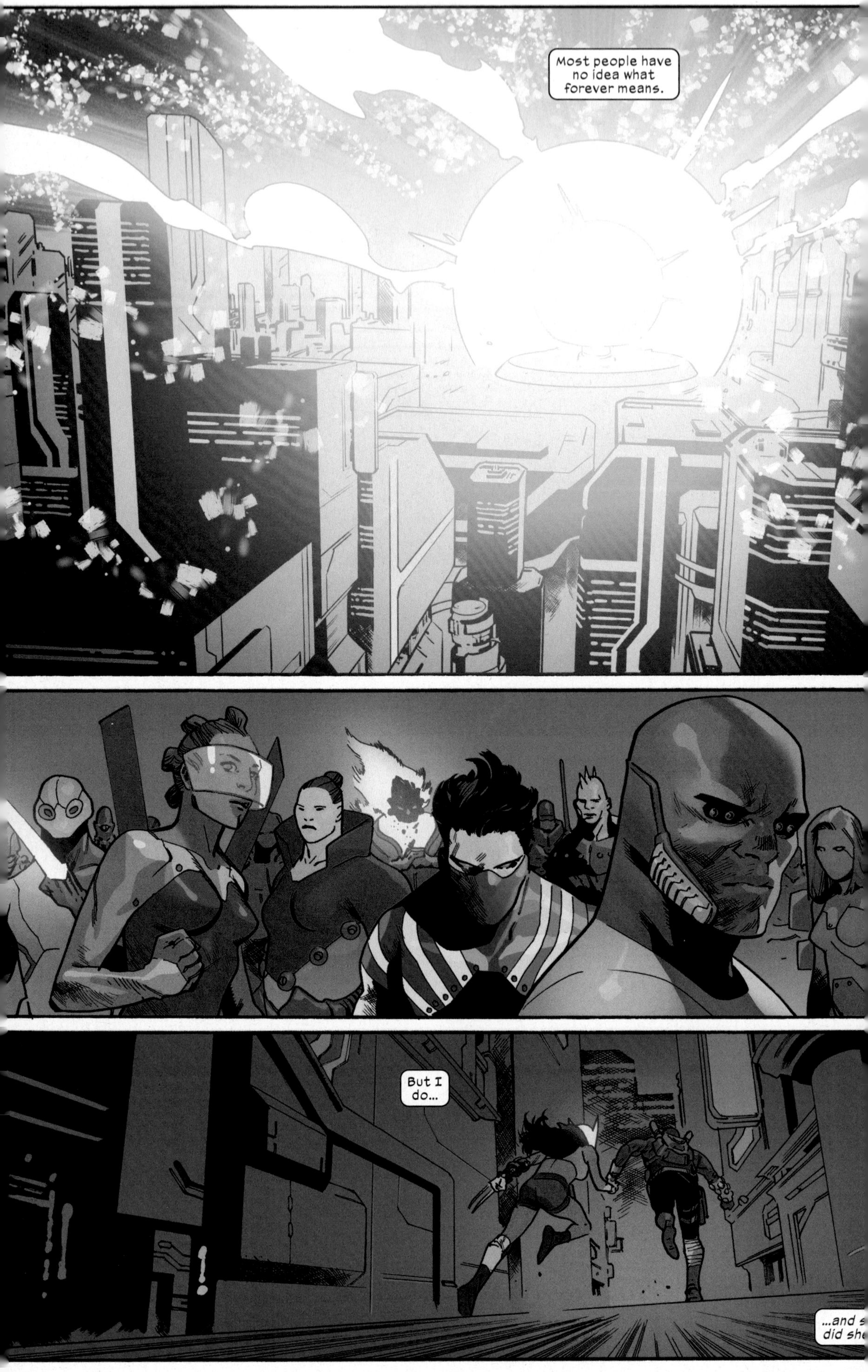
Most people have no idea what forever means.
But I do...
...and s
did sh

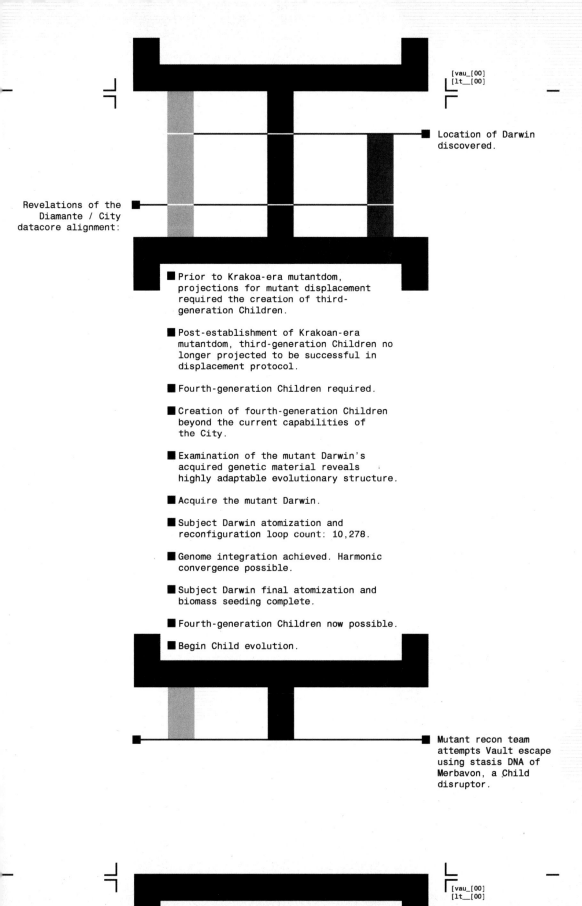

Location of Darwin
discovered.

Revelations of the
Diamante / City
datacore alignment:

■ Prior to Krakoa-era mutantdom,
projections for mutant displacement
required the creation of third-
generation Children.

■ Post-establishment of Krakoan-era
mutantdom, third-generation Children no
longer projected to be successful in
displacement protocol.

■ Fourth-generation Children required.

■ Creation of fourth-generation Children
beyond the current capabilities of
the City.

■ Examination of the mutant Darwin's
acquired genetic material reveals
highly adaptable evolutionary structure.

■ Acquire the mutant Darwin.

■ Subject Darwin atomization and
reconfiguration loop count: 10,278.

■ Genome integration achieved. Harmonic
convergence possible.

■ Subject Darwin final atomization and
biomass seeding complete.

■ Fourth-generation Children now possible.

■ Begin Child evolution.

Mutant recon team
attempts Vault escape
using stasis DNA of
Merbavon, a Child
disruptor.

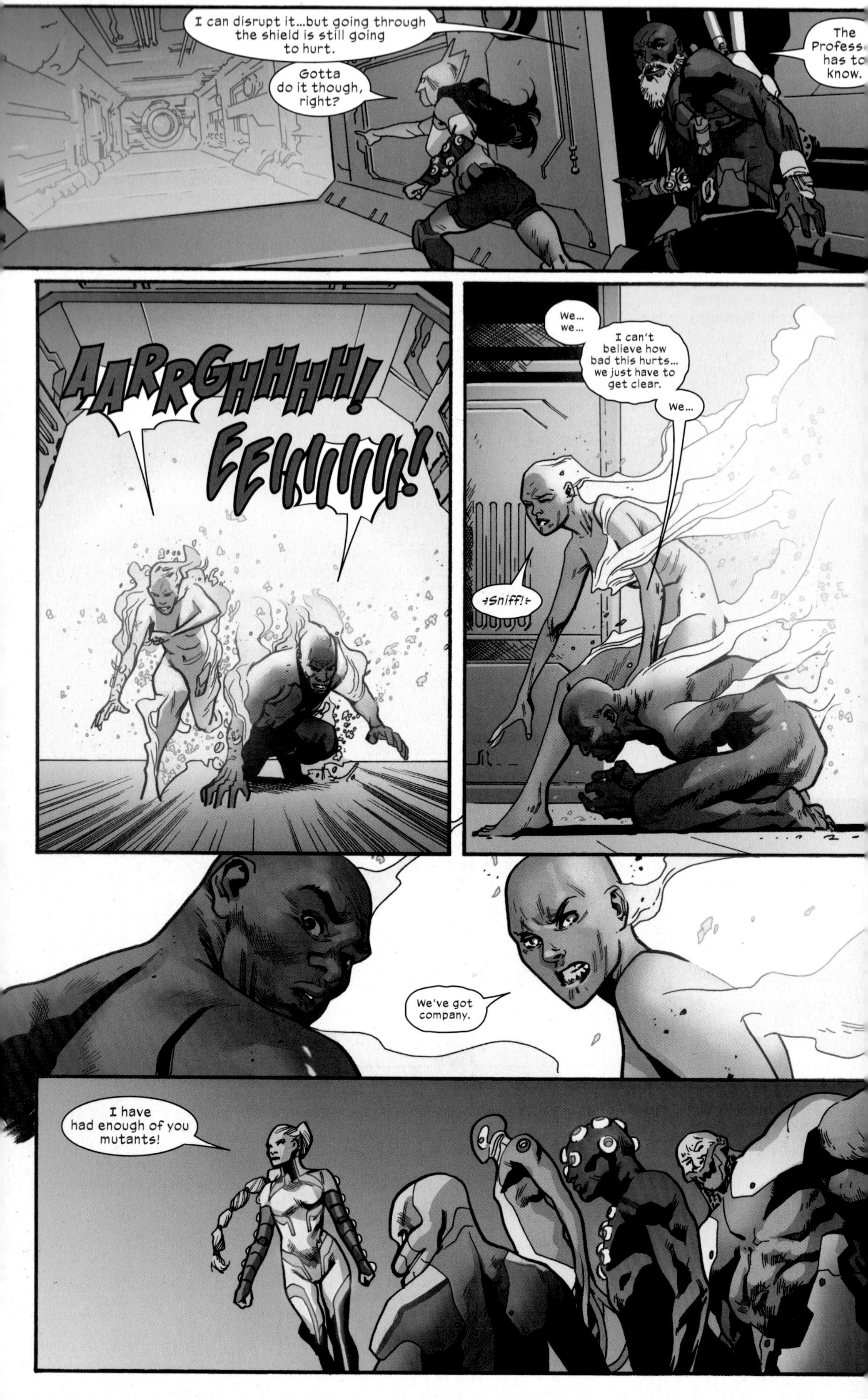
I can disrupt it...but going through the shield is still going to hurt.
Gotta do it though, right?
The Profess has to know.
AARRGHHHHH!
EEIIIIIII!
We... we...
I can't believe how bad this hurts... we just have to get clear.
We...
Sniff!
We've got company.
I have had enough of you mutants!

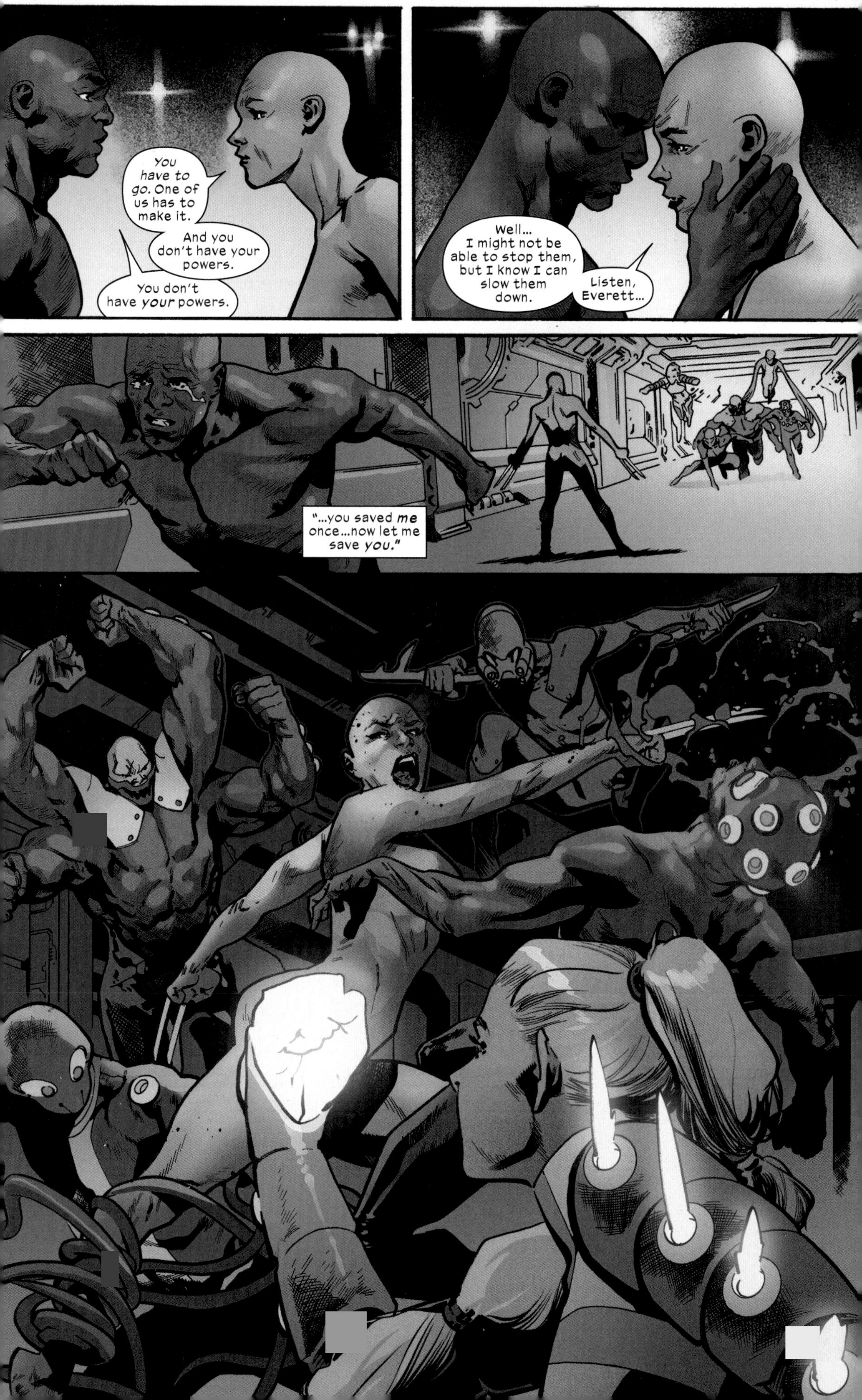
You have to go. One of us has to make it.
And you don't have your powers.
You don't have *your* powers.
Well... I might not be able to stop them, but I know I can slow them down.
Listen, Everett...
"...you saved *me* once...now let me save *you*."

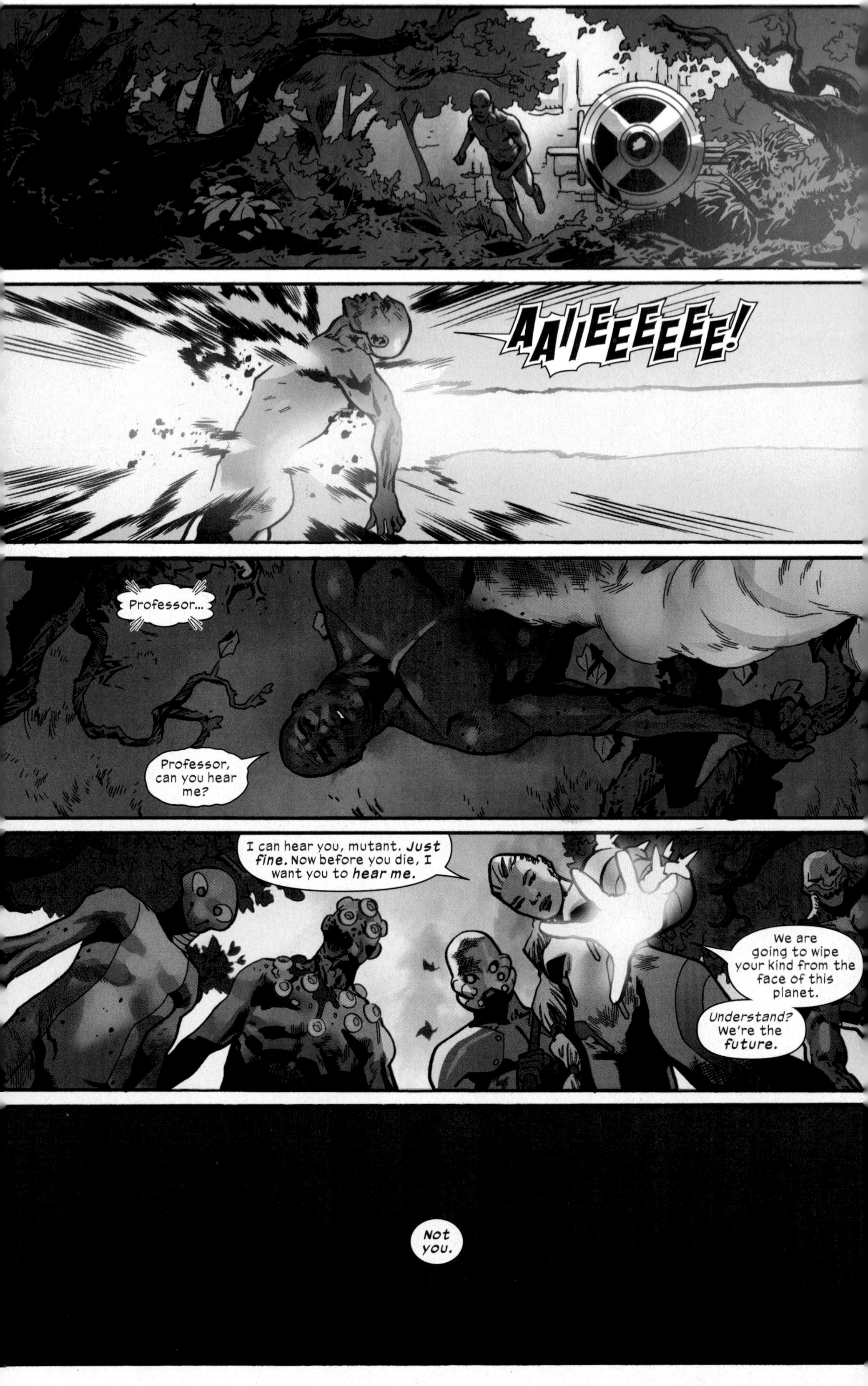
AAIIEEEEEE!
Professor...
Professor, can you hear me?
I can hear you, mutant. Just fine. Now before you die, I want you to hear me.
We are going to wipe your kind from the face of this planet.
Understand? We're the future.
Not you.

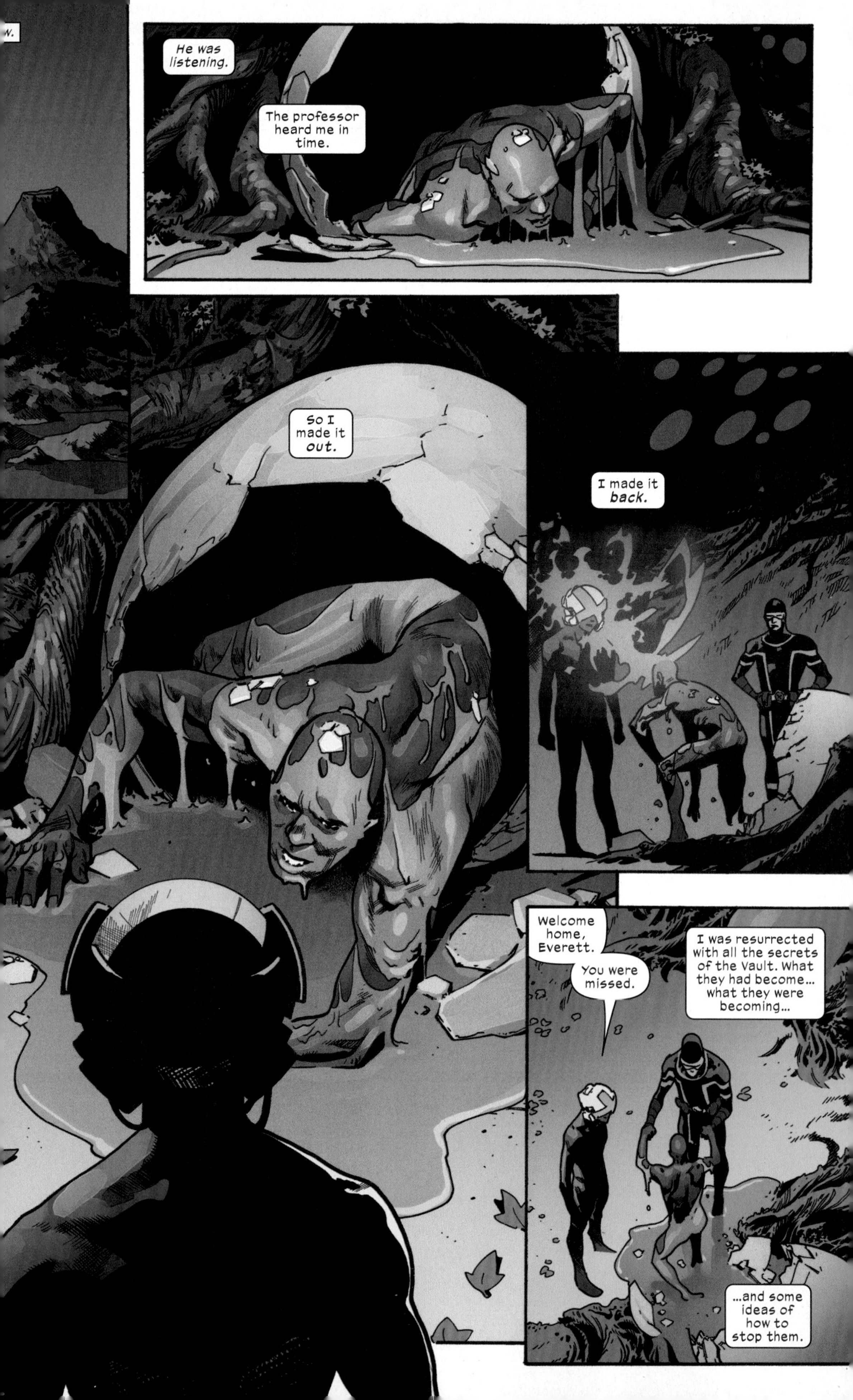
N.
He was listening.
The professor heard me in time.
So I made it *out.*
I made it *back.*
Welcome home, Everett.
You were missed.
I was resurrected with all the secrets of the Vault. What they had become... what they were becoming...
...and some ideas of how to stop them.

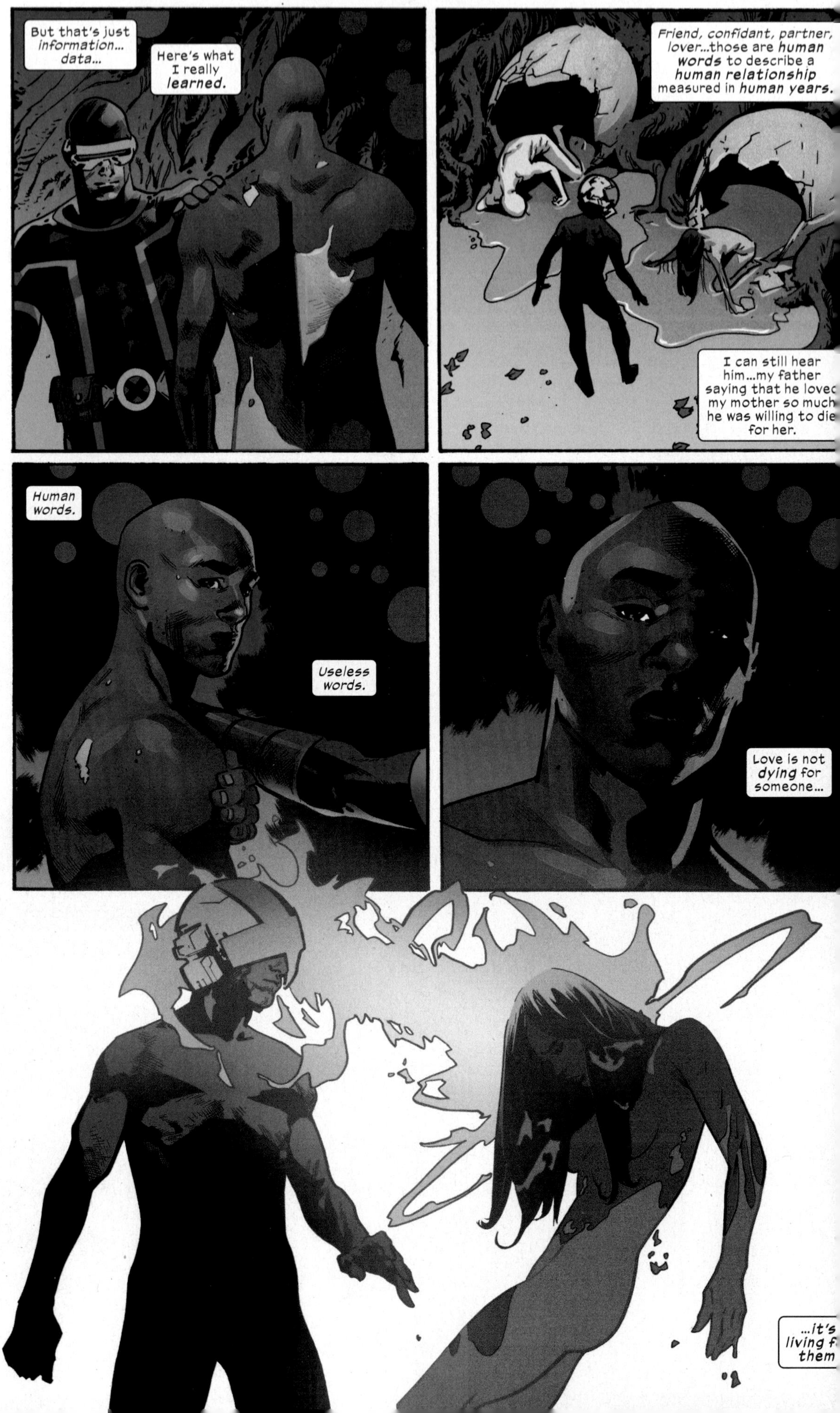

But that's just information... data...
Here's what I really learned.
Friend, confidant, partner, lover...those are human words to describe a human relationship measured in human years.
I can still hear him...my father saying that he lovec my mother so much he was willing to die for her.
Human words.
Useless words.
Love is not dying for someone...
...it's living f them

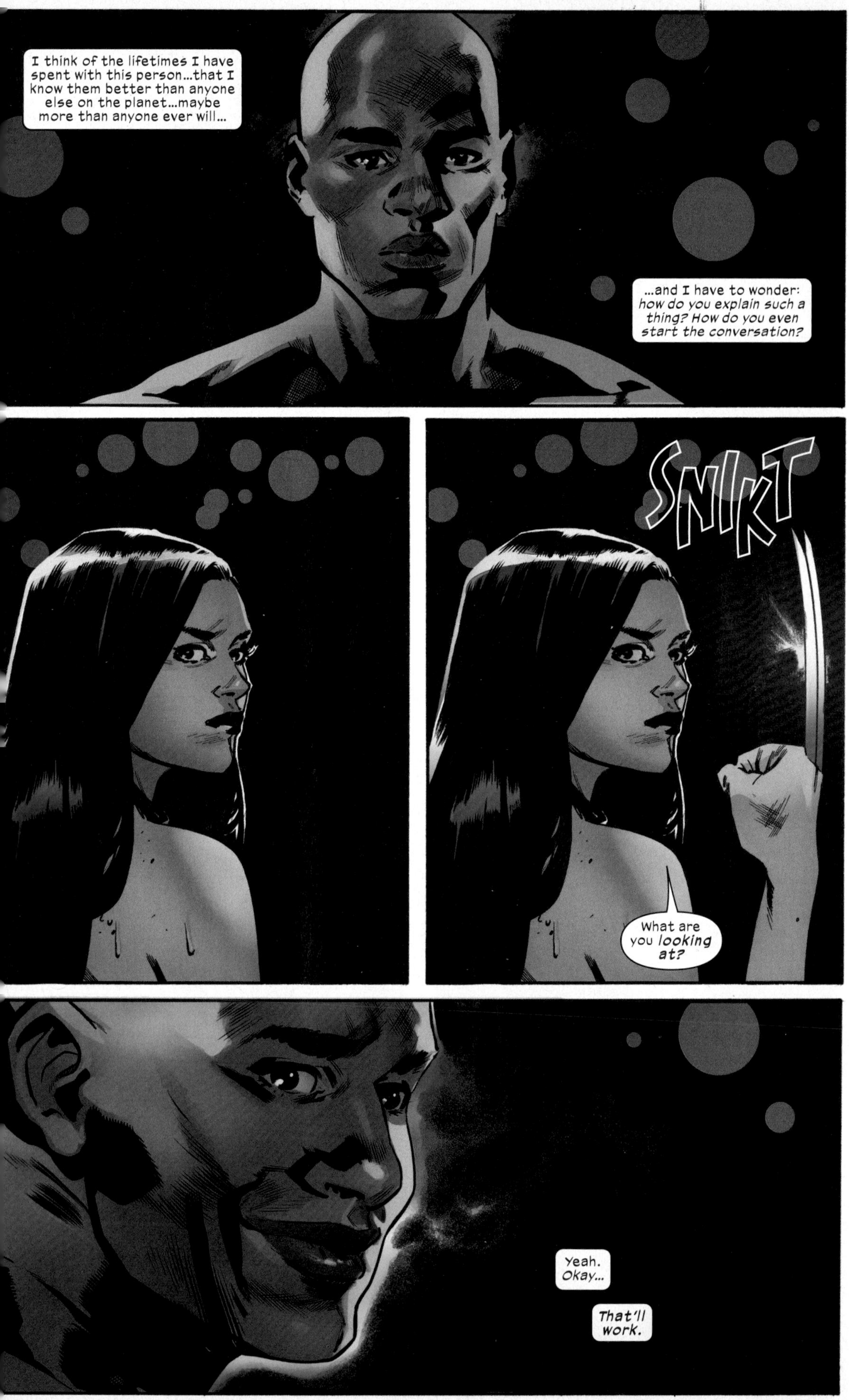
I think of the lifetimes I have spent with this person...that I know them better than anyone else on the planet...maybe more than anyone ever will...
...and I have to wonder: how do you explain such a thing? How do you even start the conversation?
SNIKT
What are you looking at?
Yeah. Okay...
That'll work.

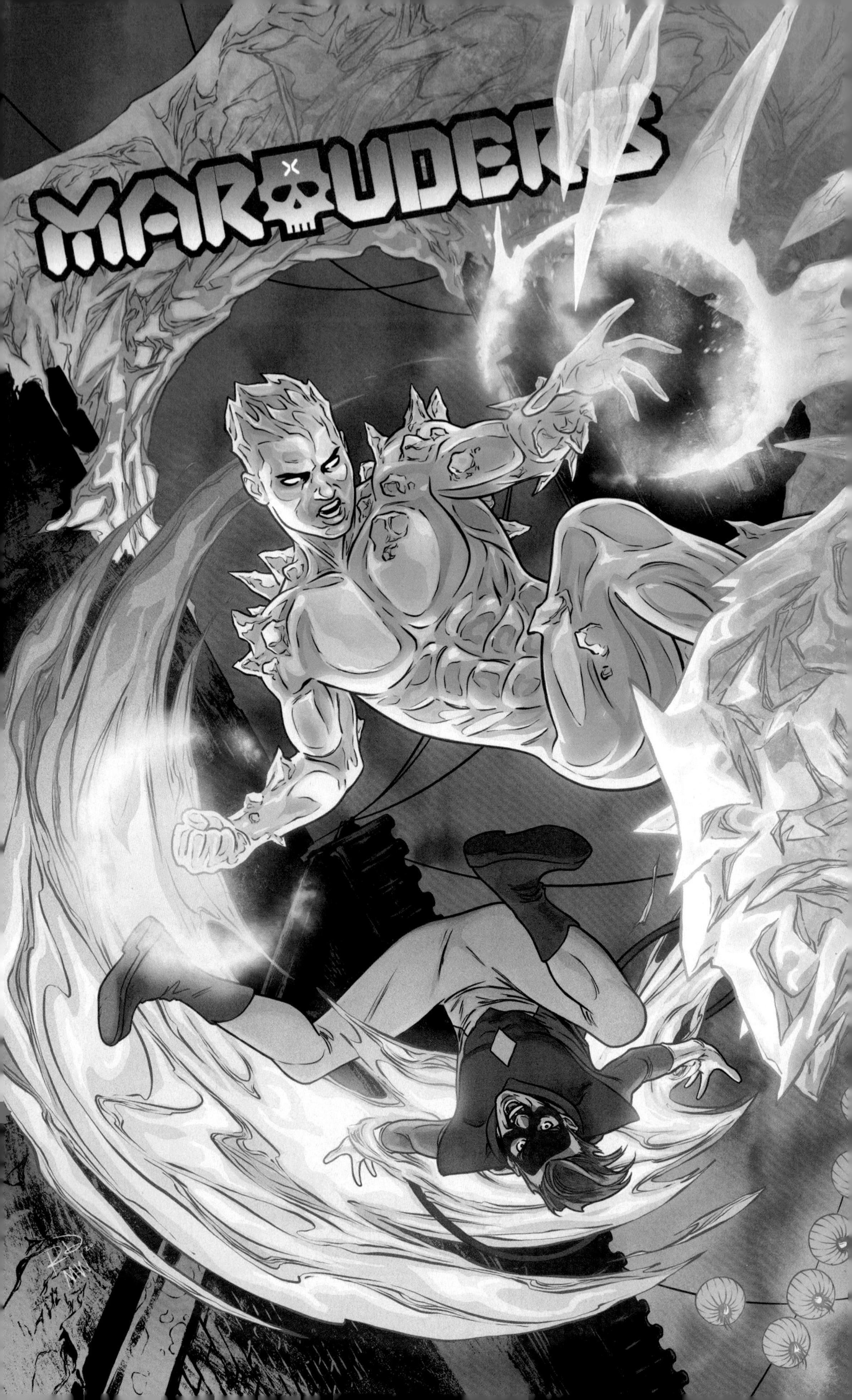
MARAUDERS

[mara.....[1.8]
[uders....[1.8]

Madripoor has earned its lawless and corrupt reputation, and its people wouldn't have it any other way.

-- UNITED NATIONS AMBASSADOR (WISHES TO REMAIN ANONYMOUS)

[mara.....[1.8]
[uders....[1.8]

[marauders_18]

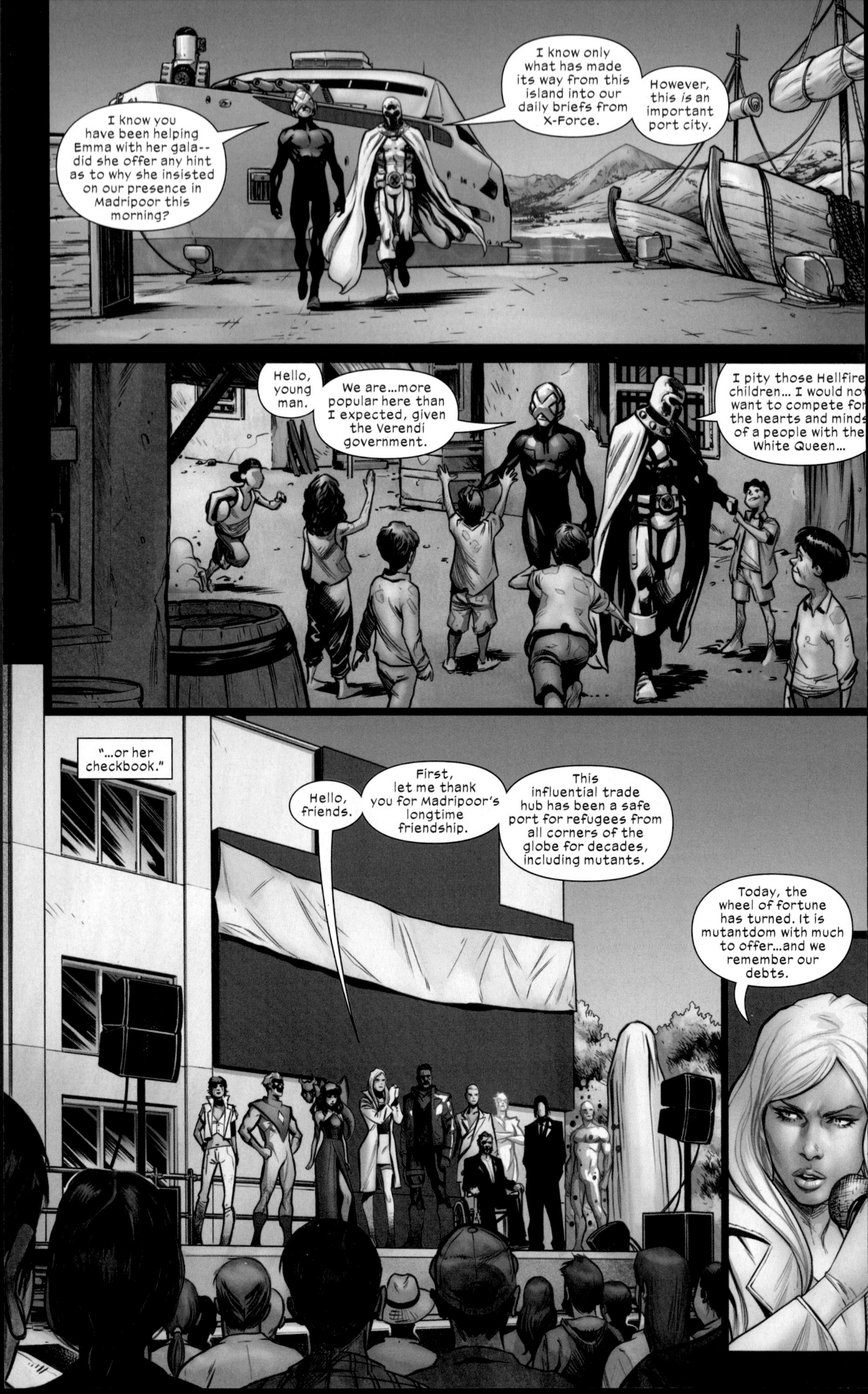
I know you have been helping Emma with her gala--did she offer any hint as to why she insisted on our presence in Madripoor this morning?
I know only what has made its way from this island into our daily briefs from X-Force.
However, this *is* an important port city.
Hello, young man.
We are...more popular here than I expected, given the Verendi government.
I pity those Hellfire children... I would not want to compete for the hearts and minds of a people with the White Queen...
"...or her checkbook."
Hello, friends.
First, let me thank you for Madripoor's longtime friendship.
This influential trade hub has been a safe port for refugees from all corners of the globe for decades, including mutants.
Today, the wheel of fortune has turned. It is mutantdom with much to offer...and we remember our debts.

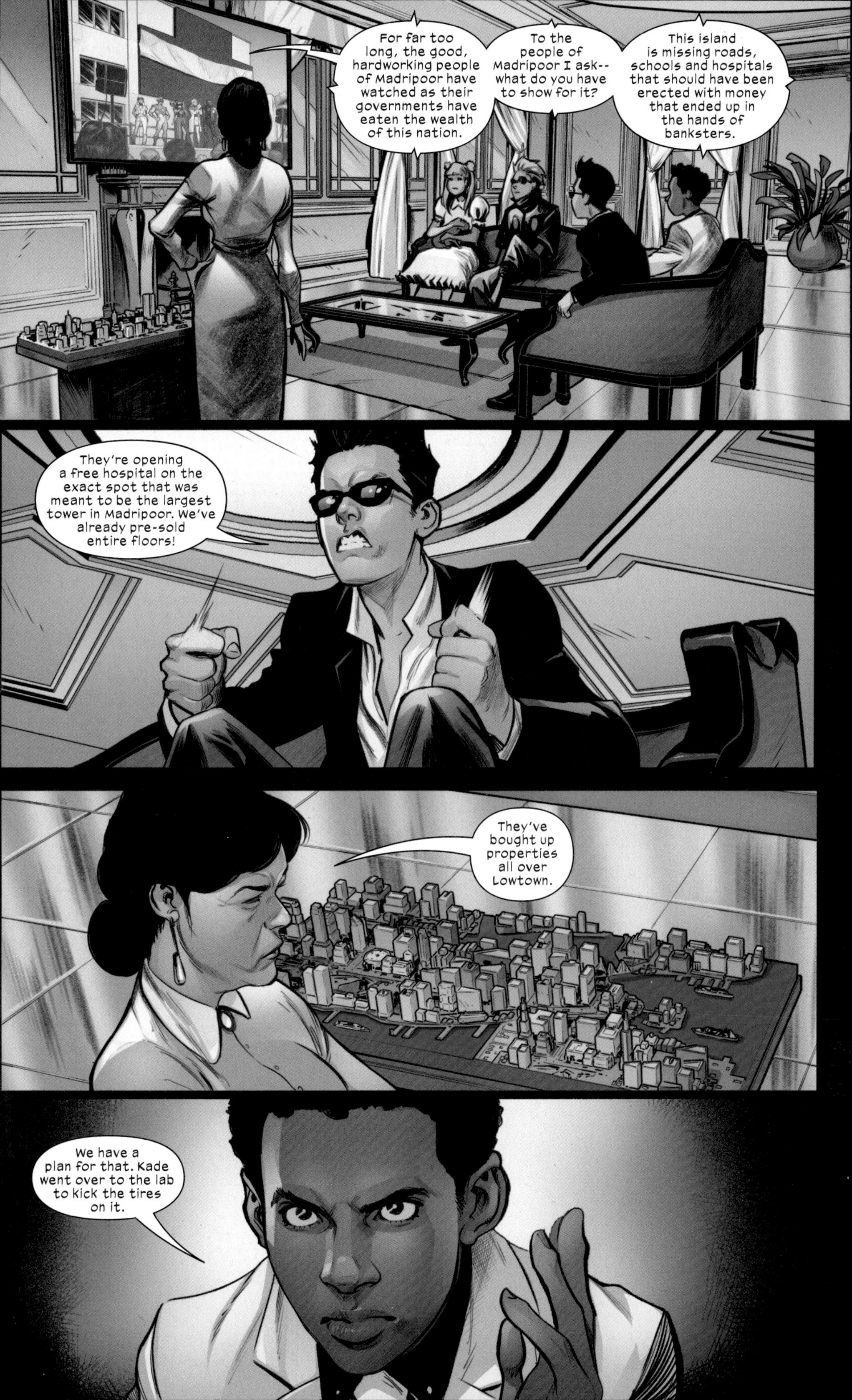
For far too long, the good, hardworking people of Madripoor have watched as their governments have eaten the wealth of this nation.
To the people of Madripoor I ask-- what do you have to show for it?
This island is missing roads, schools and hospitals that should have been erected with money that ended up in the hands of banksters.
They're opening a free hospital on the exact spot that was meant to be the largest tower in Madripoor. We've already pre-sold entire floors!
They've bought up properties all over Lowtown.
We have a plan for that. Kade went over to the lab to kick the tires on it.

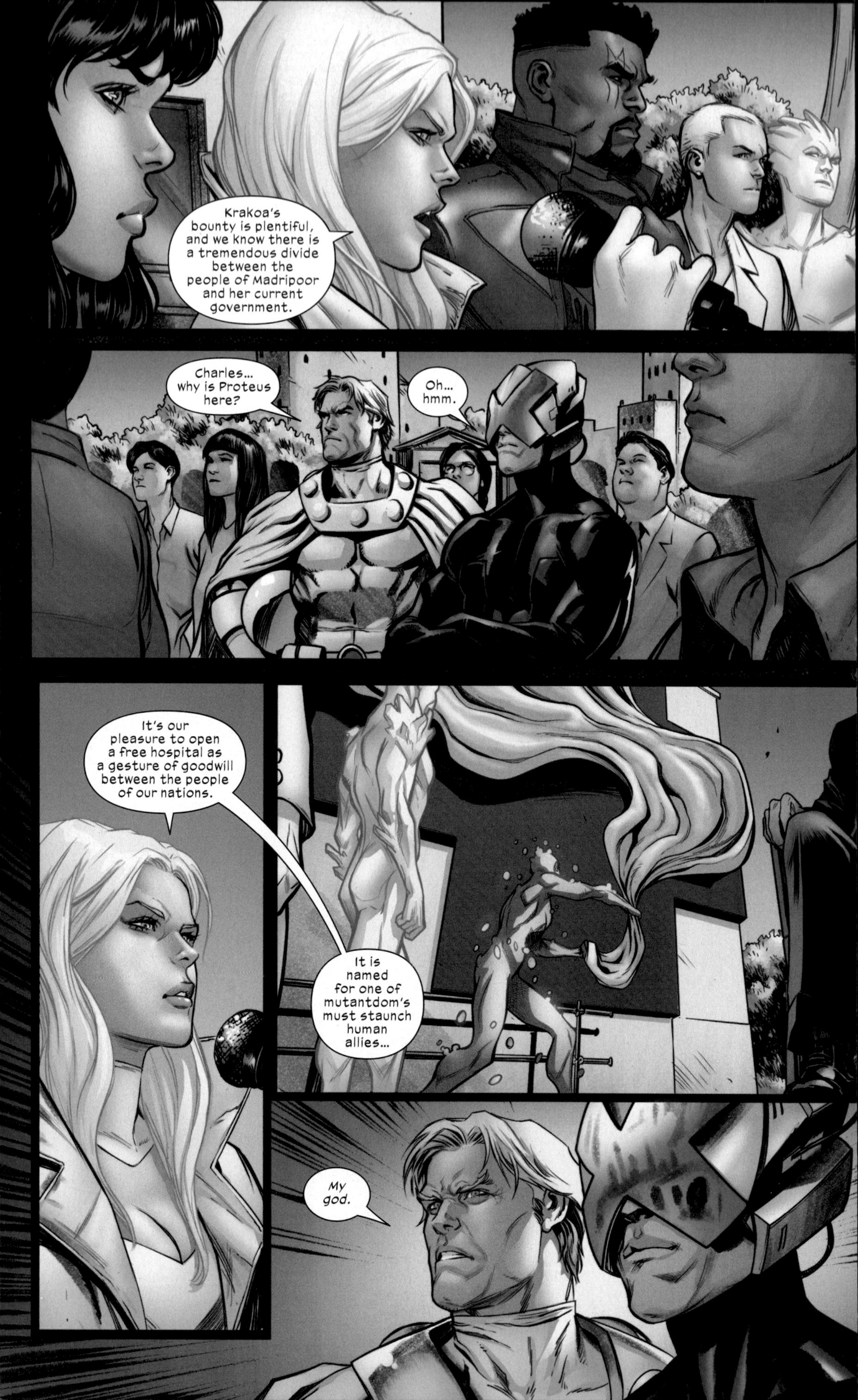
Krakoa's bounty is plentiful, and we know there is a tremendous divide between the people of Madripoor and her current government.
Charles... why is Proteus here?
Oh... hmm.
It's our pleasure to open a free hospital as a gesture of goodwill between the people of our nations.
It is named for one of mutantdom's must staunch human allies...
My god.

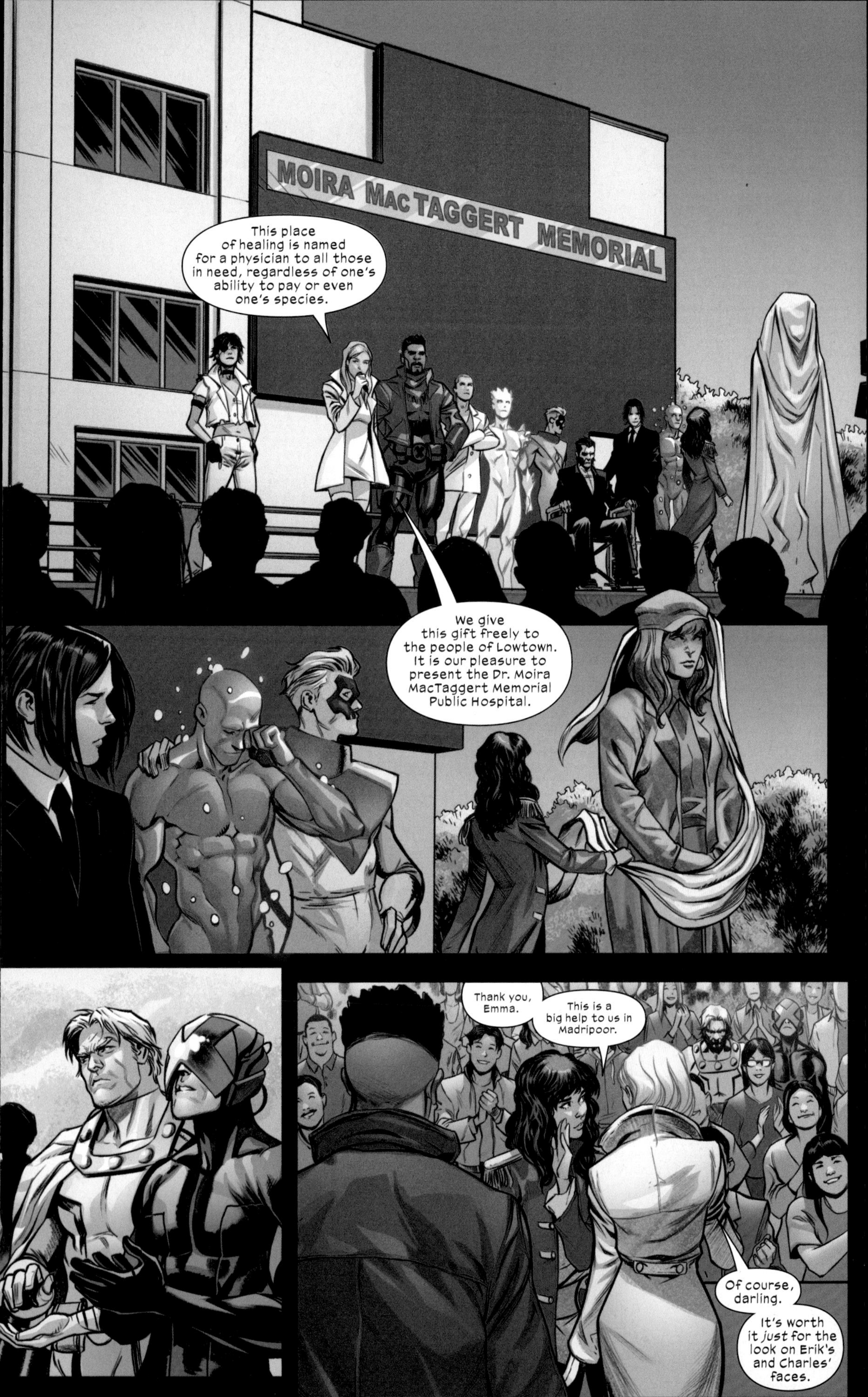
MOIRA MacTAGGERT MEMORIAL
This place of healing is named for a physician to all those in need, regardless of one's ability to pay or even one's species.
We give this gift freely to the people of Lowtown. It is our pleasure to present the Dr. Moira MacTaggert Memorial Public Hospital.
Thank you, Emma.
This is a big help to us in Madripoor.
Of course, darling.
It's worth it *just* for the look on Erik's and Charles' faces.

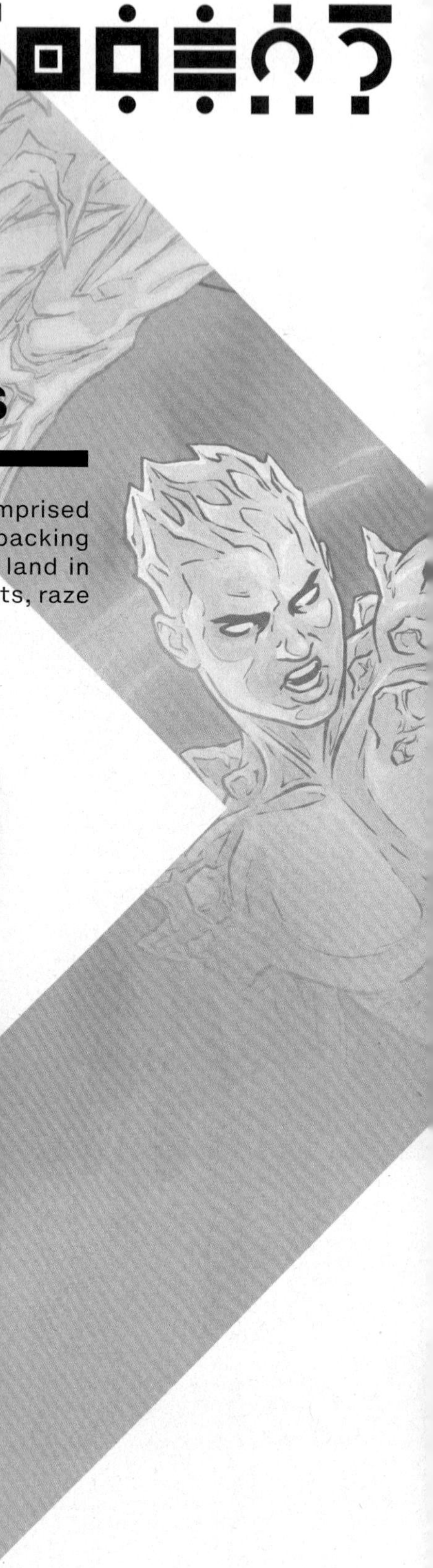

STRATEGIC HOLDINGS

The organization known as Homines Verendi -- comprised of anti-mutant children and with the financial backing of billionaire Chen Zhao -- has been buying up land in Madripoo's Lowtown, planning to evict its residents, raze their homes and build high-rises in their place.

The MARAUDERS won't stand for that.

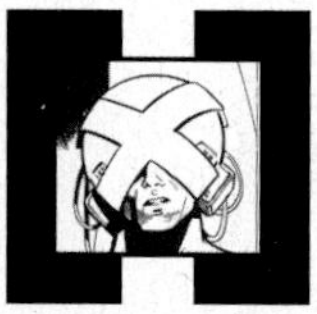

Professor X

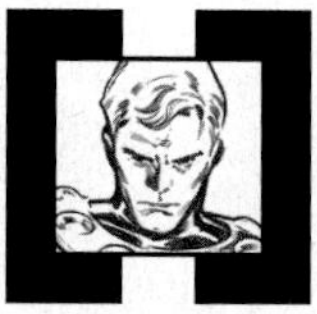

Magneto

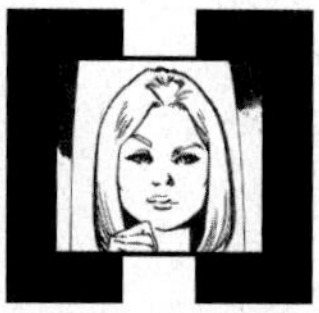

Emma Frost

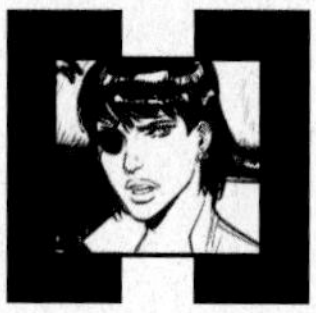

Callisto

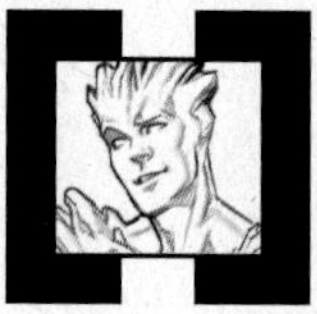

Iceman

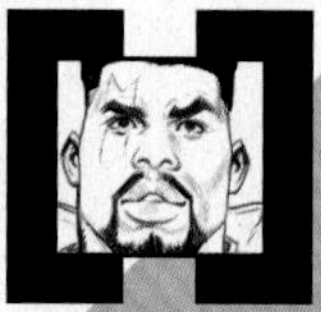

Bishop

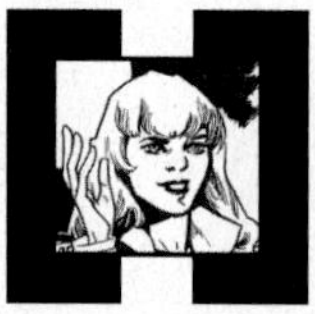

Kate Pryde

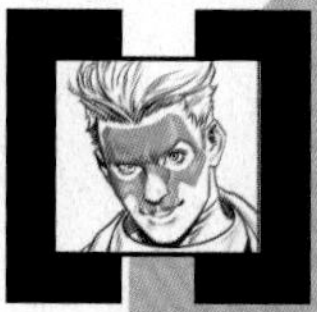

Pyro

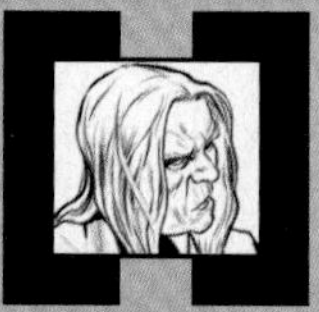

Masque

MARAUDERS

[X_18]

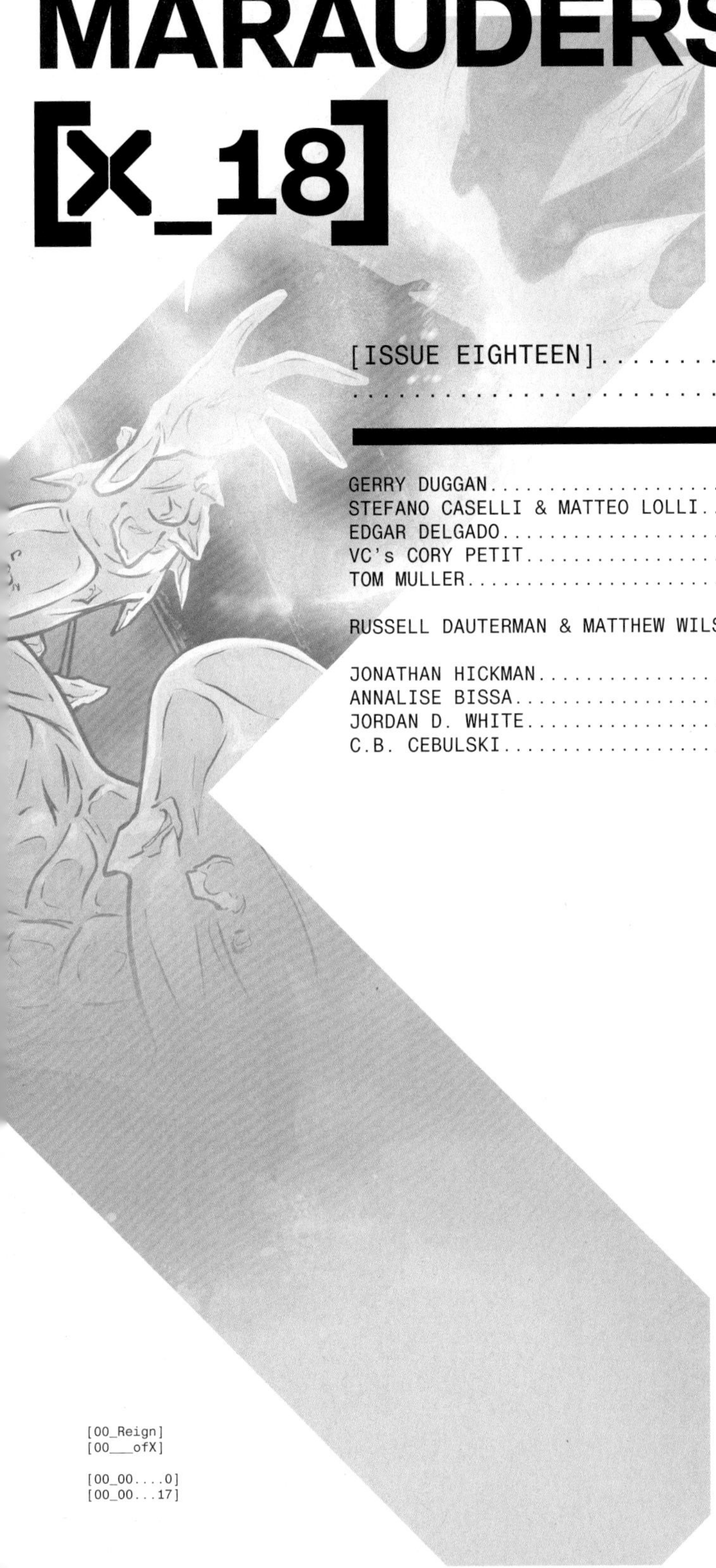

[ISSUE EIGHTEEN]................................SAVING FACE

GERRY DUGGAN..[WRITER]
STEFANO CASELLI & MATTEO LOLLI....................[ARTISTS]
EDGAR DELGADO.............................[COLOR ARTIST]
VC's CORY PETIT...................[LETTERER & PRODUCTION]
TOM MULLER...[DESIGN]

RUSSELL DAUTERMAN & MATTHEW WILSON..........[COVER ARTISTS]

JONATHAN HICKMAN.............................[HEAD OF X]
ANNALISE BISSA.........................[ASSOCIATE EDITOR]
JORDAN D. WHITE...................................[EDITOR]
C.B. CEBULSKI...........................[EDITOR IN CHIEF]

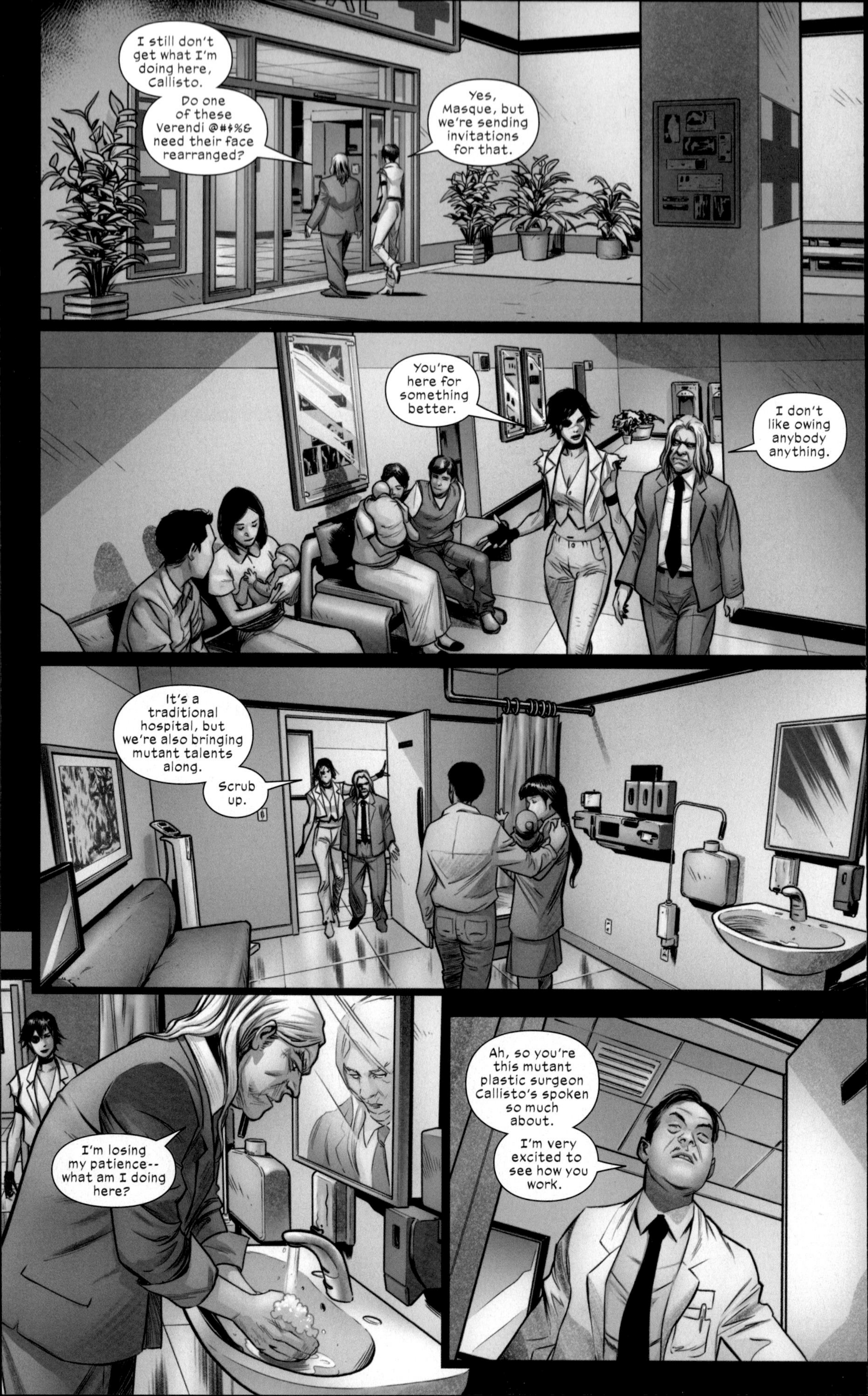

I still don't get what I'm doing here, Callisto.
Do one of these Verendi @#$%& need their face rearranged?
Yes, Masque, but we're sending invitations for that.
You're here for something better.
I don't like owing anybody anything.
It's a traditional hospital, but we're also bringing mutant talents along.
Scrub up.
I'm losing my patience--what am I doing here?
Ah, so you're this mutant plastic surgeon Callisto's spoken so much about.
I'm very excited to see how you work.

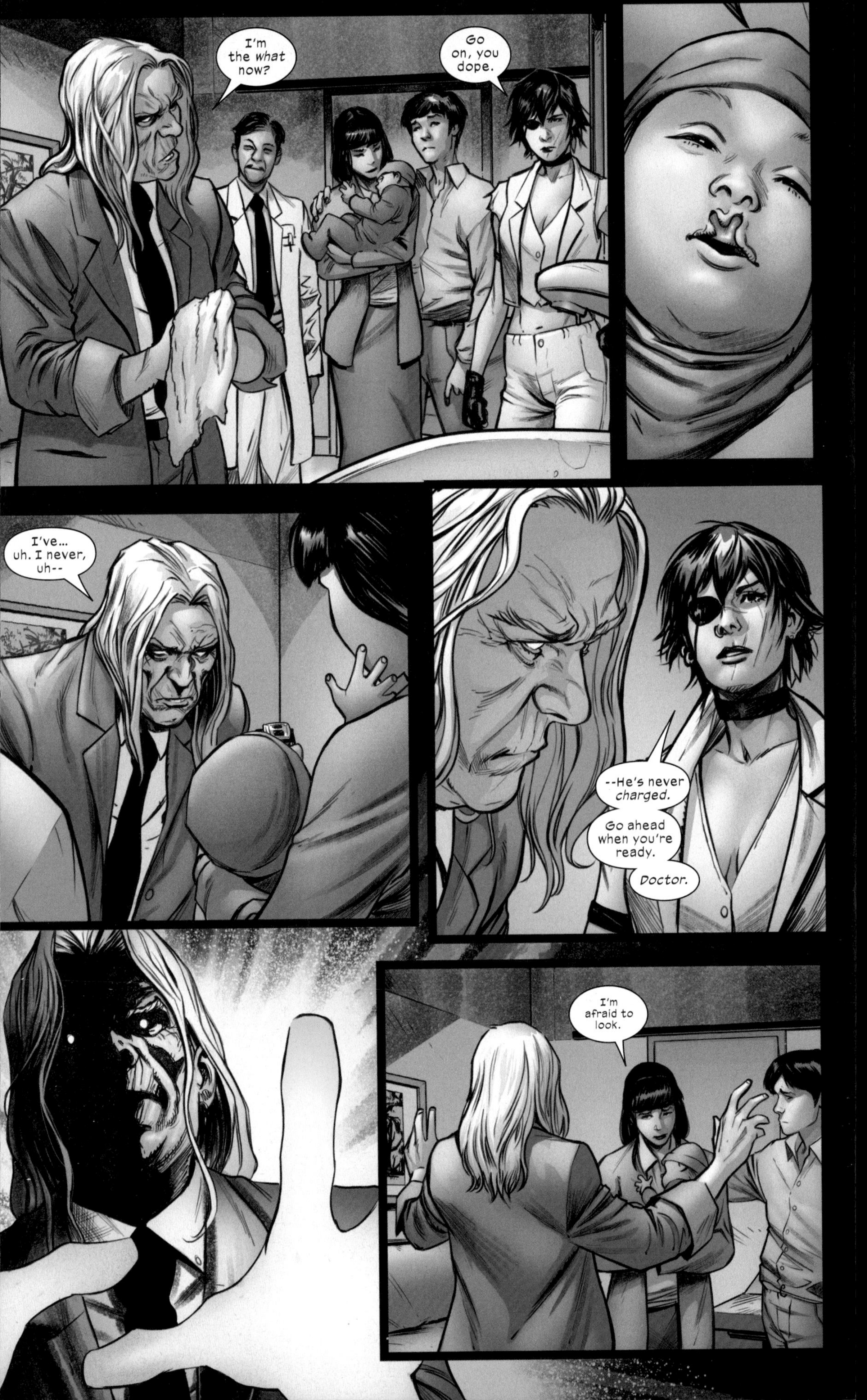
I'm the *what* now?
Go on, you dope.
I've... uh. I never, uh--
--He's never *charged*.
Go ahead when you're ready.
Doctor.
I'm afraid to look.

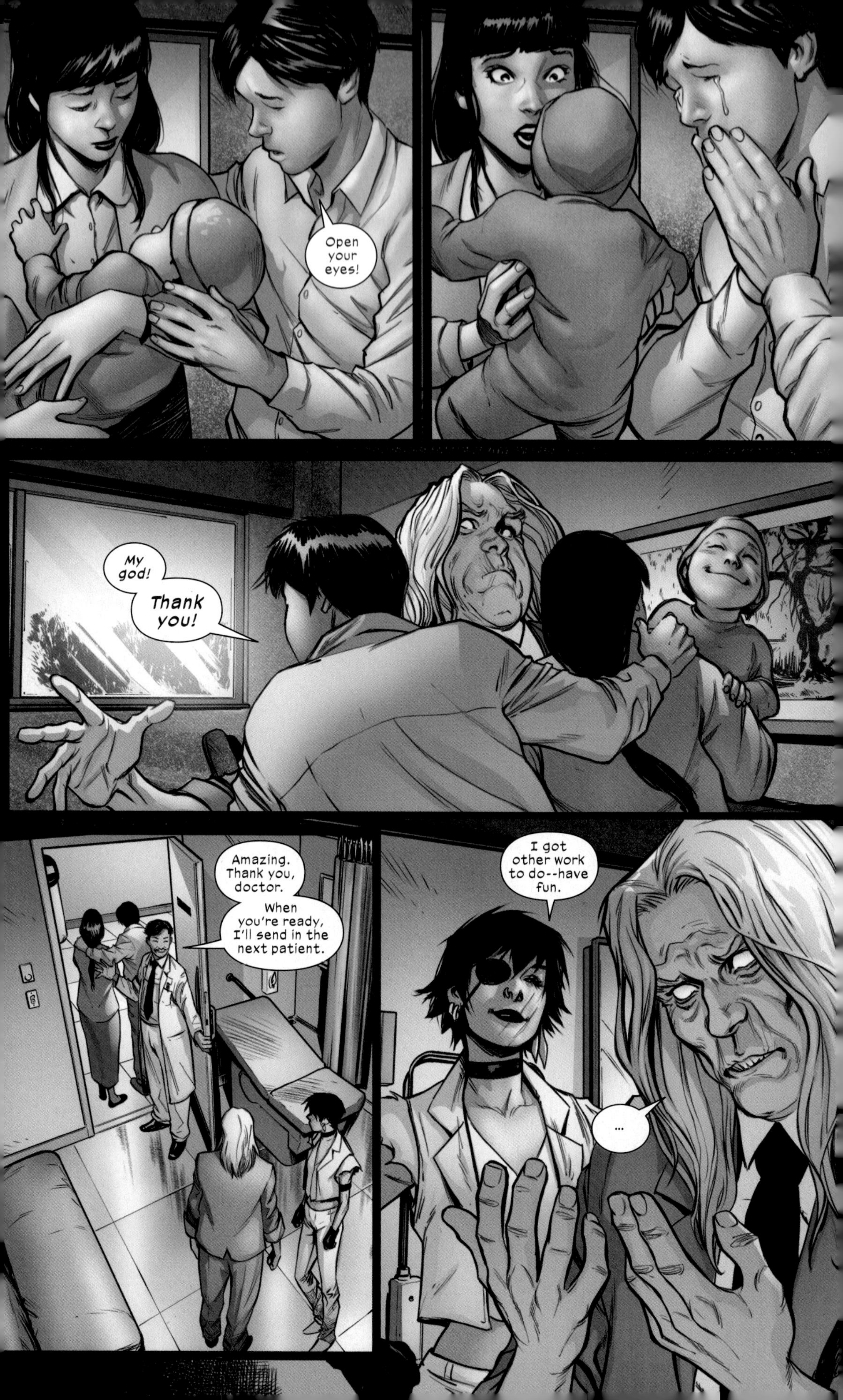
Open your eyes!
My god!
Thank you!
Amazing. Thank you, doctor.
When you're ready, I'll send in the next patient.
I got other work to do--have fun.
...

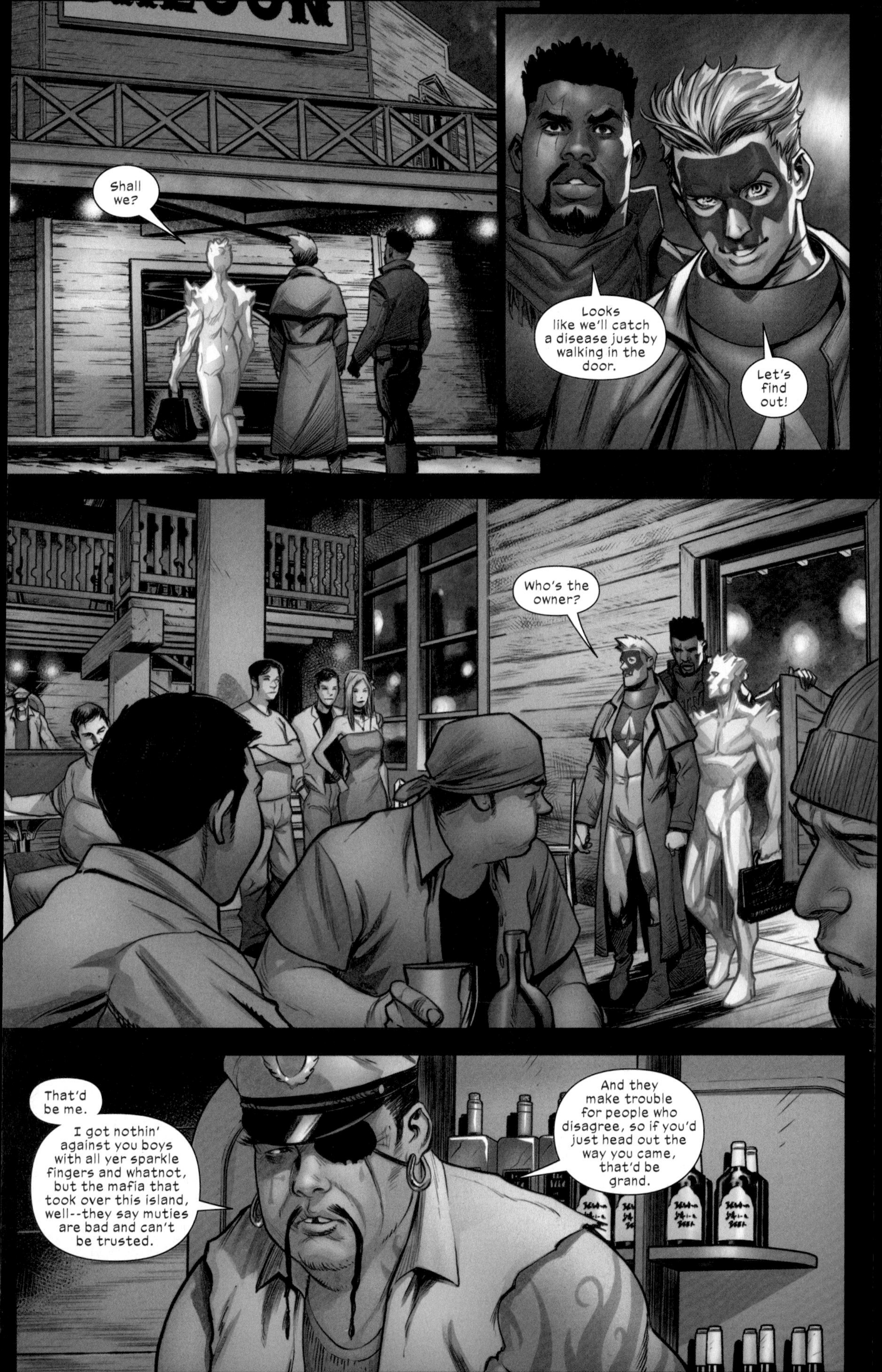

Shall we?
Looks like we'll catch a disease just by walking in the door.
Let's find out!
Who's the owner?
That'd be me.
I got nothin' against you boys with all yer sparkle fingers and whatnot, but the mafia that took over this island, well--they say muties are bad and can't be trusted.
And they make trouble for people who disagree, so if you'd just head out the way you came, that'd be grand.

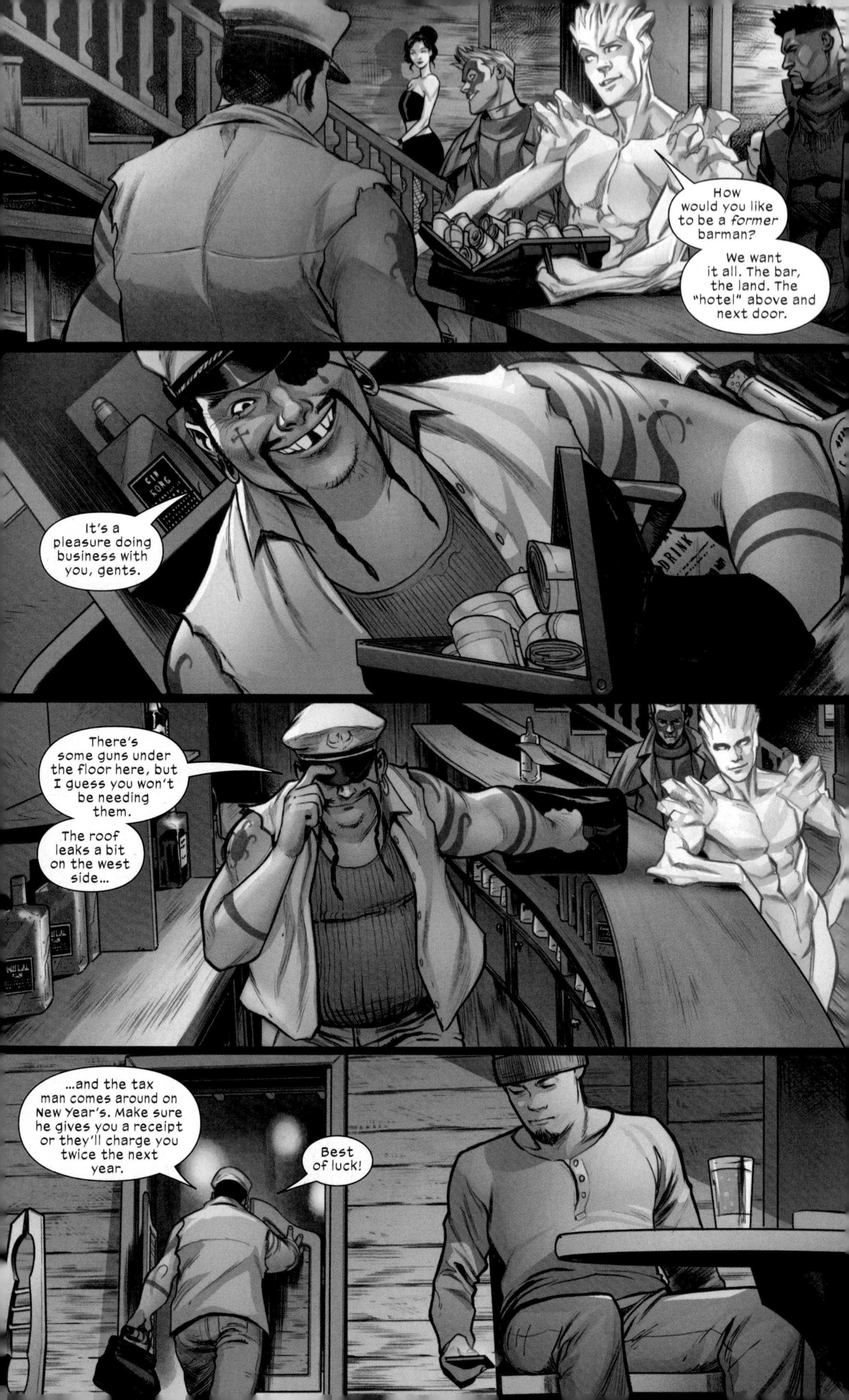
How would you like to be a *former* barman?
We want it all. The bar, the land. The "hotel" above and next door.
It's a pleasure doing business with you, gents.
There's some guns under the floor here, but I guess you won't be needing them.
The roof leaks a bit on the west side...
...and the tax man comes around on New Year's. Make sure he gives you a receipt or they'll charge you twice the next year.
Best of luck!

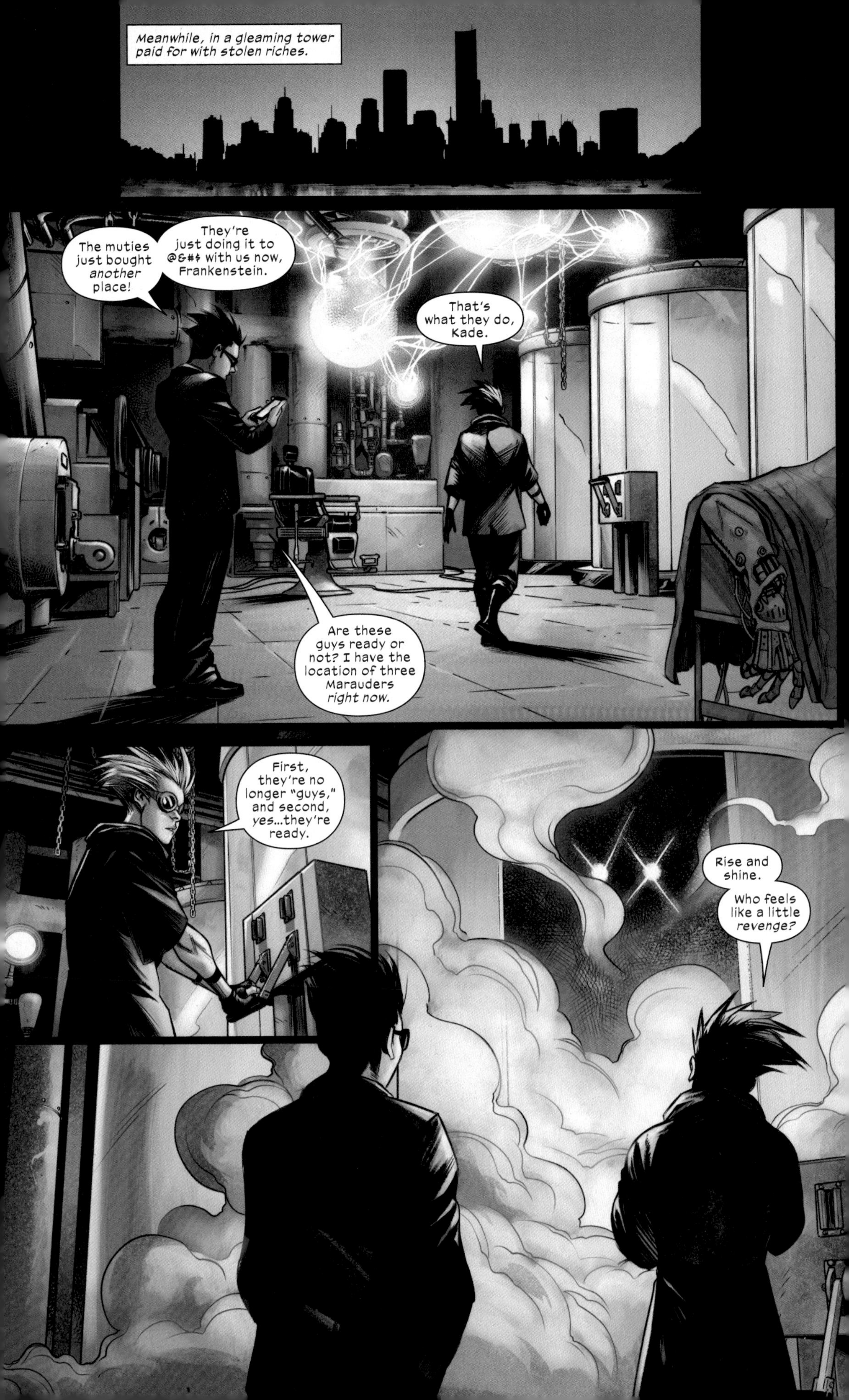
Meanwhile, in a gleaming tower paid for with stolen riches.
The muties just bought another place!
They're just doing it to @&#$ with us now, Frankenstein.
That's what they do, Kade.
Are these guys ready or not? I have the location of three Marauders right now.
First, they're no longer "guys," and second, yes...they're ready.
Rise and shine.
Who feels like a little revenge?

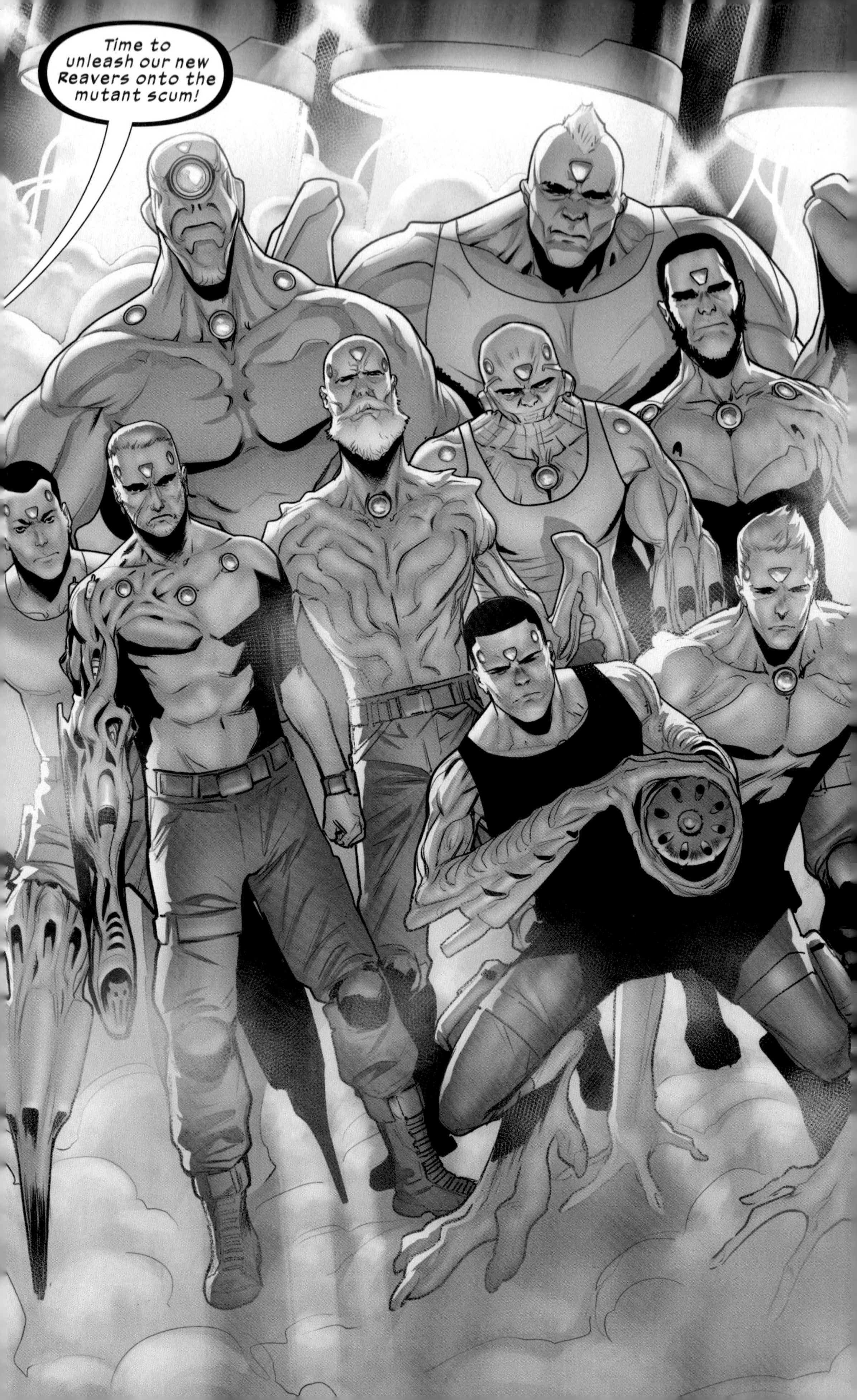
Time to unleash our new Reavers onto the mutant scum!

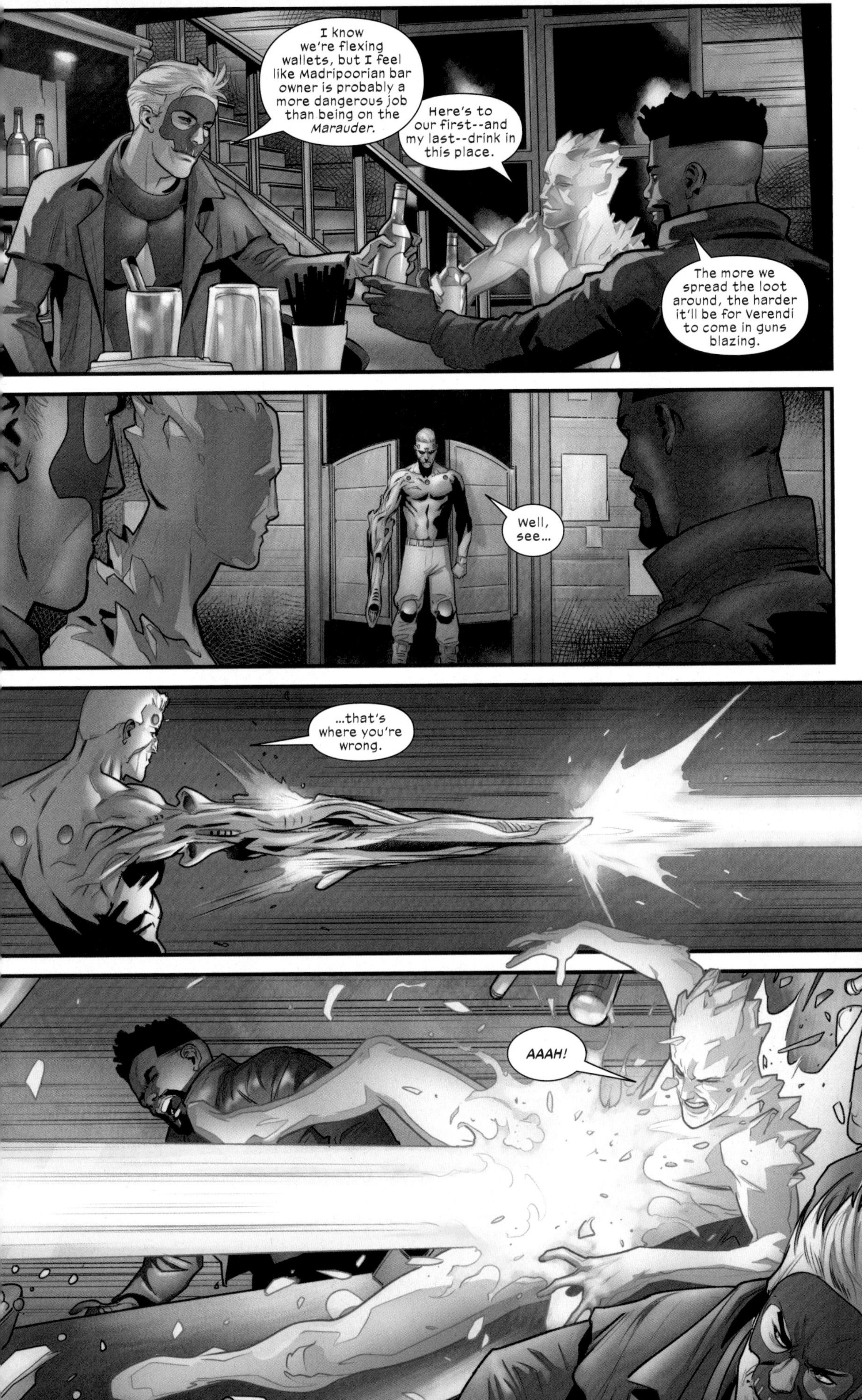
I know we're flexing wallets, but I feel like Madripoorian bar owner is probably a more dangerous job than being on the *Marauder*.
Here's to our first--and my last--drink in this place.
The more we spread the loot around, the harder it'll be for Verendi to come in guns blazing.
Well, see...
...that's where you're wrong.
AAAH!

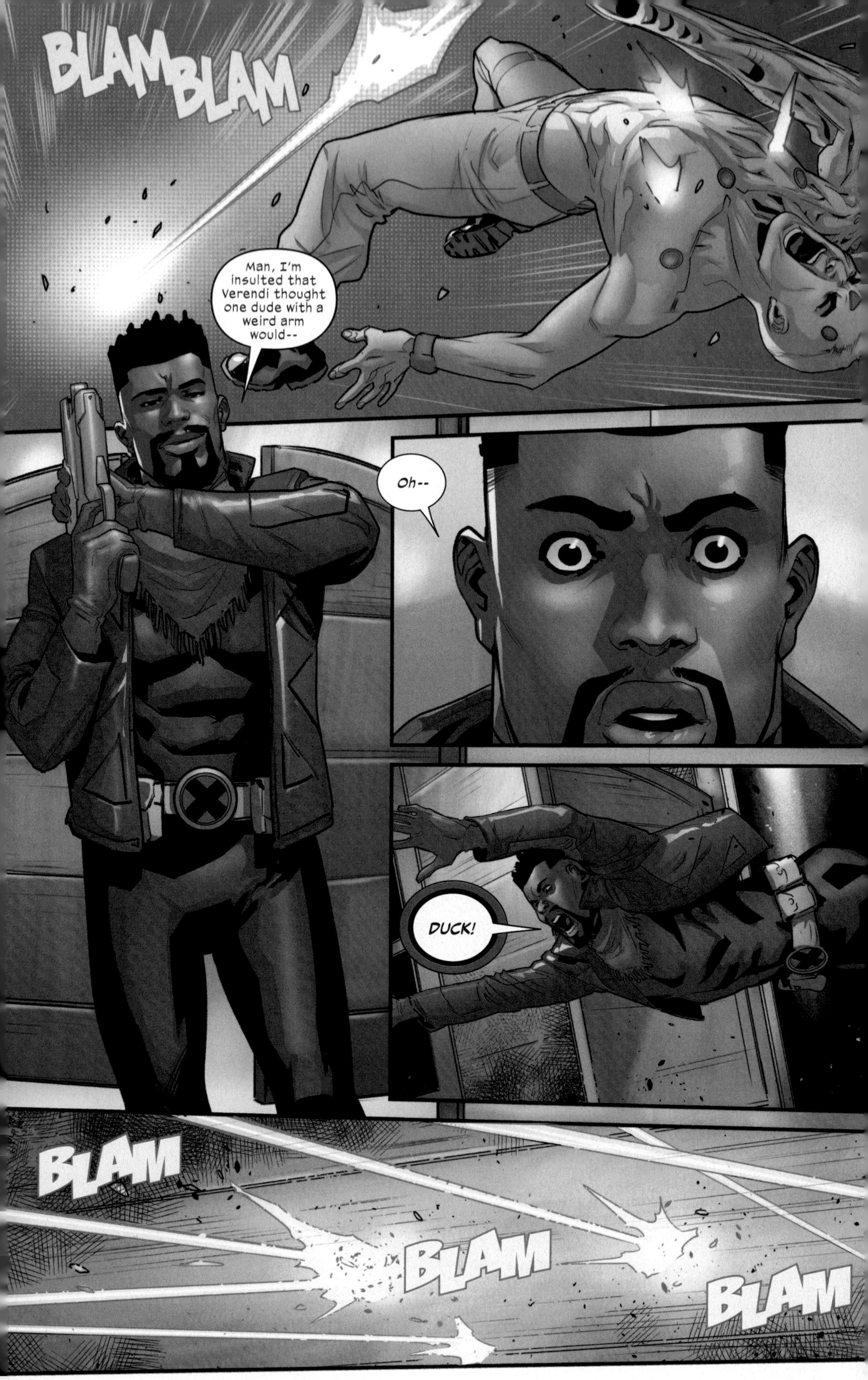
BLAM BLAM
Man, I'm insulted that Verendi thought one dude with a weird arm would--
Oh--
DUCK!
BLAM
BLAM
BLAM

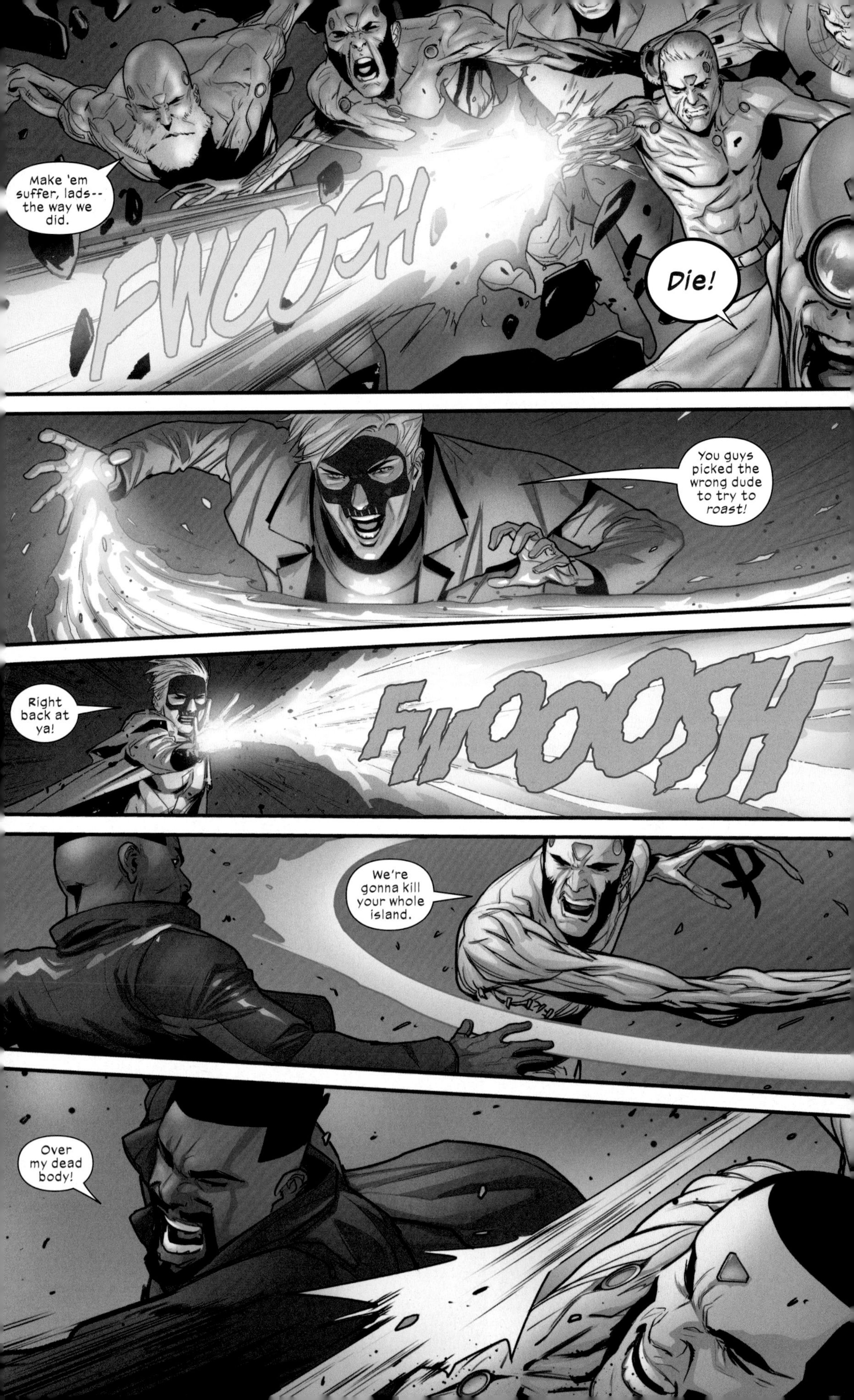
Make 'em suffer, lads-- the way we did.
FWOOSH
Die!
You guys picked the wrong dude to try to *roast!*
Right back at ya!
FWOOOSH
We're gonna kill your whole island.
Over my dead body!

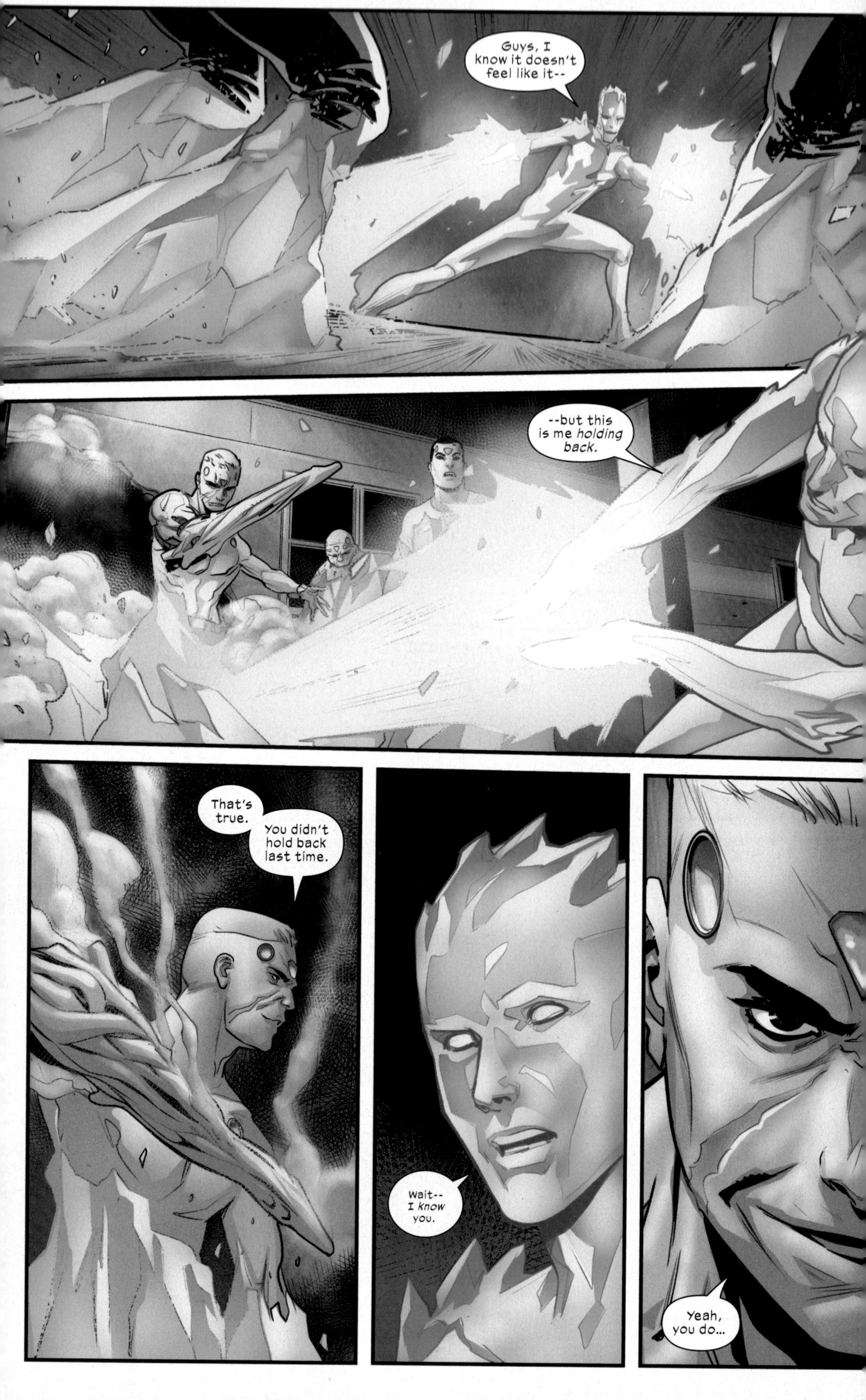
Guys, I know it doesn't feel like it--
--but this is me *holding* back.
That's true.
You didn't hold back last time.
Wait-- I *know* you.
Yeah, you do...

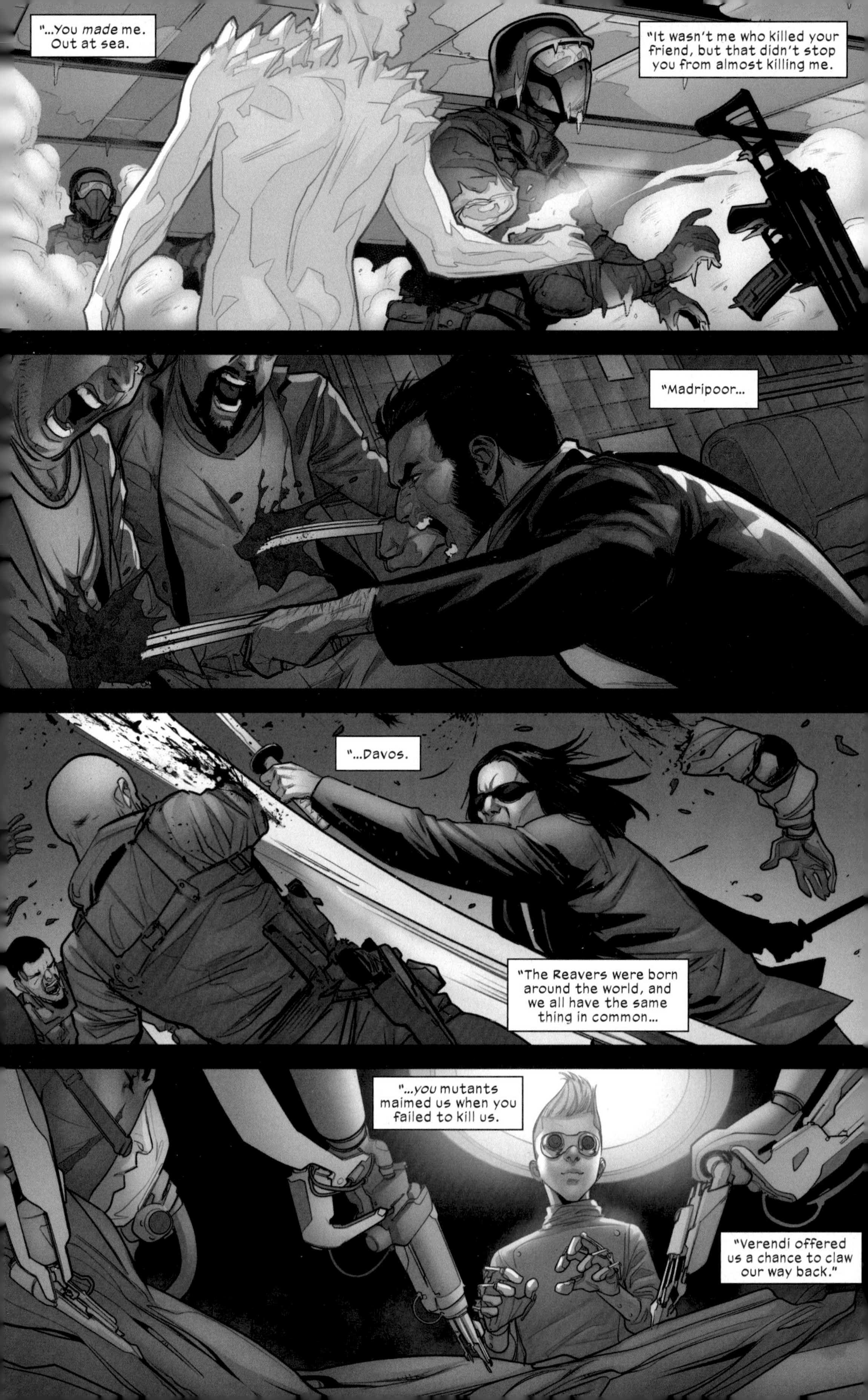
"...You *made* me. Out at sea.
"It wasn't me who killed your friend, but that didn't stop you from almost killing me.
"Madripoor...
"...Davos.
"The Reavers were born around the world, and we all have the same thing in common...
"...*you* mutants maimed us when you failed to kill us.
"Verendi offered us a chance to claw our way back."

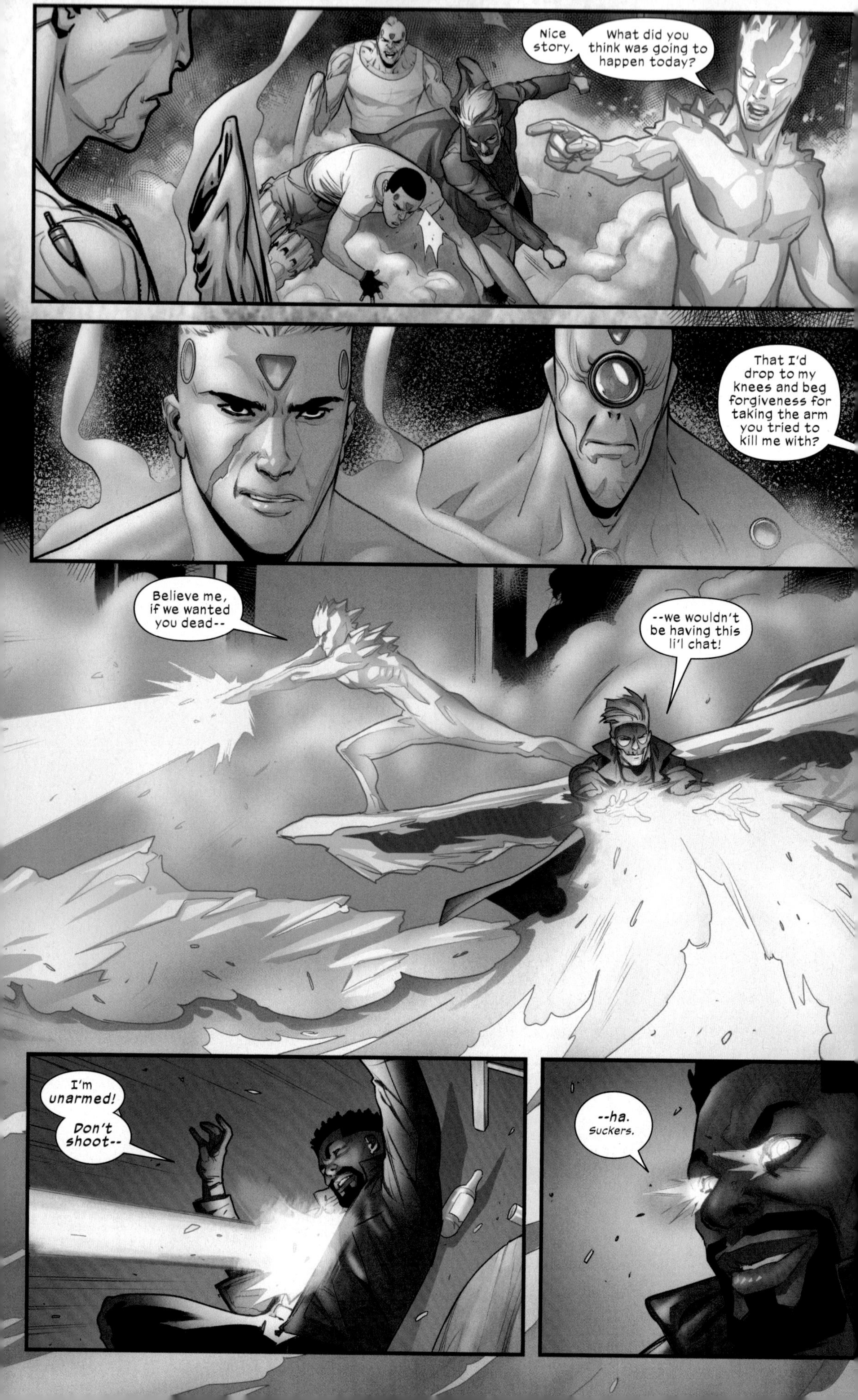
Nice story.
What did you think was going to happen today?
That I'd drop to my knees and beg forgiveness for taking the arm you tried to kill me with?
Believe me, if we wanted you dead--
--we wouldn't be having this li'l chat!
I'm unarmed!
Don't shoot--
--ha.
Suckers.

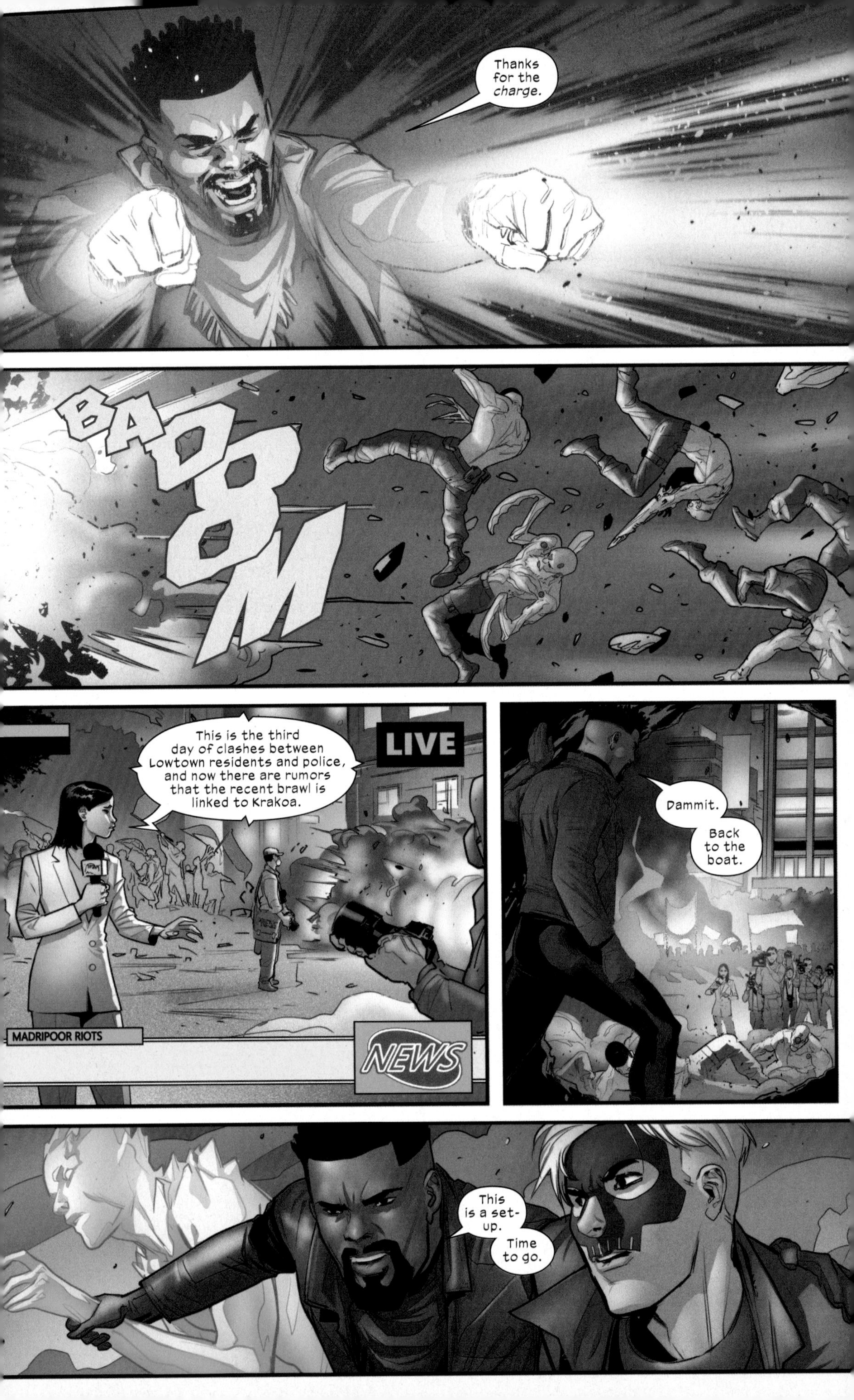
Thanks for the charge.
BADOOM
This is the third day of clashes between Lowtown residents and police, and now there are rumors that the recent brawl is linked to Krakoa.
LIVE
MADRIPOOR RIOTS
NEWS
Dammit.
Back to the boat.
This is a set-up.
Time to go.

MISSION REPORT

Beast -

Heads up: got a situation in Madripoor. We were spreading around some of Emma's money in Lowtown -- enough that some of the locals started calling it "Mutietown". The goal was to force Verendi to spend more money, and they did -- but not in the way we expected.

They have a new group of Reavers, I recognized that some of them were mercs injured by Iceman back when we discovered the Red Queen had gone down with the ship, and I know Gorgon made quite a mess at Davos -- wouldn't surprise me if some of them were in the mix here.

I didn't get photos, but they won't be hard for you to find, because we got suckered into a street fight that was well-photographed -- no doubt in my mind that was the objective.

Those images will probably be used against us -- if not in a court of law, at least to shape public opinion.

The Reavers seemed to be willing participants in their transformation. Suggest a review of injuries caused by mutants off Krakoa.

There may be more of them.

- Bishop

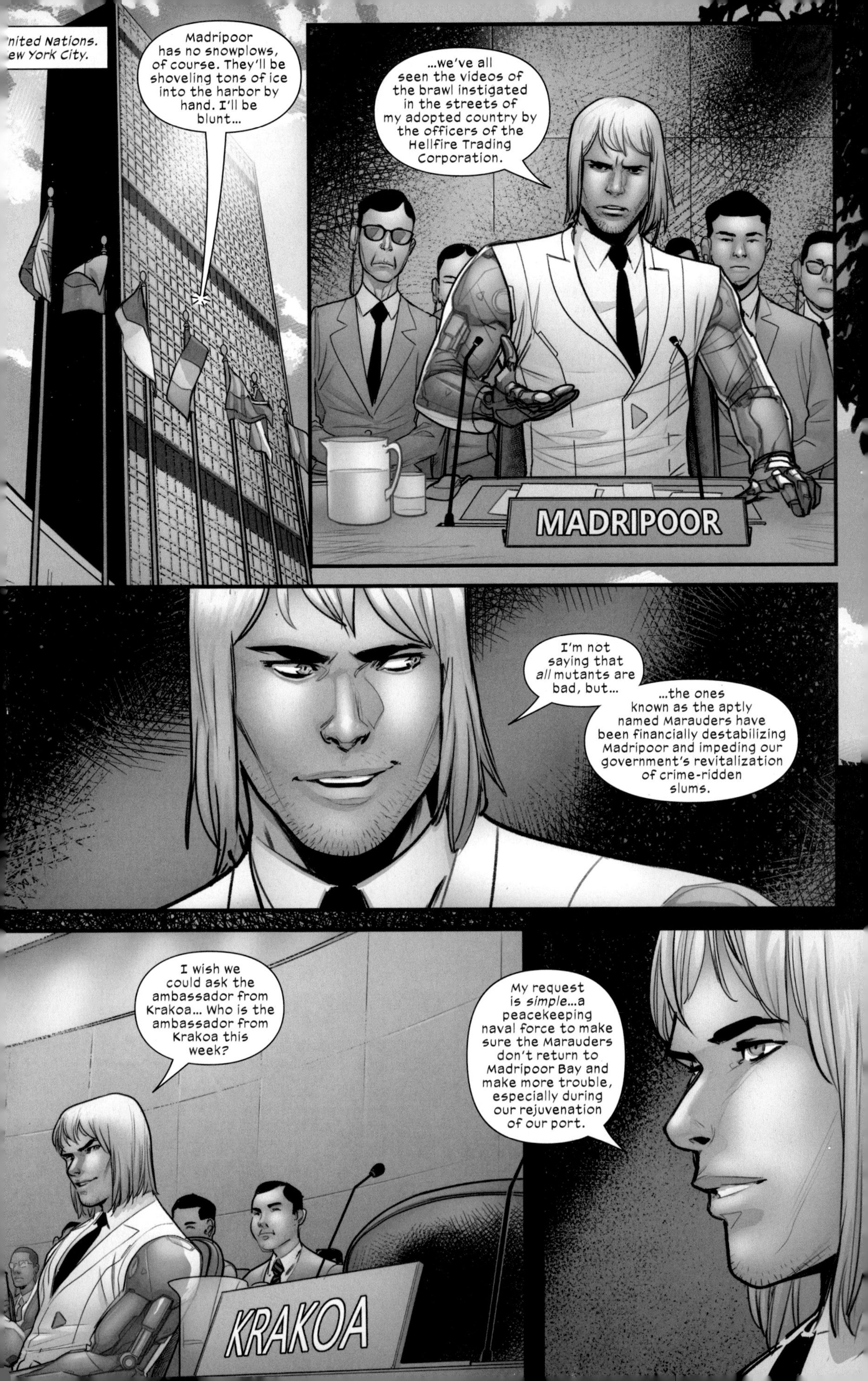
nited Nations. ew York City.
Madripoor has no snowplows, of course. They'll be shoveling tons of ice into the harbor by hand. I'll be blunt...
...we've all seen the videos of the brawl instigated in the streets of my adopted country by the officers of the Hellfire Trading Corporation.
MADRIPOOR
I'm not saying that *all* mutants are bad, but...
...the ones known as the aptly named Marauders have been financially destabilizing Madripoor and impeding our government's revitalization of crime-ridden slums.
I wish we could ask the ambassador from Krakoa... Who is the ambassador from Krakoa this week?
My request is *simple*...a peacekeeping naval force to make sure the Marauders don't return to Madripoor Bay and make more trouble, especially during our rejuvenation of our port.
KRAKOA

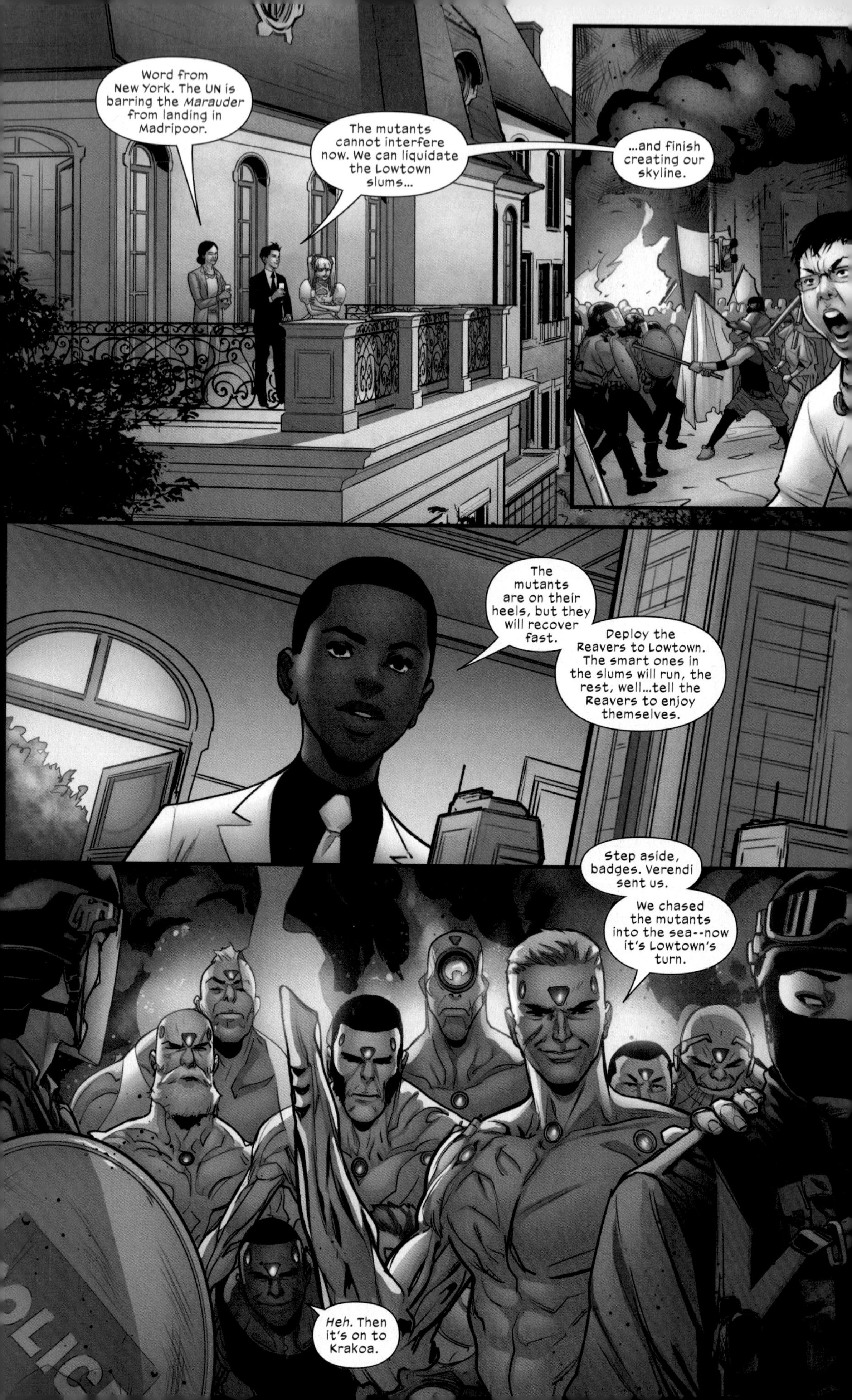
Word from New York. The UN is barring the *Marauder* from landing in Madripoor.
The mutants cannot interfere now. We can liquidate the Lowtown slums...
...and finish creating our skyline.
The mutants are on their heels, but they will recover fast.
Deploy the Reavers to Lowtown. The smart ones in the slums will run, the rest, well...tell the Reavers to enjoy themselves.
Step aside, badges. Verendi sent us.
We chased the mutants into the sea--now it's Lowtown's turn.
Heh. Then it's on to Krakoa.

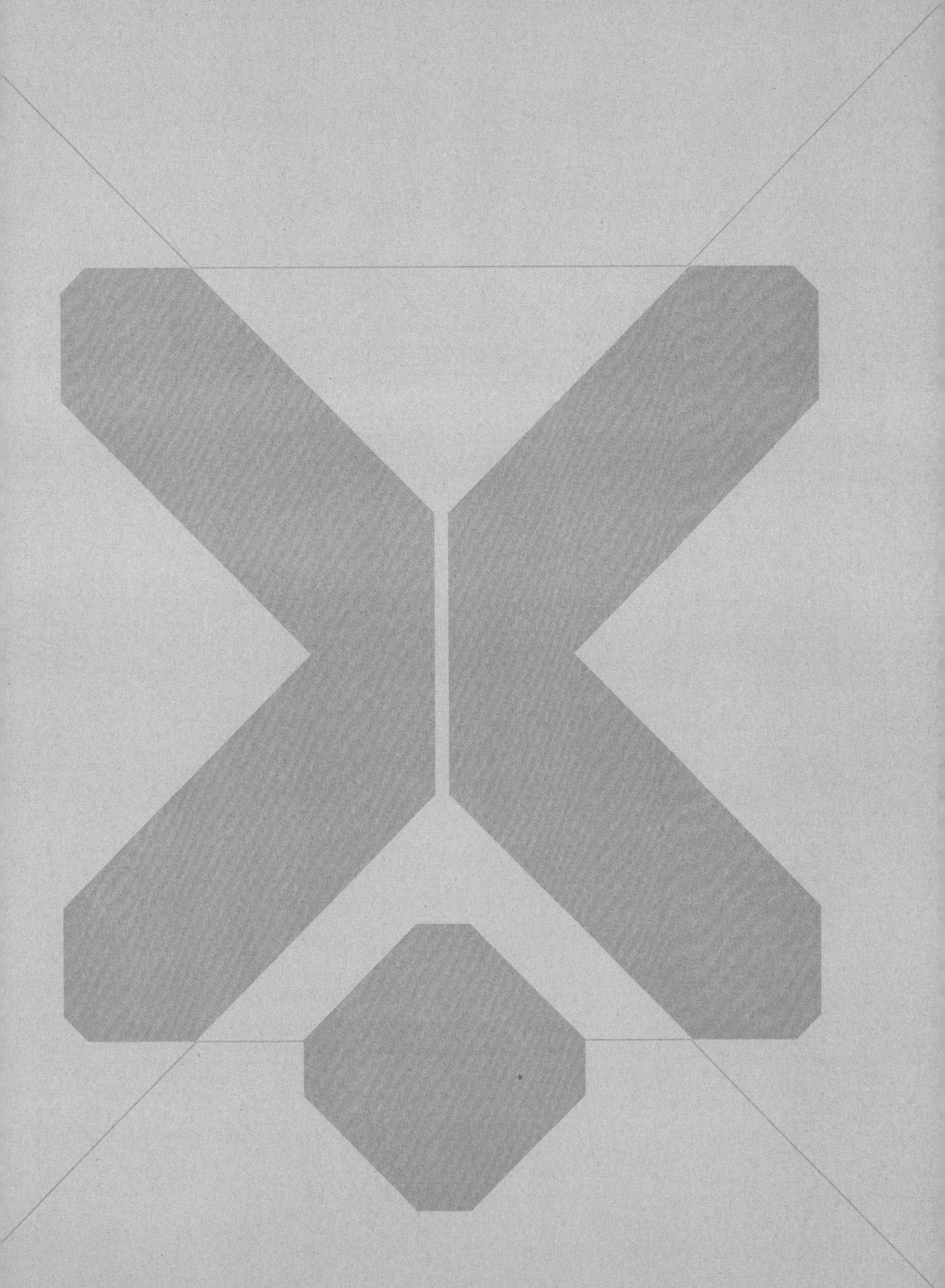

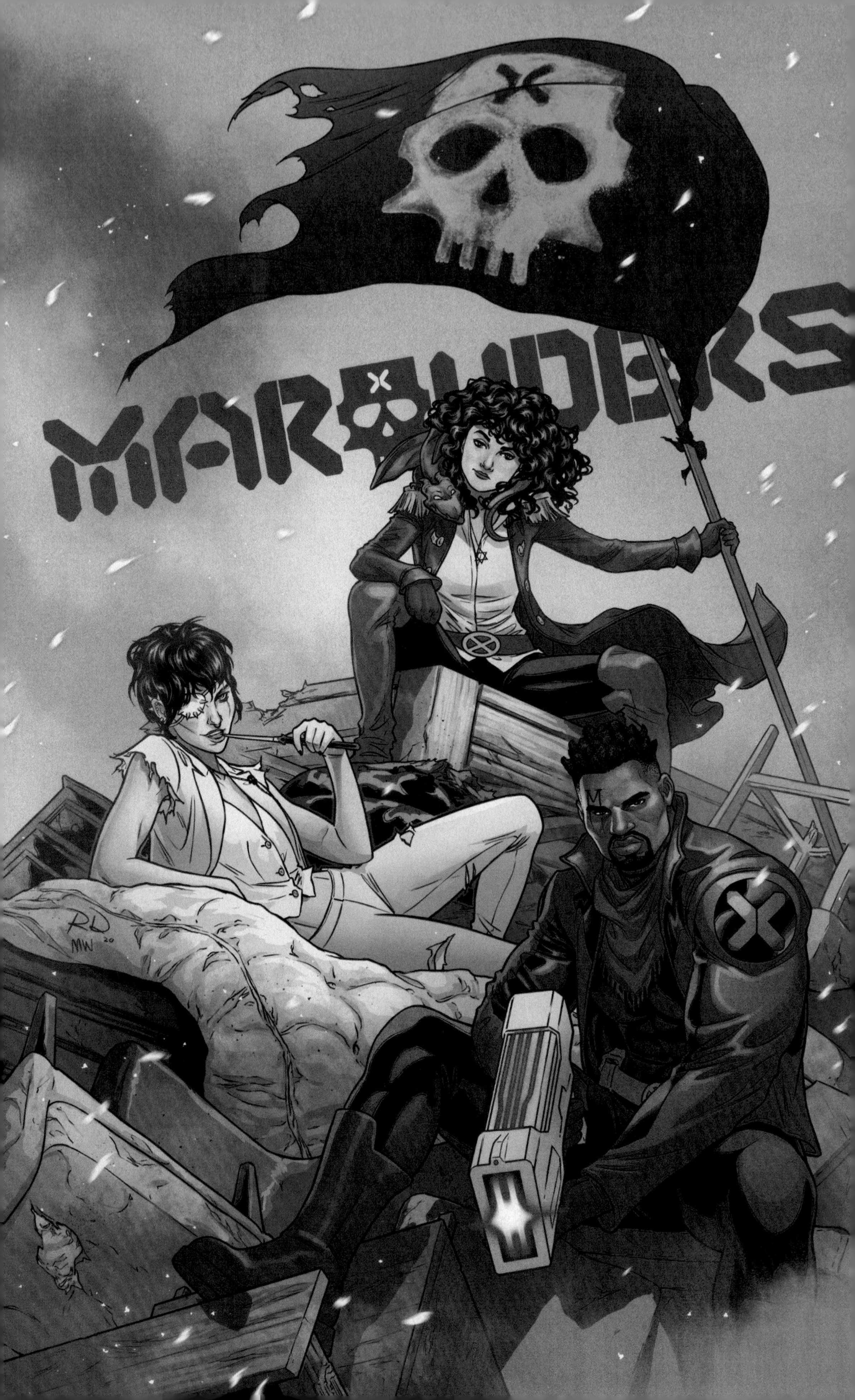
MARAUDERS

Only two types of people in Madripoor:
the rich, and those willing to kill you
to become rich.

-- PATCH

[marauders_19]

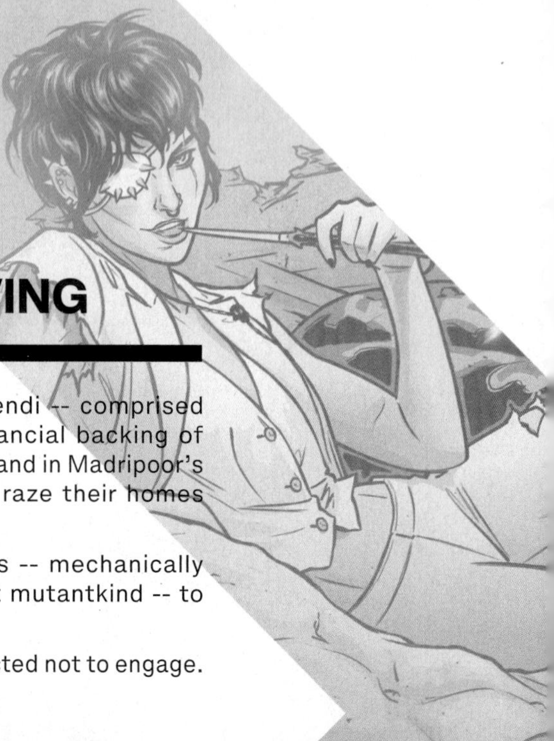

SOWING & REAVING

The organization known as Homines Verendi -- comprised of anti-mutant children and with the financial backing of billionaire Chen Zhao -- has been buying up land in Madripoor's Lowtown, planning to evict its residents, raze their homes and build high-rises in their place.

Now they've sent a new team of Reavers -- mechanically augmented humans with a grudge against mutantkind -- to clear the streets of Lowtown.

The MARAUDERS have been explicitly instructed not to engage.

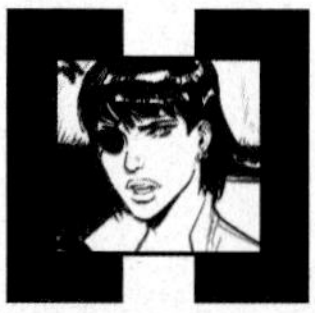
Callisto

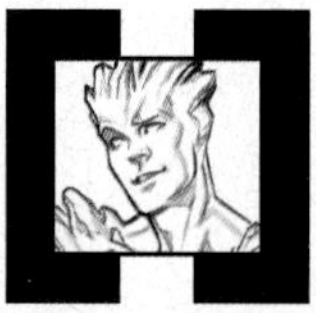
Iceman

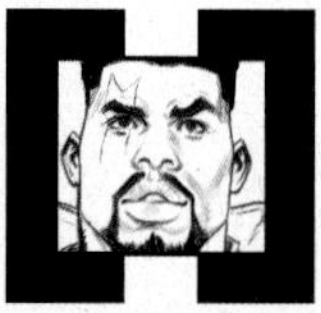
Bishop

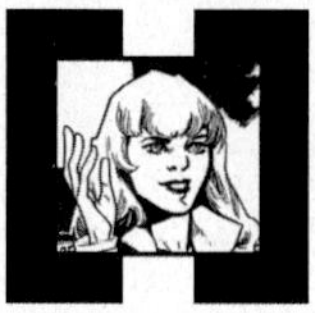
Kate Pryde

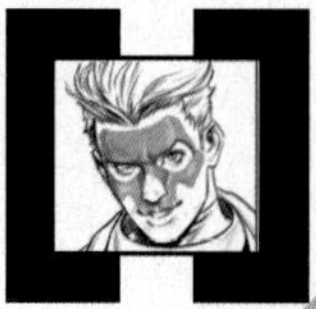
Pyro

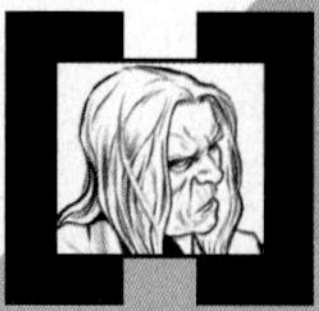
Masque

[00_Reign]
[00___ofX]

MARAUDERS

[X_19]

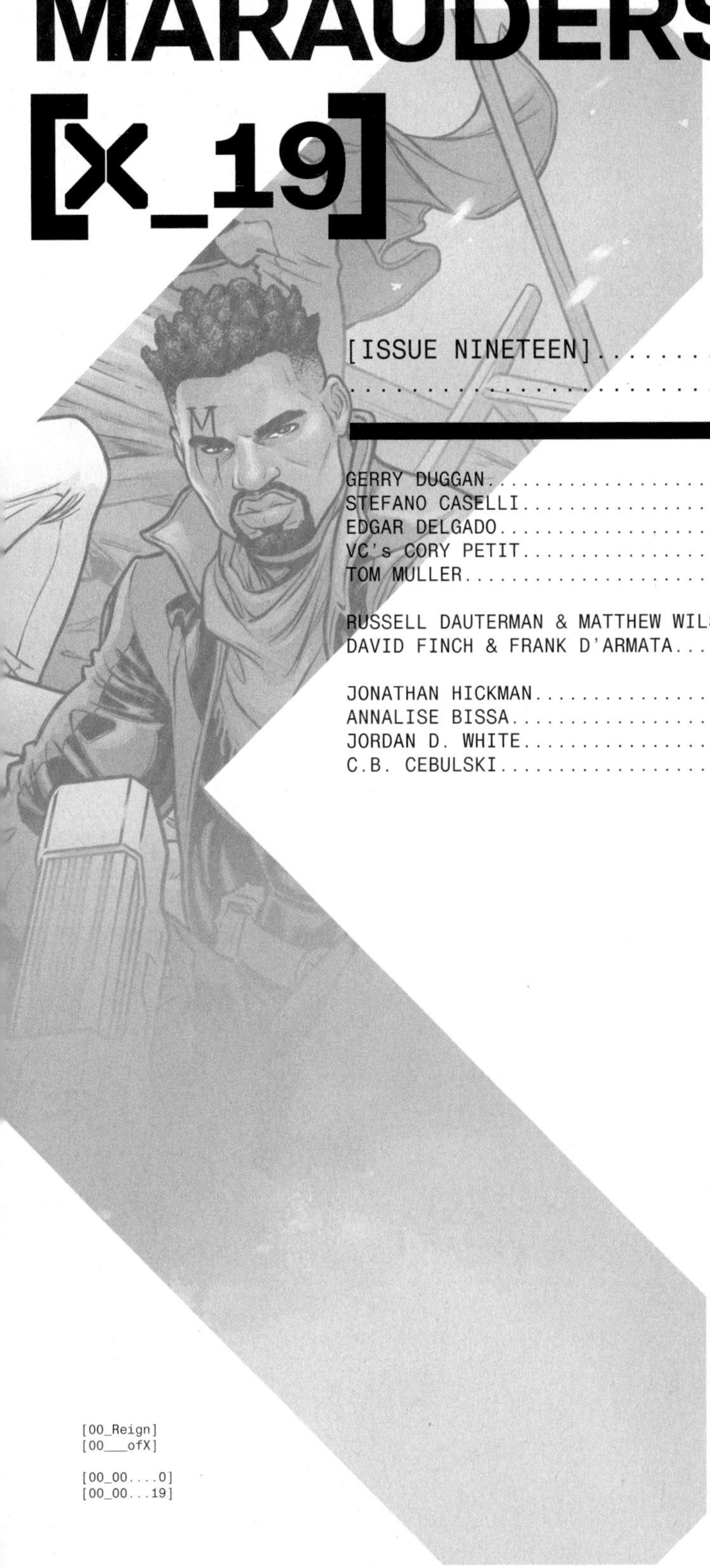

[ISSUE NINETEEN]..............................
..................................FIRE & ICE

GERRY DUGGAN.......................................[WRITER]
STEFANO CASELLI....................................[ARTIST]
EDGAR DELGADO...............................[COLOR ARTIST]
VC's CORY PETIT.....................[LETTERER & PRODUCTION]
TOM MULLER...[DESIGN]

RUSSELL DAUTERMAN & MATTHEW WILSON..........[COVER ARTISTS]
DAVID FINCH & FRANK D'ARMATA........[VARIANT COVER ARTISTS]

JONATHAN HICKMAN...............................[HEAD OF X]
ANNALISE BISSA........................[ASSOCIATE EDITOR]
JORDAN D. WHITE....................................[EDITOR]
C.B. CEBULSKI.............................[EDITOR IN CHIEF]

[00_Reign]
[00___ofX]

[00_00....0]
[00_00...19]

[00_Reign_]
[00_______]

[00___of__]

[00_______X]

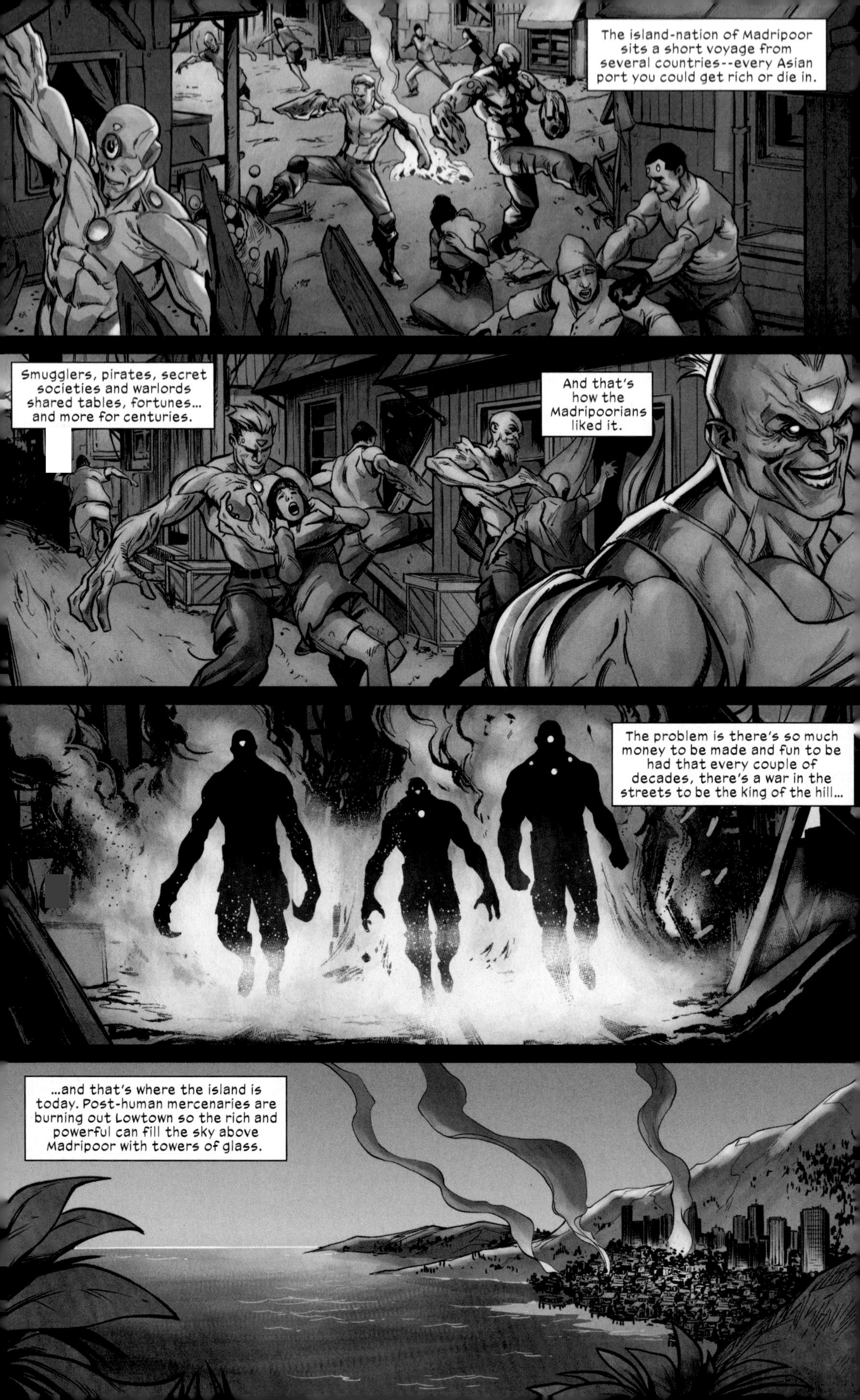
The island-nation of Madripoor sits a short voyage from several countries--every Asian port you could get rich or die in.
Smugglers, pirates, secret societies and warlords shared tables, fortunes... and more for centuries.
And that's how the Madripoorians liked it.
The problem is there's so much money to be made and fun to be had that every couple of decades, there's a war in the streets to be the king of the hill...
...and that's where the island is today. Post-human mercenaries are burning out Lowtown so the rich and powerful can fill the sky above Madripoor with towers of glass.

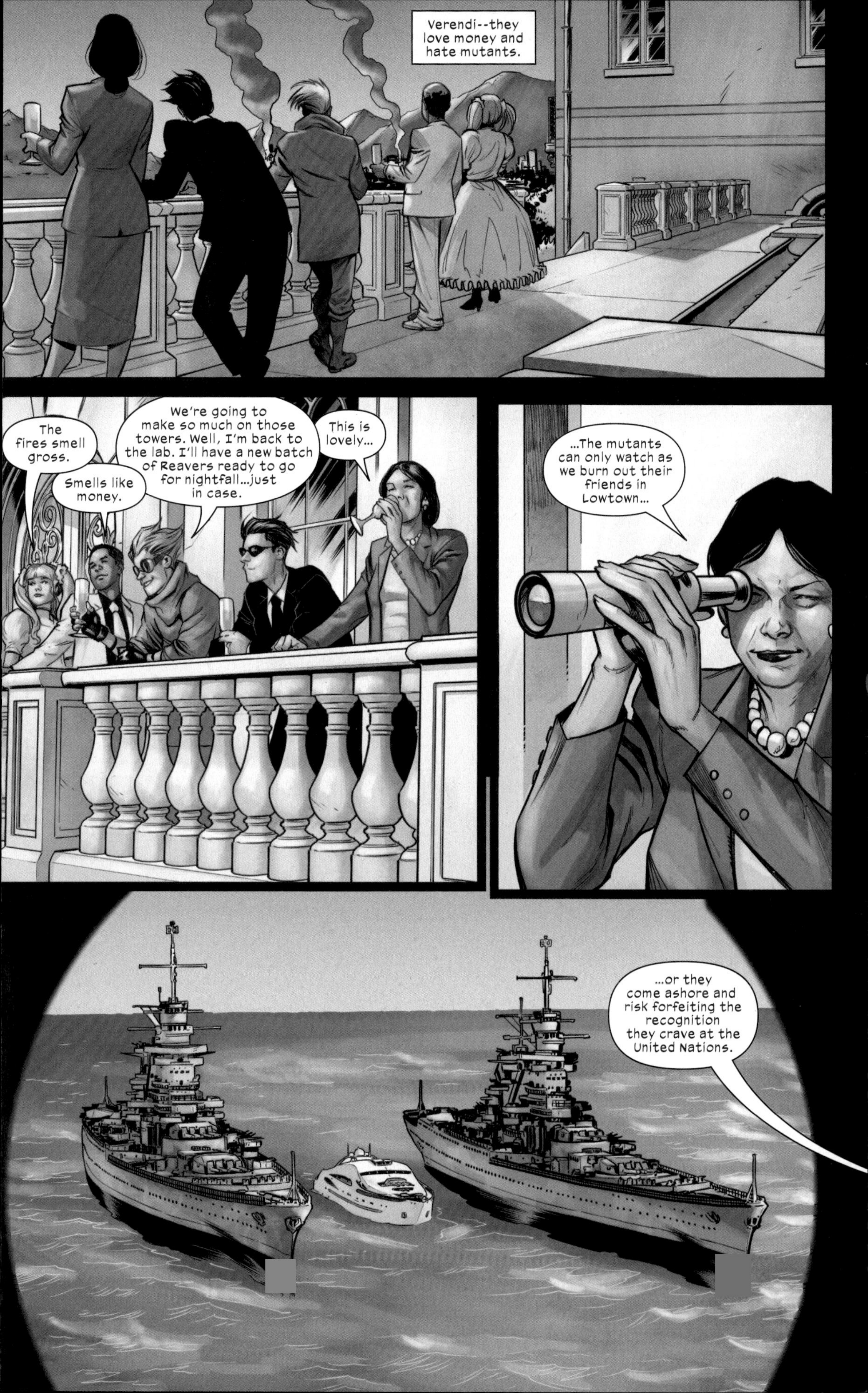
Verendi--they love money and hate mutants.
The fires smell gross.
Smells like money.
We're going to make so much on those towers. Well, I'm back to the lab. I'll have a new batch of Reavers ready to go for nightfall...just in case.
This is lovely...
...The mutants can only watch as we burn out their friends in Lowtown...
...or they come ashore and risk forfeiting the recognition they crave at the United Nations.

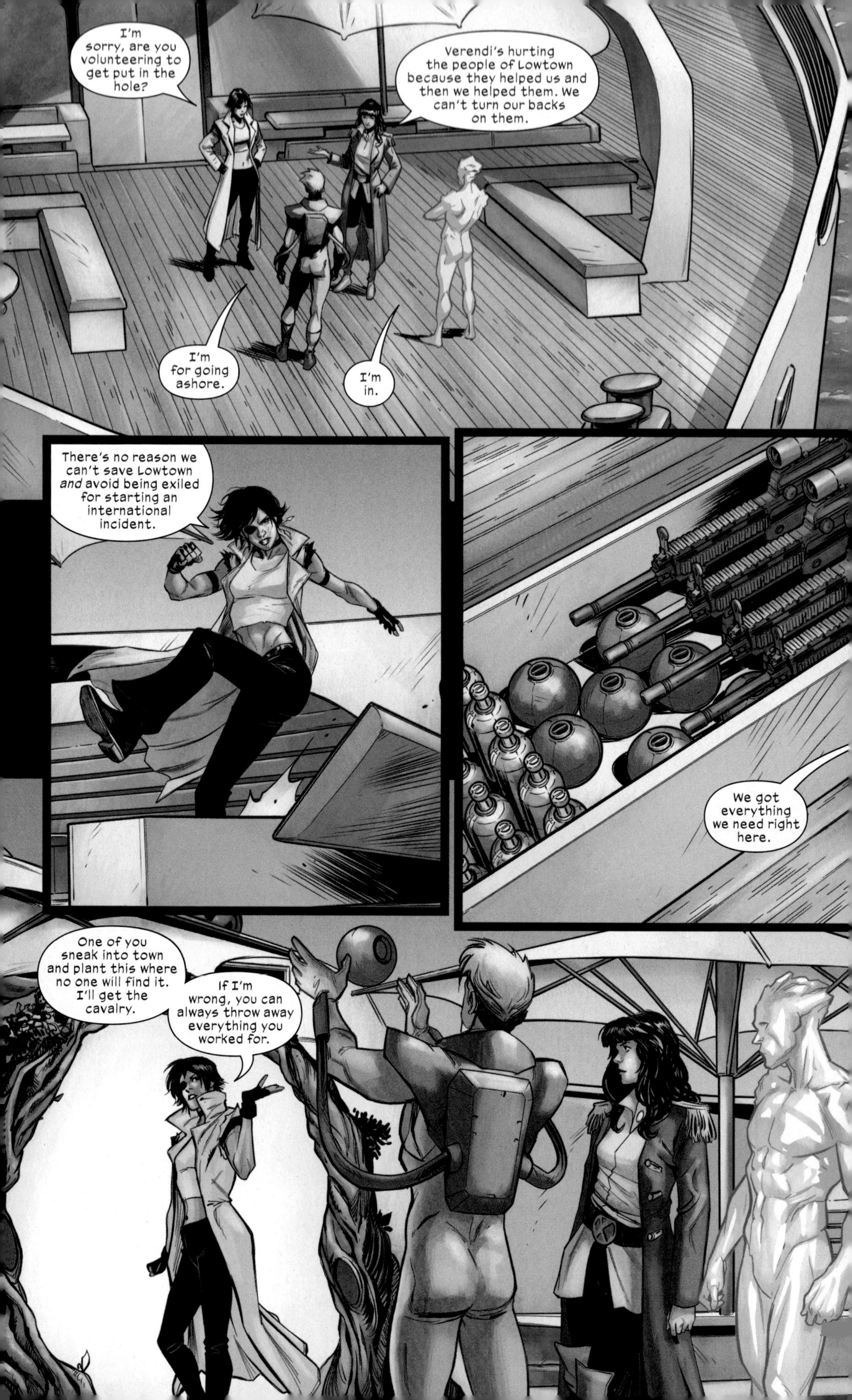
I'm sorry, are you volunteering to get put in the hole?
Verendi's hurting the people of Lowtown because they helped us and then we helped them. We can't turn our backs on them.
I'm for going ashore.
I'm in.
There's no reason we can't save Lowtown *and* avoid being exiled for starting an international incident.
We got everything we need right here.
One of you sneak into town and plant this where no one will find it. I'll get the cavalry.
If I'm wrong, you can always throw away everything you worked for.

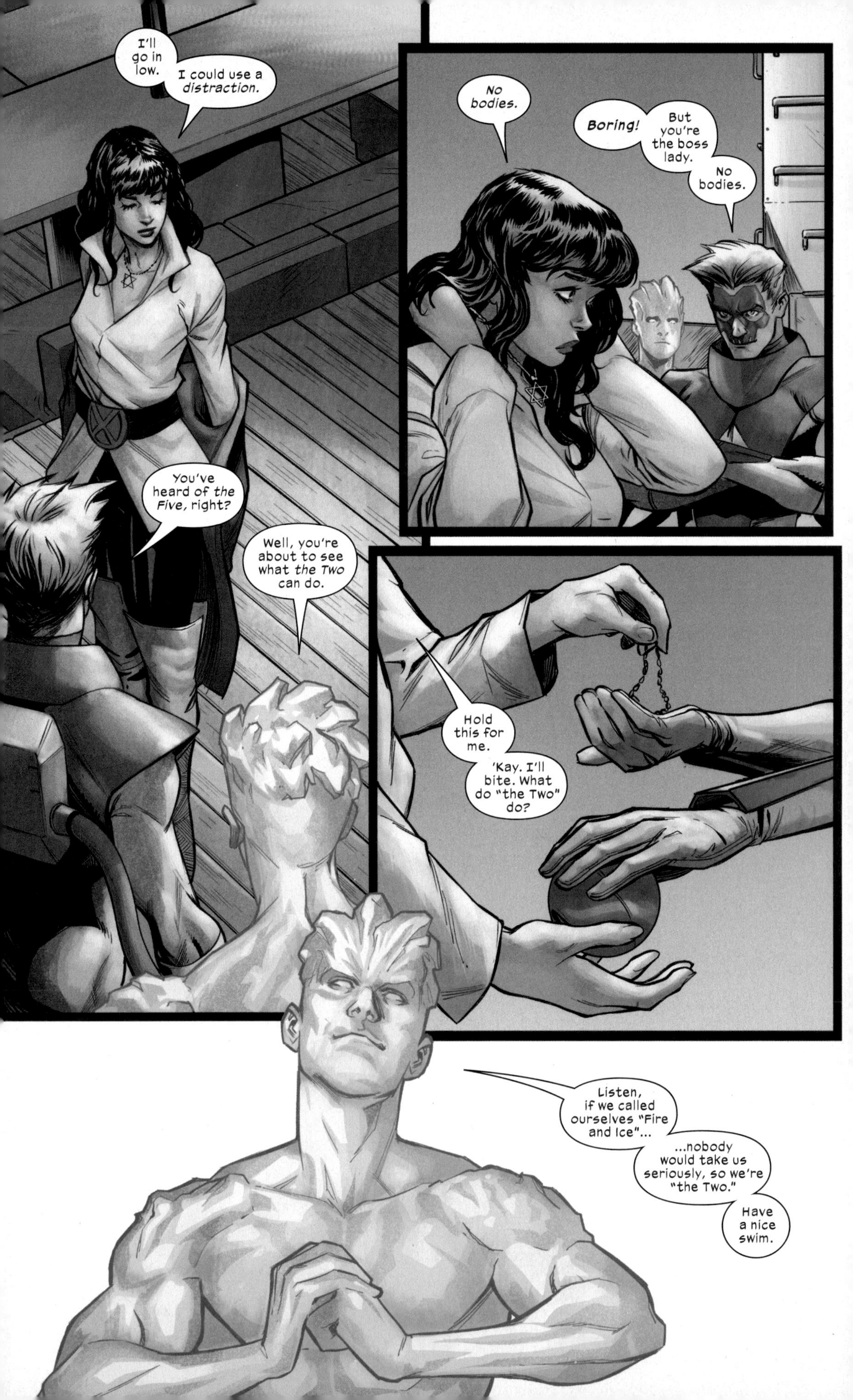
I'll go in low.
I could use a *distraction.*
No bodies.
Boring!
But you're the boss lady.
No bodies.
You've heard of *the Five,* right?
Well, you're about to see what *the Two* can do.
Hold this for me.
'Kay. I'll bite. What do "the Two" do?
Listen, if we called ourselves "Fire and Ice"...
...nobody would take us seriously, so we're "the Two."
Have a nice swim.

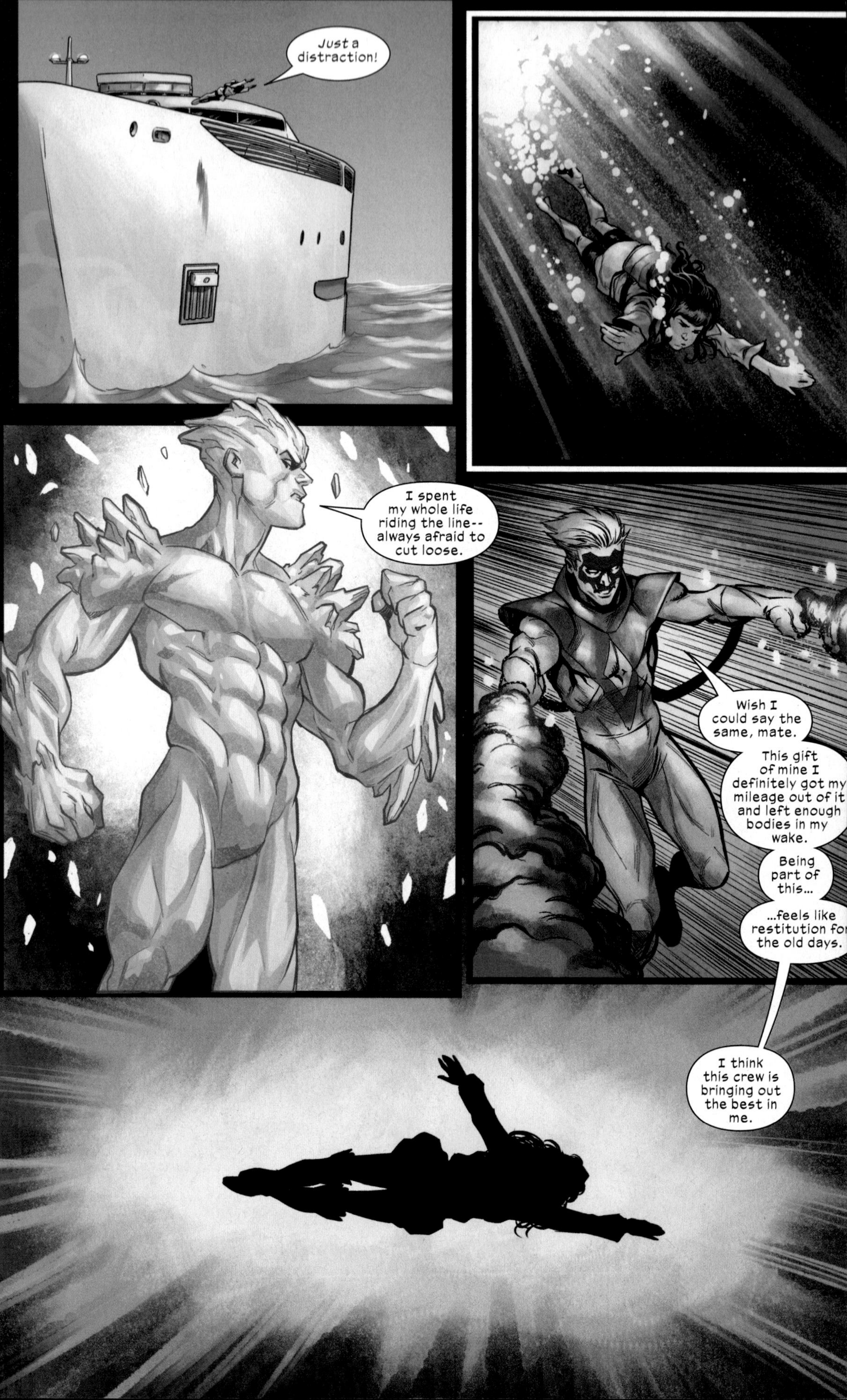
Just a distraction!
I spent my whole life riding the line-- always afraid to cut loose.
Wish I could say the same, mate.
This gift of mine I definitely got my mileage out of it and left enough bodies in my wake.
Being part of this...
...feels like restitution for the old days.
I think this crew is bringing out the best in me.

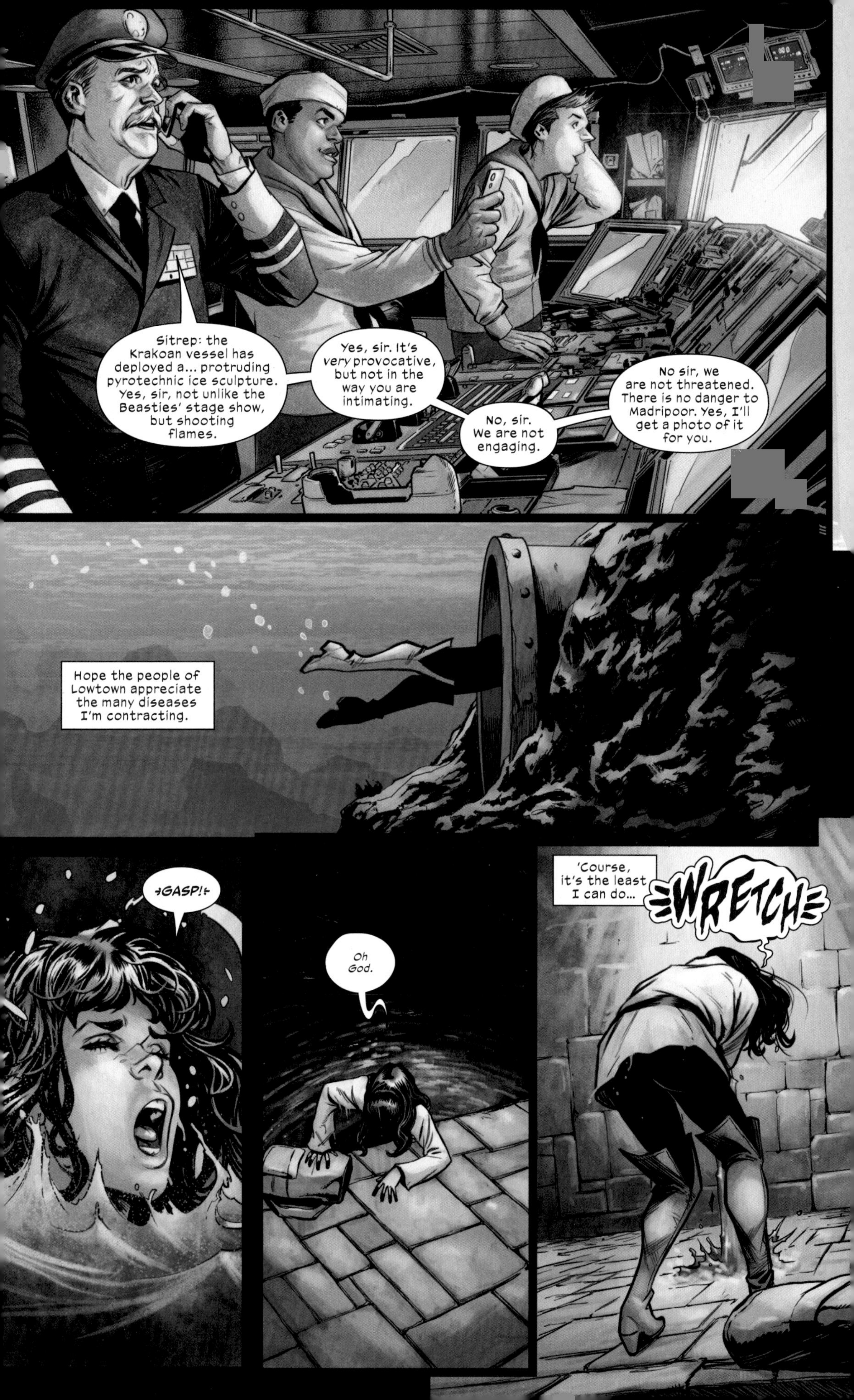

Sitrep: the Krakoan vessel has deployed a... protruding pyrotechnic ice sculpture. Yes, sir, not unlike the Beasties' stage show, but shooting flames.
Yes, sir. It's *very* provocative, but not in the way you are intimating.
No, sir. We are not engaging.
No sir, we are not threatened. There is no danger to Madripoor. Yes, I'll get a photo of it for you.
Hope the people of Lowtown appreciate the many diseases I'm contracting.
GASP!
Oh God.
'Course, it's the least I can do...
WRETCH

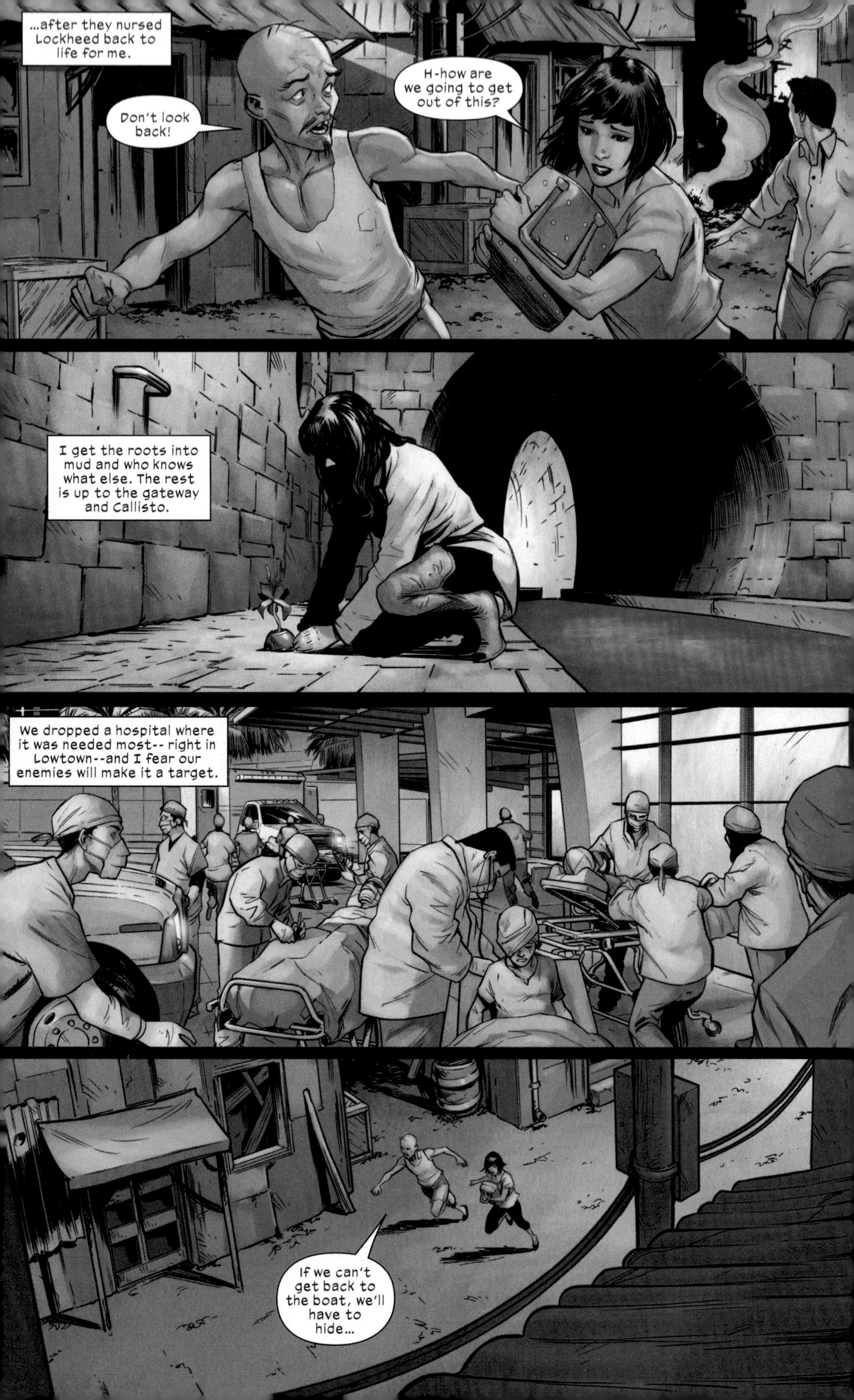
...after they nursed Lockheed back to life for me.
Don't look back!
H-how are we going to get out of this?
I get the roots into mud and who knows what else. The rest is up to the gateway and Callisto.
We dropped a hospital where it was needed most-- right in Lowtown--and I fear our enemies will make it a target.
If we can't get back to the boat, we'll have to hide...

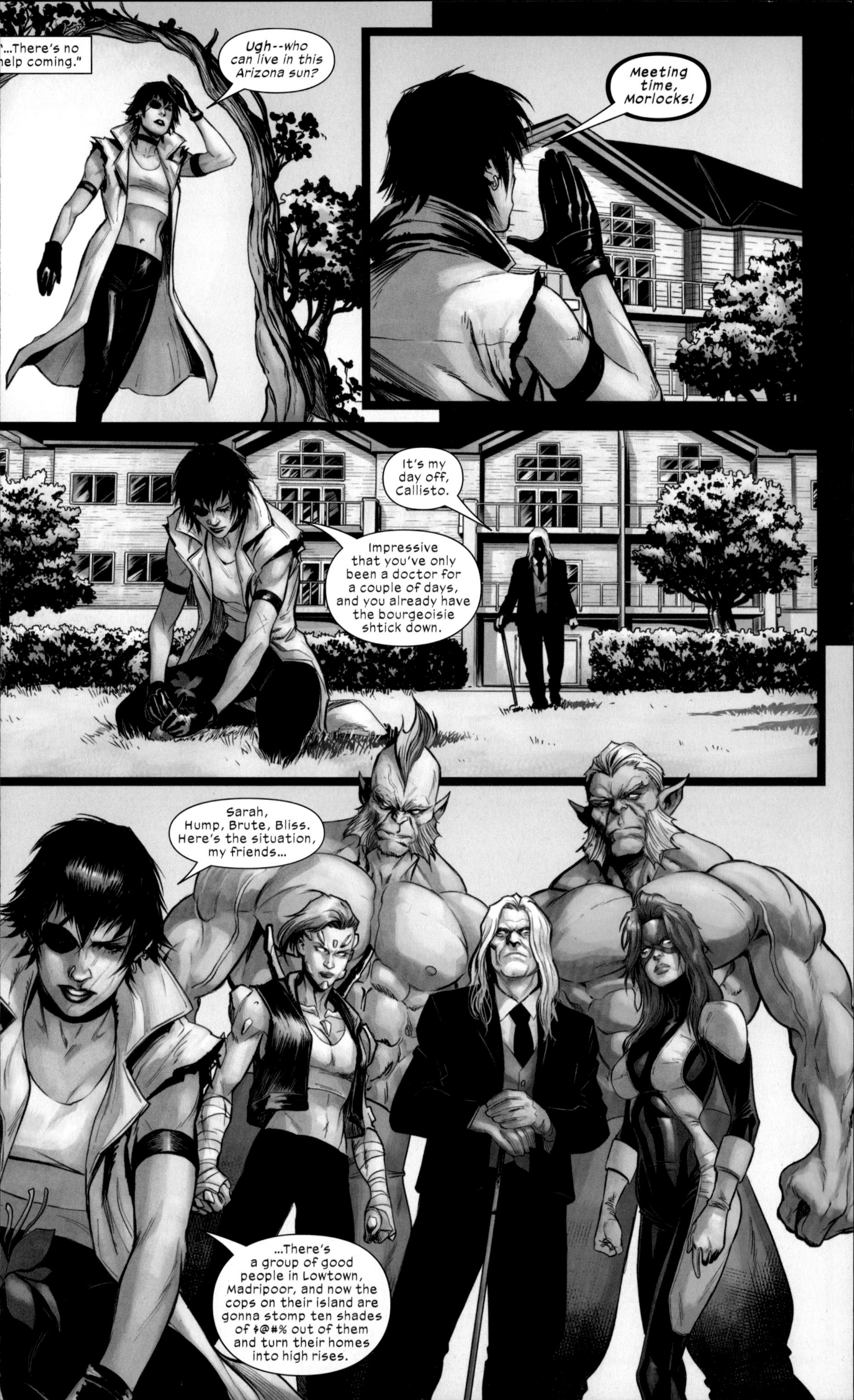
"...There's no help coming."
Ugh--who can live in this Arizona sun?
Meeting time, Morlocks!
It's my day off, Callisto.
Impressive that you've only been a doctor for a couple of days, and you already have the bourgeoisie shtick down.
Sarah, Hump, Brute, Bliss. Here's the situation, my friends...
...There's a group of good people in Lowtown, Madripoor, and now the cops on their island are gonna stomp ten shades of $@#% out of them and turn their homes into high rises.

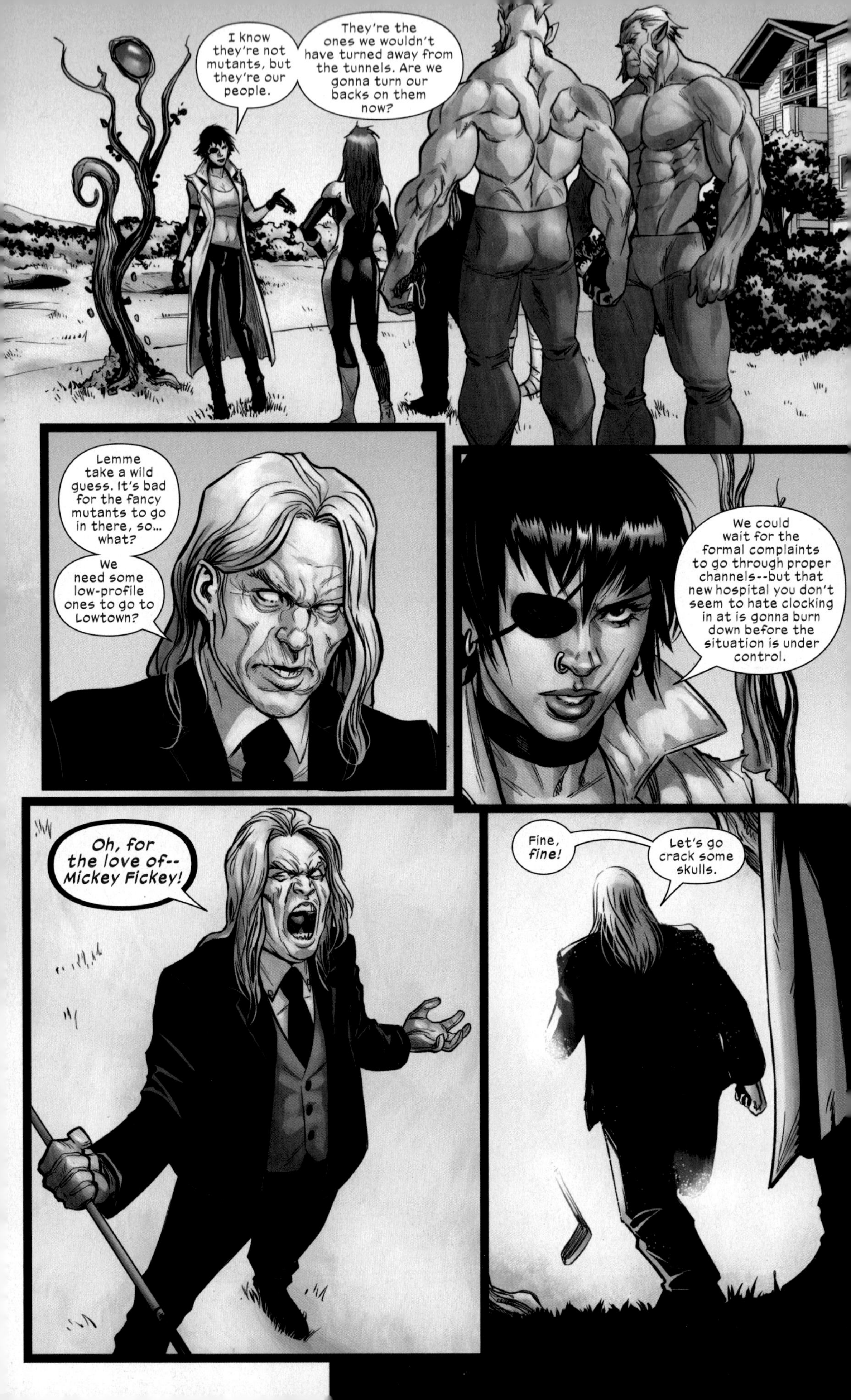
I know they're not mutants, but they're our people.
They're the ones we wouldn't have turned away from the tunnels. Are we gonna turn our backs on them now?
Lemme take a wild guess. It's bad for the fancy mutants to go in there, so... what?
We need some low-profile ones to go to Lowtown?
We could wait for the formal complaints to go through proper channels--but that new hospital you don't seem to hate clocking in at is gonna burn down before the situation is under control.
Oh, for the love of-- Mickey Fickey!
Fine, fine!
Let's go crack some skulls.

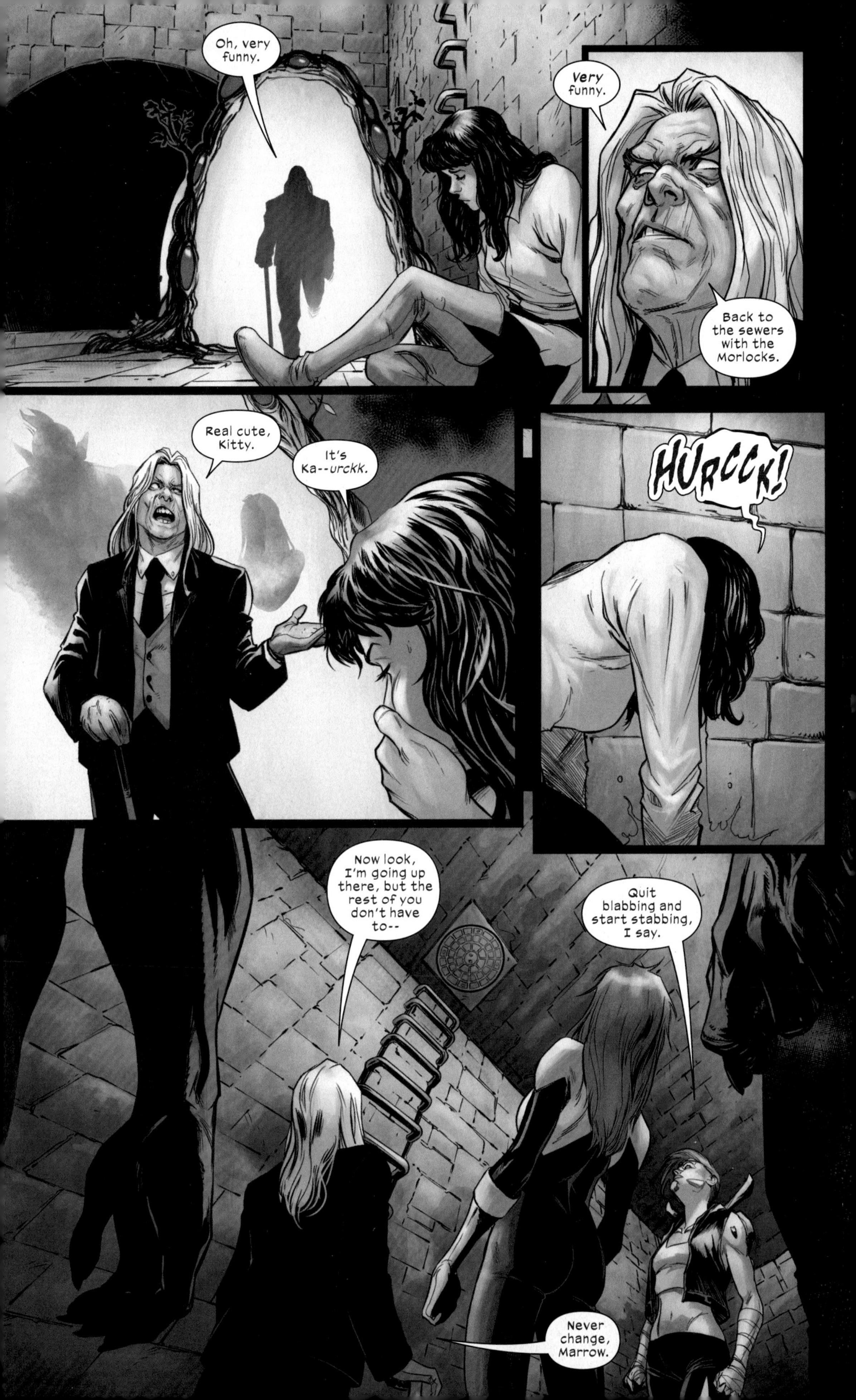
Oh, very funny.
Very funny.
Back to the sewers with the Morlocks.
Real cute, Kitty.
It's Ka--urckk.
HURCCK!
Now look, I'm going up there, but the rest of you don't have to--
Quit blabbing and start stabbing, I say.
Never change, Marrow.

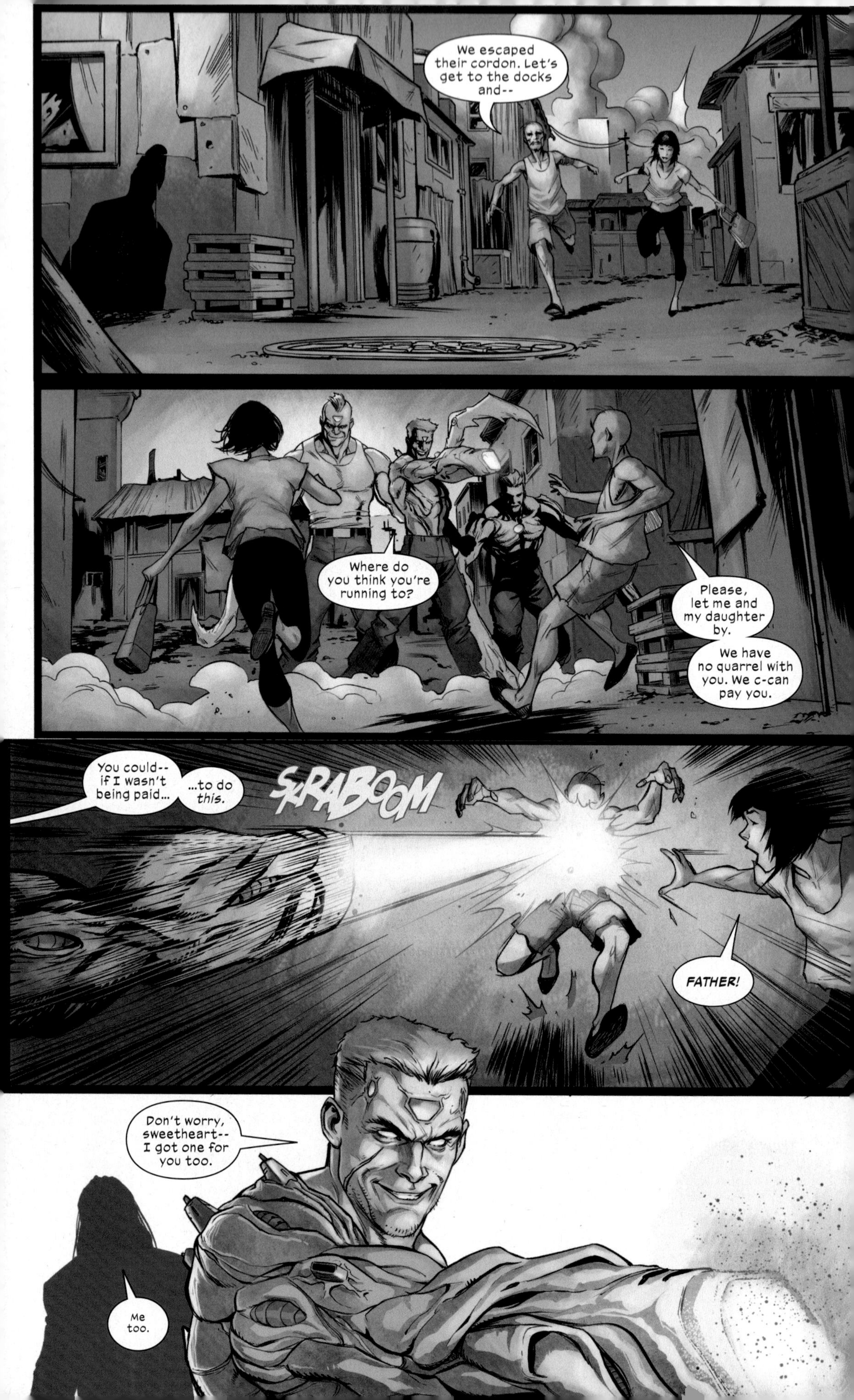
We escaped their cordon. Let's get to the docks and--
Where do you think you're running to?
Please, let me and my daughter by.
We have no quarrel with you. We c-can pay you.
You could--if I wasn't being paid...
...to do *this.*
SKRABOOM
FATHER!
Don't worry, sweetheart--I got one for you too.
Me too.

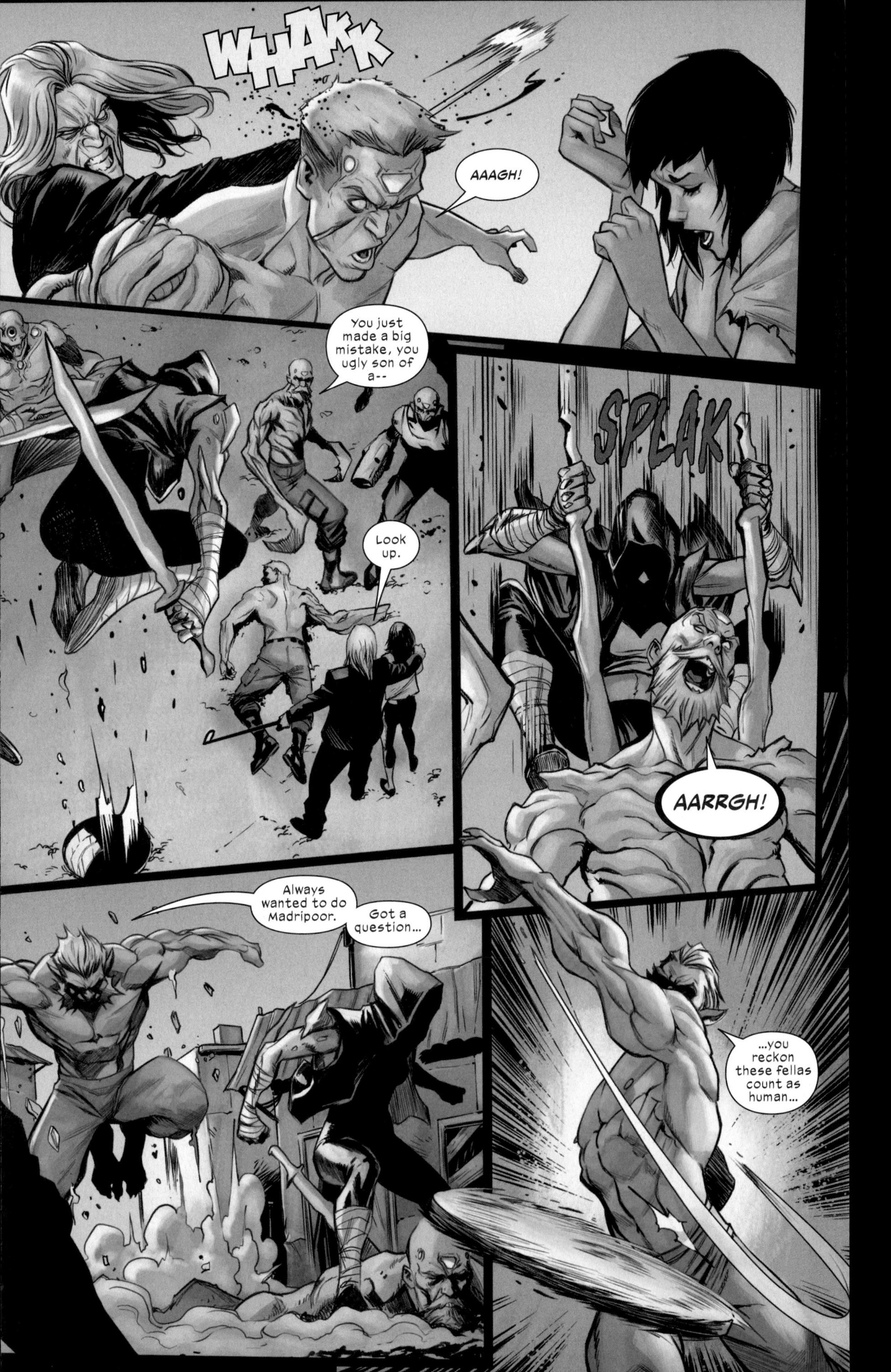
WHAKK
AAAGH!
You just made a big mistake, you ugly son of a--
Look up.
SPLAK
AARRGH!
Always wanted to do Madripoor.
Got a question...
...you reckon these fellas count as human...

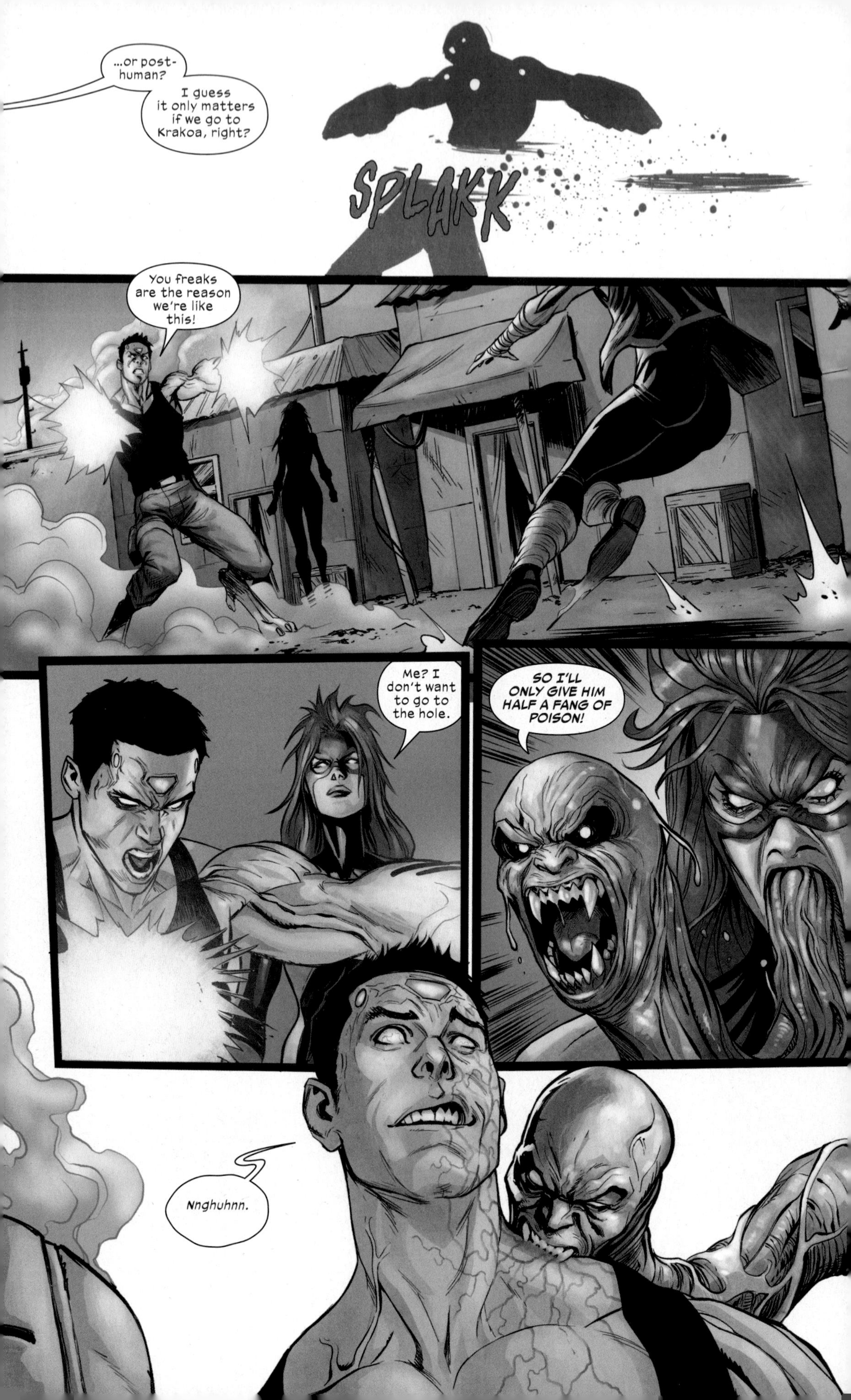
...or post-human?
I guess it only matters if we go to Krakoa, right?
SPLAKK
You freaks are the reason we're like this!
Me? I don't want to go to the hole.
SO I'LL ONLY GIVE HIM HALF A FANG OF POISON!
Nnghuhnn.

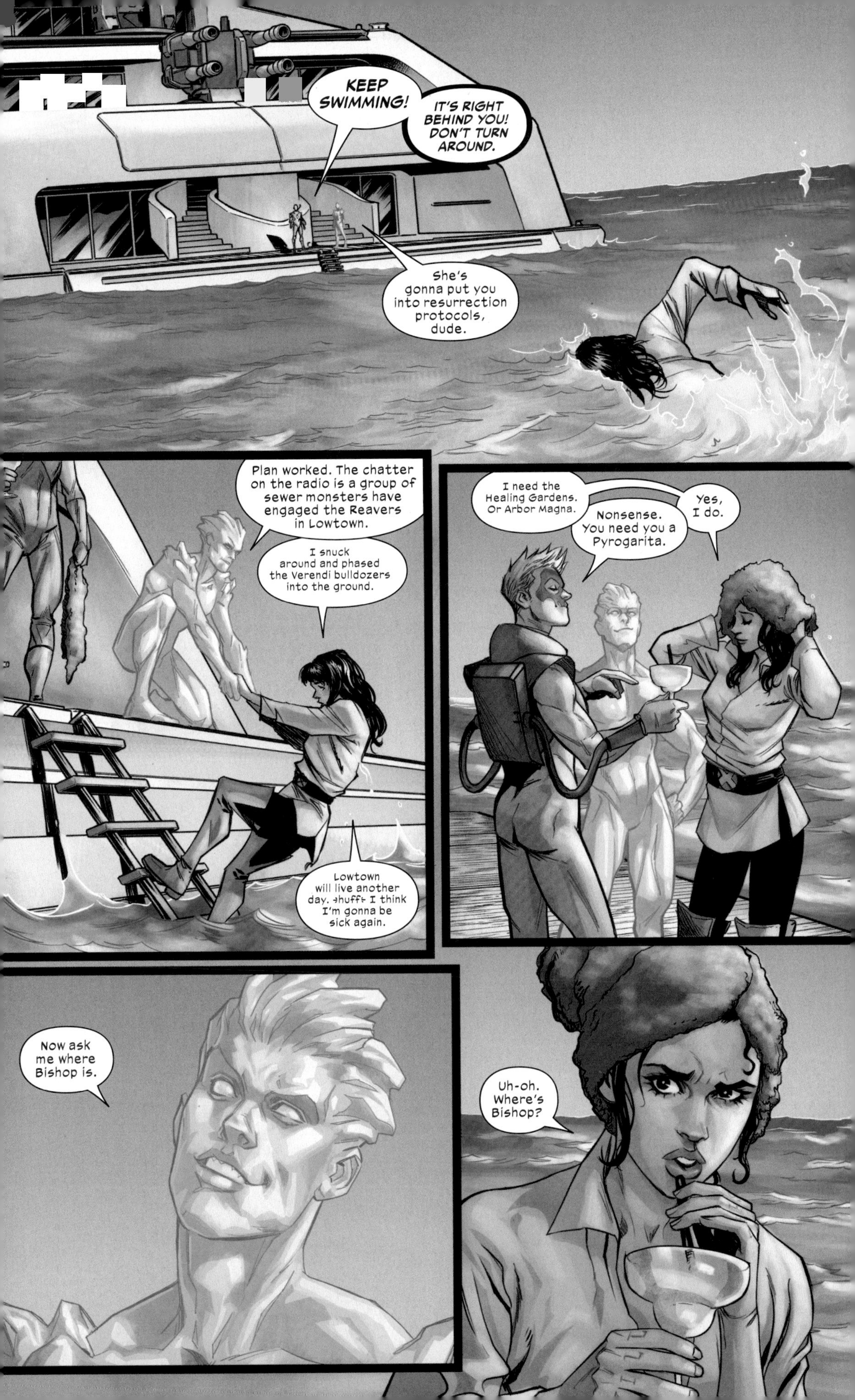
KEEP SWIMMING!
IT'S RIGHT BEHIND YOU! DON'T TURN AROUND.
She's gonna put you into resurrection protocols, dude.
Plan worked. The chatter on the radio is a group of sewer monsters have engaged the Reavers in Lowtown.
I snuck around and phased the Verendi bulldozers into the ground.
Lowtown will live another day. ⸗huff⸗ I think I'm gonna be sick again.
I need the Healing Gardens. Or Arbor Magna.
Nonsense. You need you a Pyrogarita.
Yes, I do.
Now ask me where Bishop is.
Uh-oh. Where's Bishop?

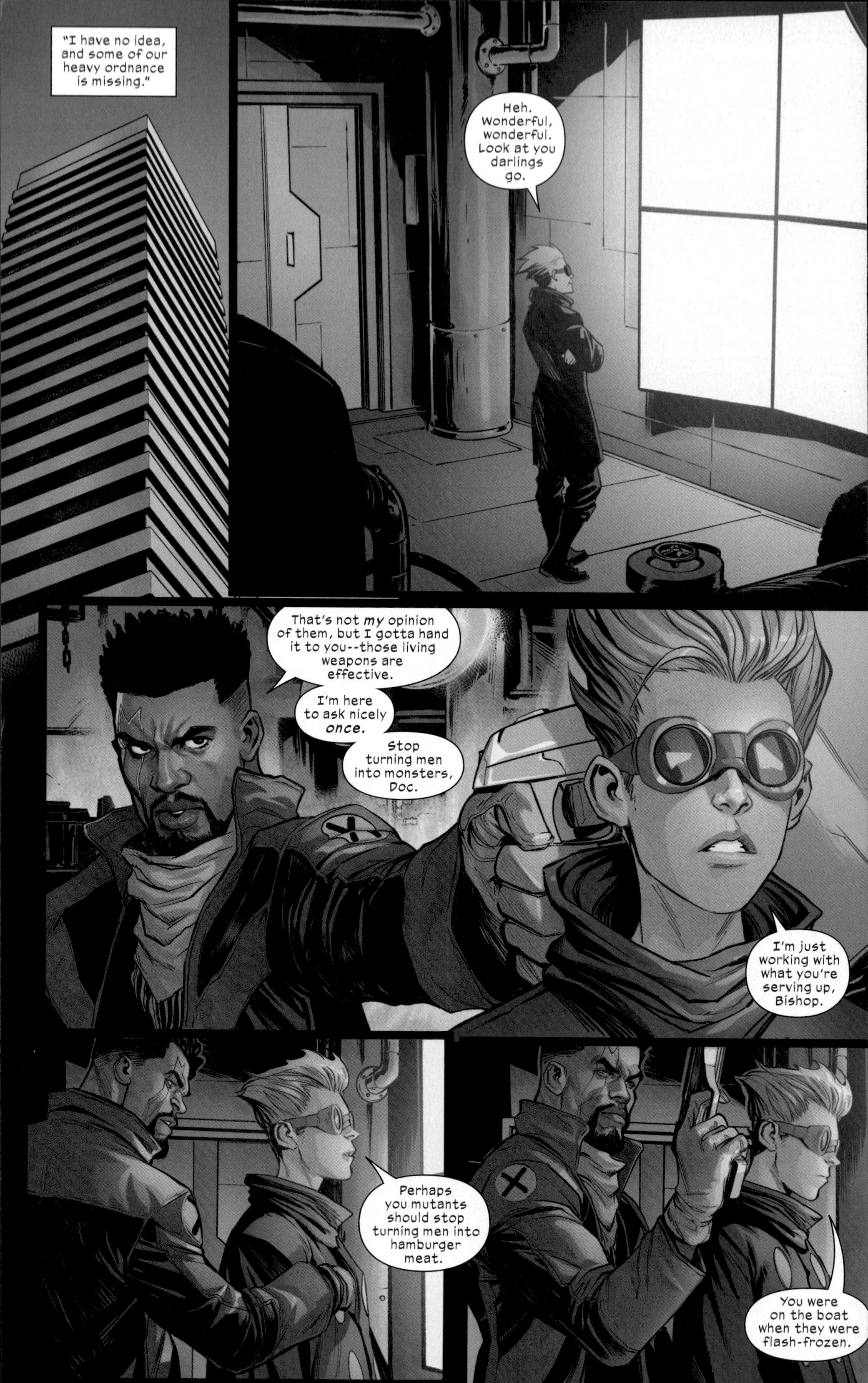
"I have no idea, and some of our heavy ordnance is missing."
Heh. Wonderful, wonderful. Look at you darlings go.
That's not *my* opinion of them, but I gotta hand it to you--those living weapons are effective.
I'm here to ask nicely *once.*
Stop turning men into monsters, Doc.
I'm just working with what you're serving up, Bishop.
Perhaps you mutants should stop turning men into hamburger meat.
You were on the boat when they were flash-frozen.

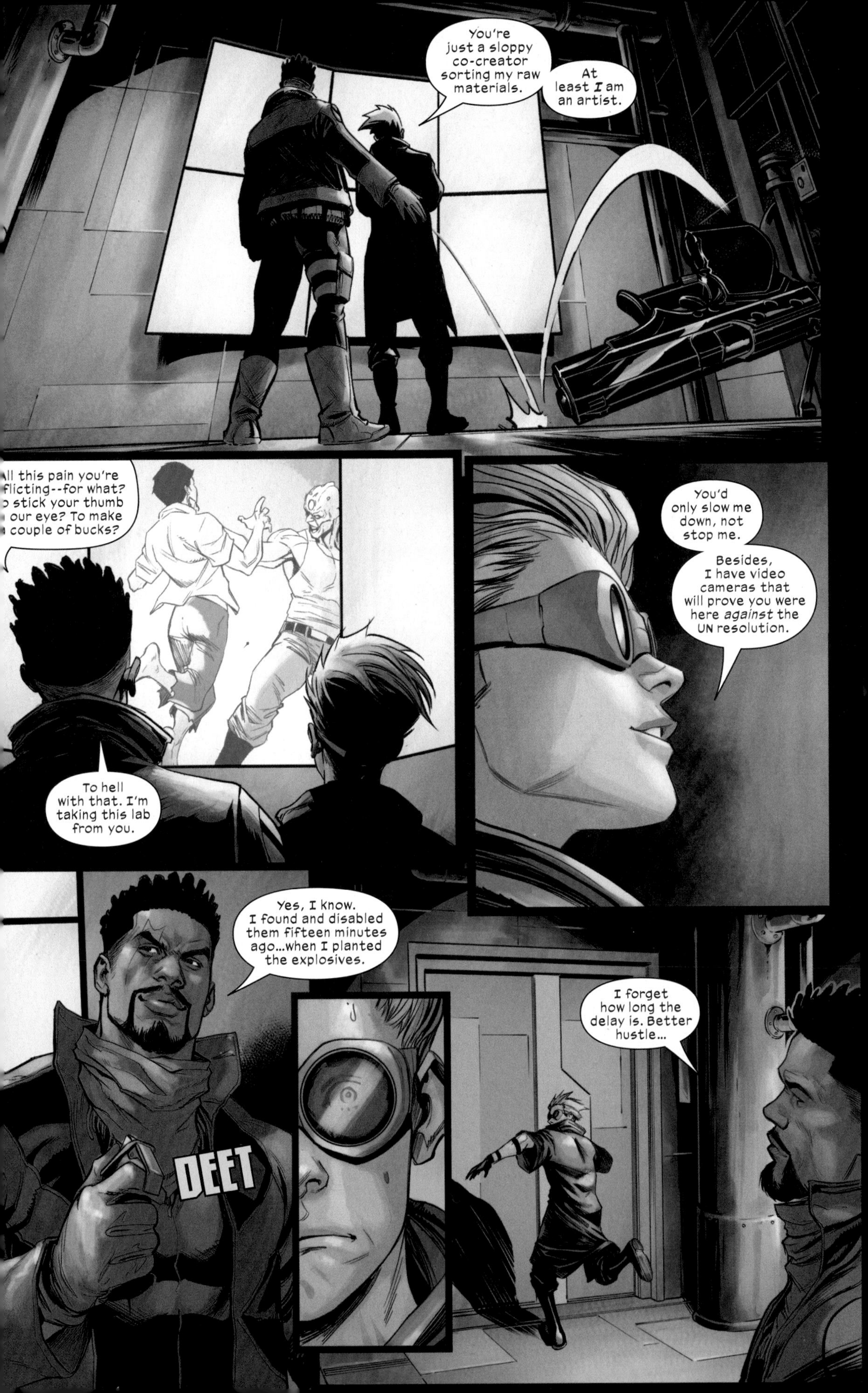
You're just a sloppy co-creator sorting my raw materials.
At least *I* am an artist.
ll this pain you're flicting--for what? o stick your thumb our eye? To make couple of bucks?
To hell with that. I'm taking this lab from you.
You'd only slow me down, not stop me.
Besides, I have video cameras that will prove you were here *against* the UN resolution.
Yes, I know. I found and disabled them fifteen minutes ago...when I planted the explosives.
DEET
I forget how long the delay is. Better hustle...

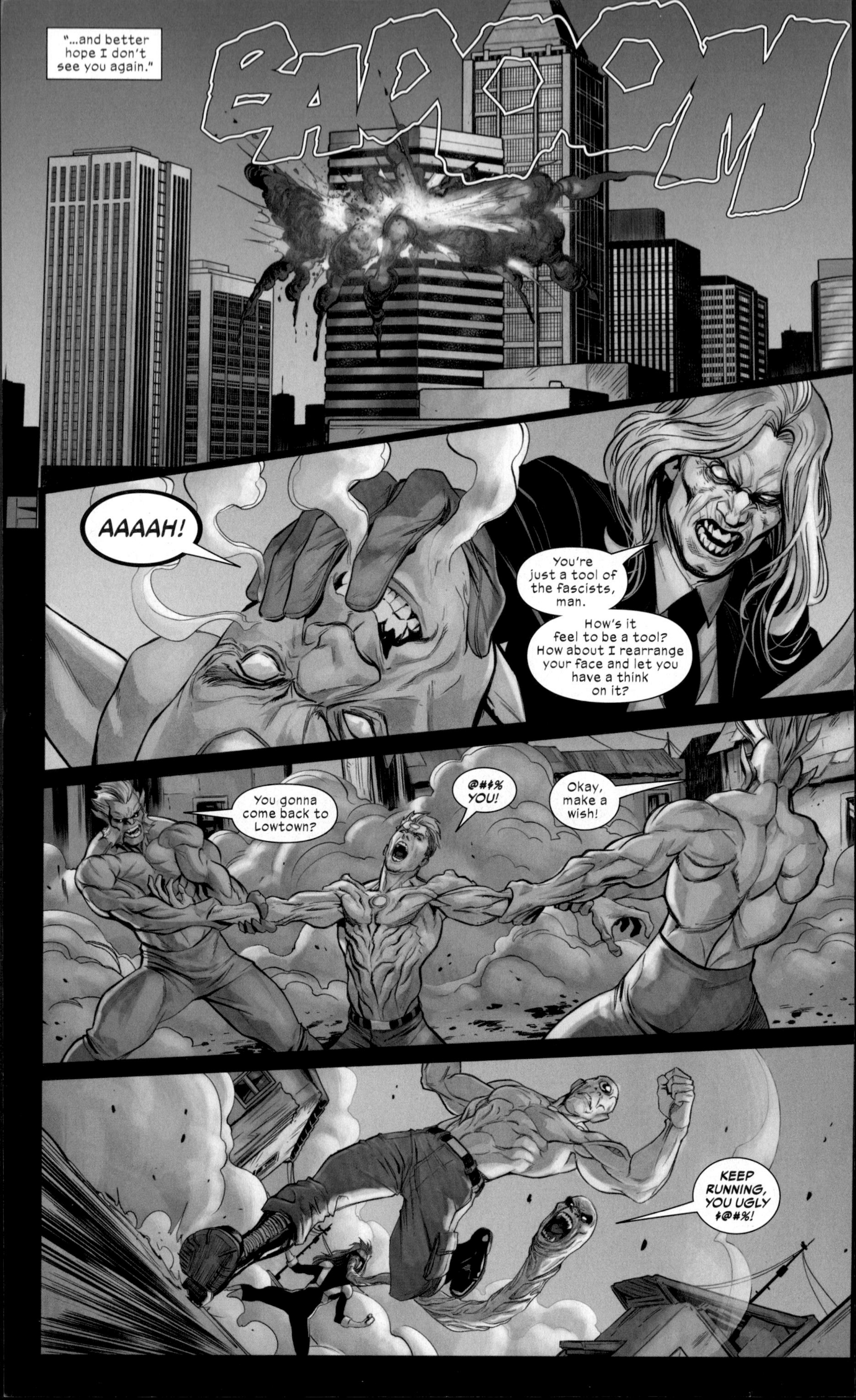
"...and better hope I don't see you again."
BADOOM
AAAAH!
You're just a tool of the fascists, man.
How's it feel to be a tool? How about I rearrange your face and let you have a think on it?
You gonna come back to Lowtown?
@#$% YOU!
Okay, make a wish!
KEEP RUNNING, YOU UGLY $@#%!

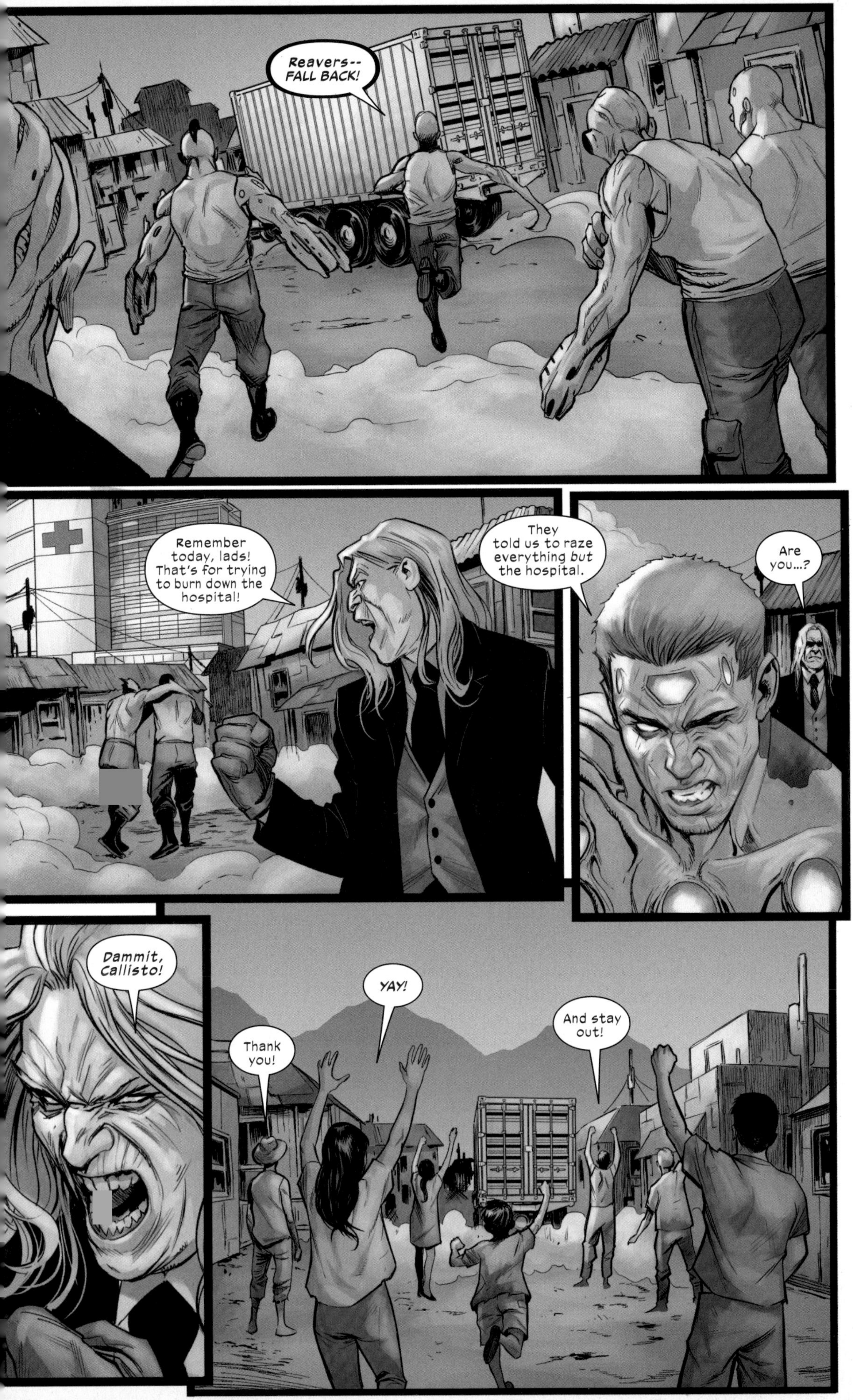
Reavers-- FALL BACK!
Remember today, lads! That's for trying to burn down the hospital!
They told us to raze everything *but* the hospital.
Are you...?
Dammit, Callisto!
Thank you!
YAY!
And stay out!

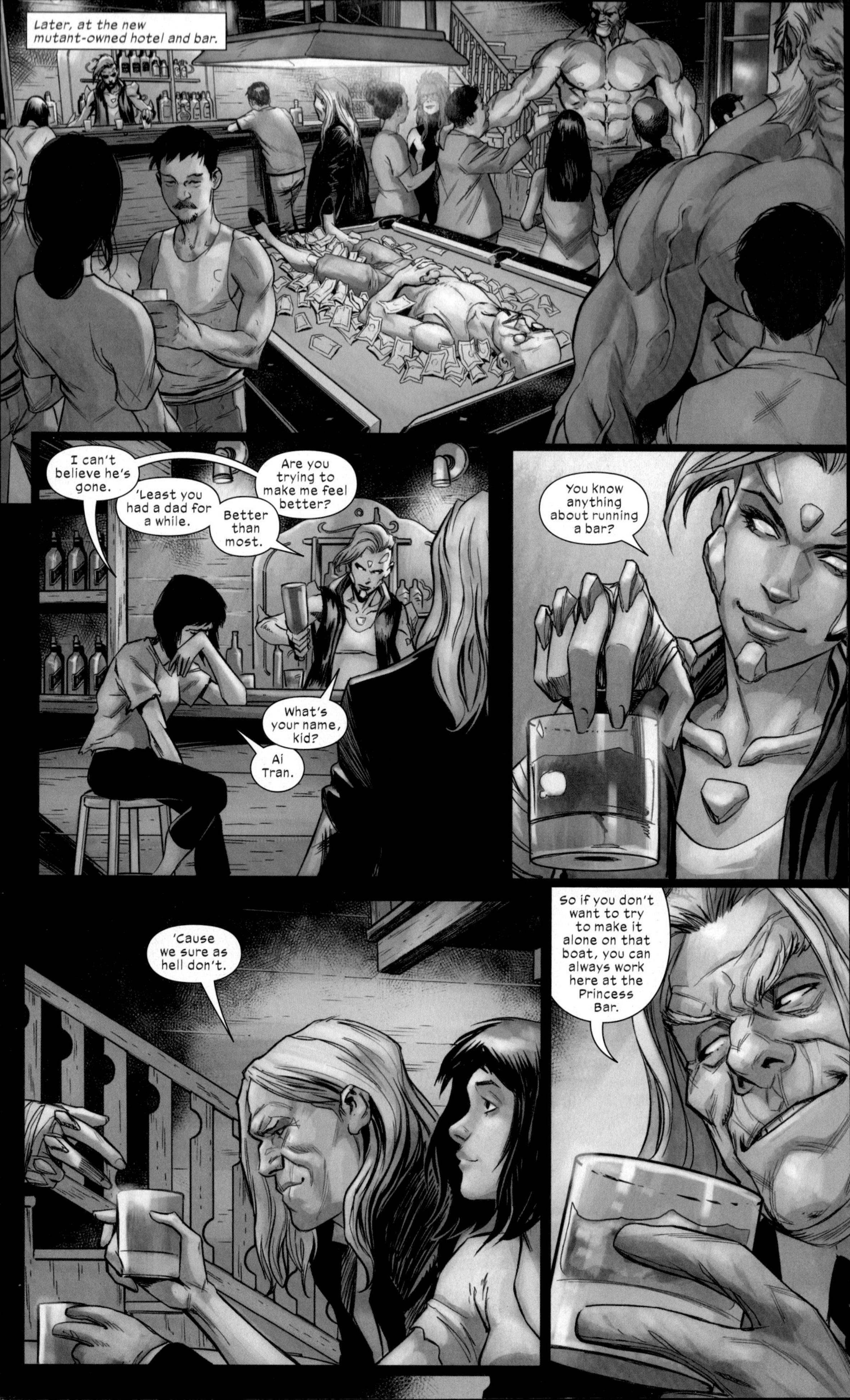
Later, at the new mutant-owned hotel and bar.
I can't believe he's gone.
'Least you had a dad for a while.
Are you trying to make me feel better?
Better than most.
What's your name, kid?
Ai Tran.
You know anything about running a bar?
'Cause we sure as hell don't.
So if you don't want to try to make it alone on that boat, you can always work here at the Princess Bar.

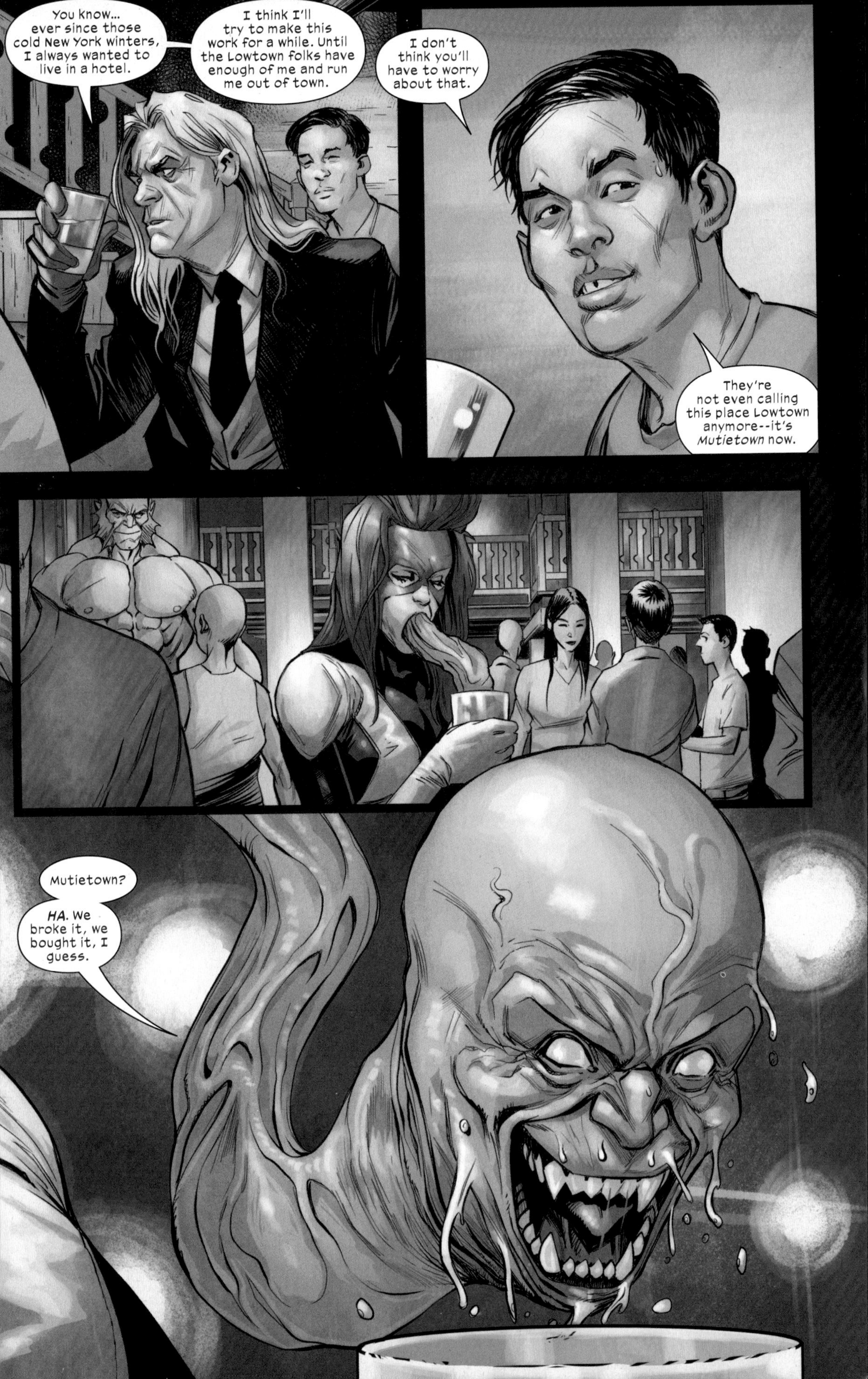

You know... ever since those cold New York winters, I always wanted to live in a hotel.
I think I'll try to make this work for a while. Until the Lowtown folks have enough of me and run me out of town.
I don't think you'll have to worry about that.
They're not even calling this place Lowtown anymore--it's *Mutietown* now.
Mutietown?
HA. We broke it, we bought it, I guess.

X-DESK MUTANT MEDIA DATA CAPTURE

DAILY BUGLE — FASHION SECTION, JUNE
BY EMMA NEWCOMER

How do you dress hundreds of mutants for the Hellfire Gala when you only have four arms? With some careful planning and by borrowing some very special mutant gifts. Jumbo Carnation, the breakout fashion star originally from New York City, set the fashion world ablaze with his inspiring work.

The *Daily Bugle* managed to get a few short minutes with him during a limousine ride from the Krakoan Gate in Midtown to the Garment District along with some very...weird assistants. When I press Jumbo on how he plans to be able to dress the mutants himself, he smiles and introduces me to Madrox, the Multiple Man (Well, hello) and the Stepford Cuckoos (WHAT?). Evidently, the Stepford Cuckoos can pluck the ideas right from Jumbo's talented mind and drop them into the Madrox minds, serving as House Carnation's cut and sew department.

Bugle readers might recall Jumbo's name from the crime blotter a few seasons back, not as a perp — but as a victim. It turns out that Jumbo cracked up a bit with all the fame, partying, attention and drugs that came with his meteoric success.

"I needed a break, and I didn't quite plan it right. I've apologized to my fans, but...it's not like I'm the first designer to fake my death...but I'm not going to name names." Jumbo laughs with a mischievous glint in his eye.

I make a joke about whether the Stepford Cuckoos are really blond, and they don't even respond. That's discipline.

I ask Jumbo if he's got a plus-one for me for the gala, and he lets me down easy.

"I've got someone on my arm that night. My patron, Emma Frost, the White Queen of the Hellfire Club."

But, Jumbo! What about your other arms?

The White Queen's Hellfire Gala, the hottest ticket anywhere on the planet this summer, and you and I are not invited. I'm not even mad.

I ask for a peek at Jumbo's designs, and once again he lets me down easy but does give me the scoop that he has inked a deal with Timely Publications to publish a limited edition book of this year's fashions, which should be under trees for the holidays.

I'll be attending the Hellfire Gala with the rest of you: watching from home in our sweatpants. I wasn't born a mutant. C'est la vie.

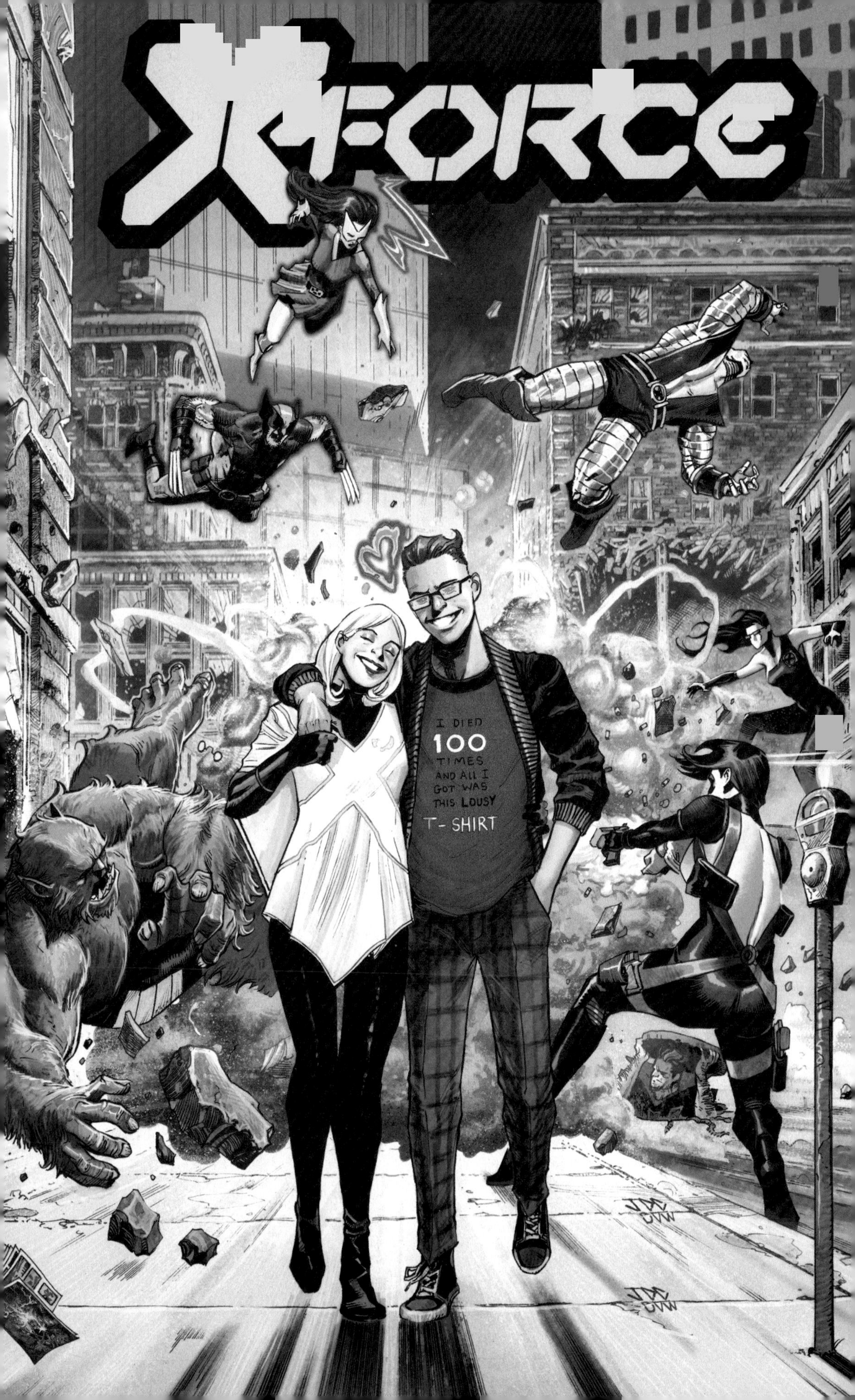
X-FORCE
I DIED 100 TIMES AND ALL I GOT WAS THIS LOUSY T-SHIRT

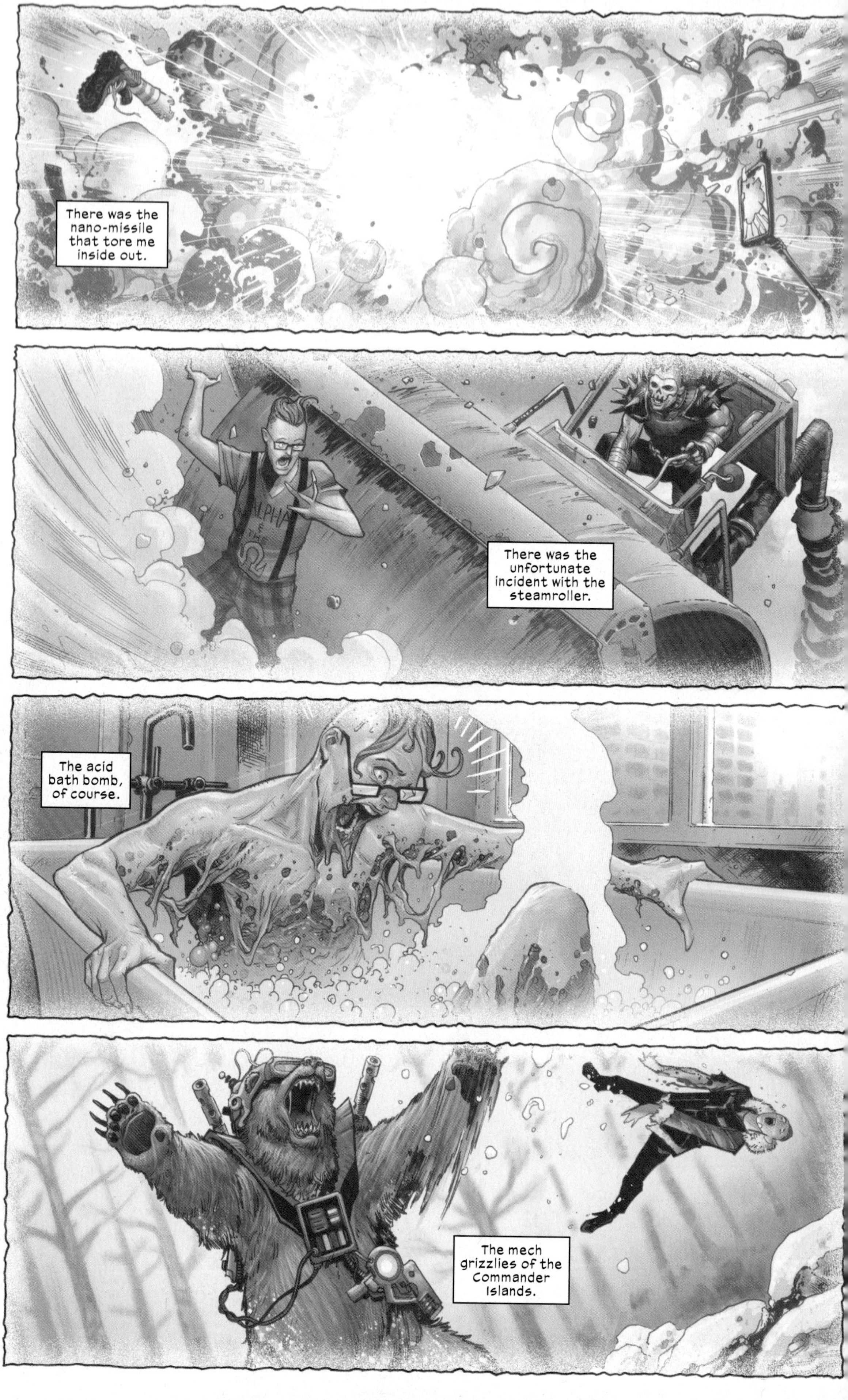
There was the nano-missile that tore me inside out.
There was the unfortunate incident with the steamroller.
The acid bath bomb, of course.
The mech grizzlies of the Commander Islands.

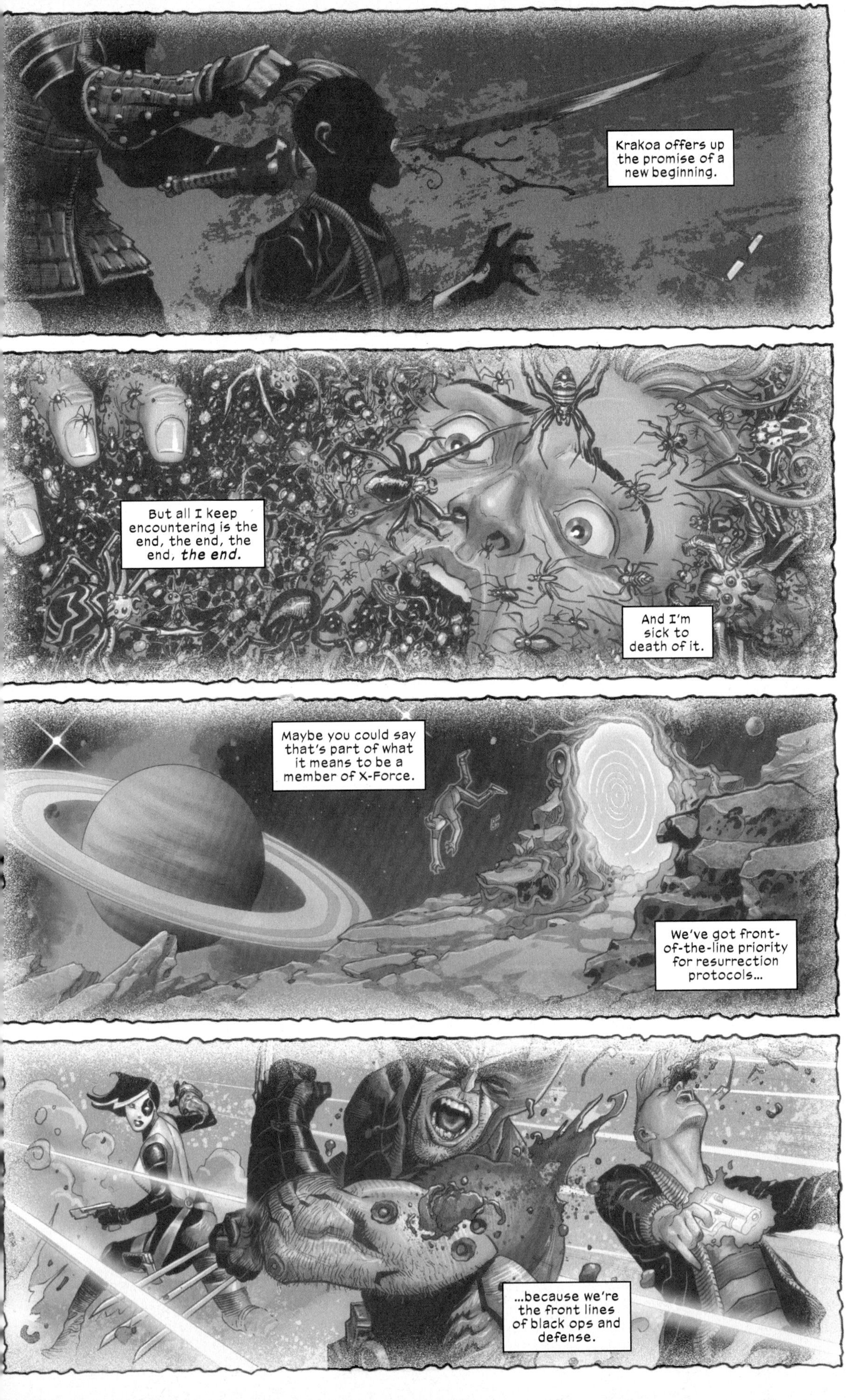

Krakoa offers up the promise of a new beginning.
But all I keep encountering is the end, the end, the end, ***the end.***
And I'm sick to death of it.
Maybe you could say that's part of what it means to be a member of X-Force.
We've got front-of-the-line priority for resurrection protocols...
...because we're the front lines of black ops and defense.

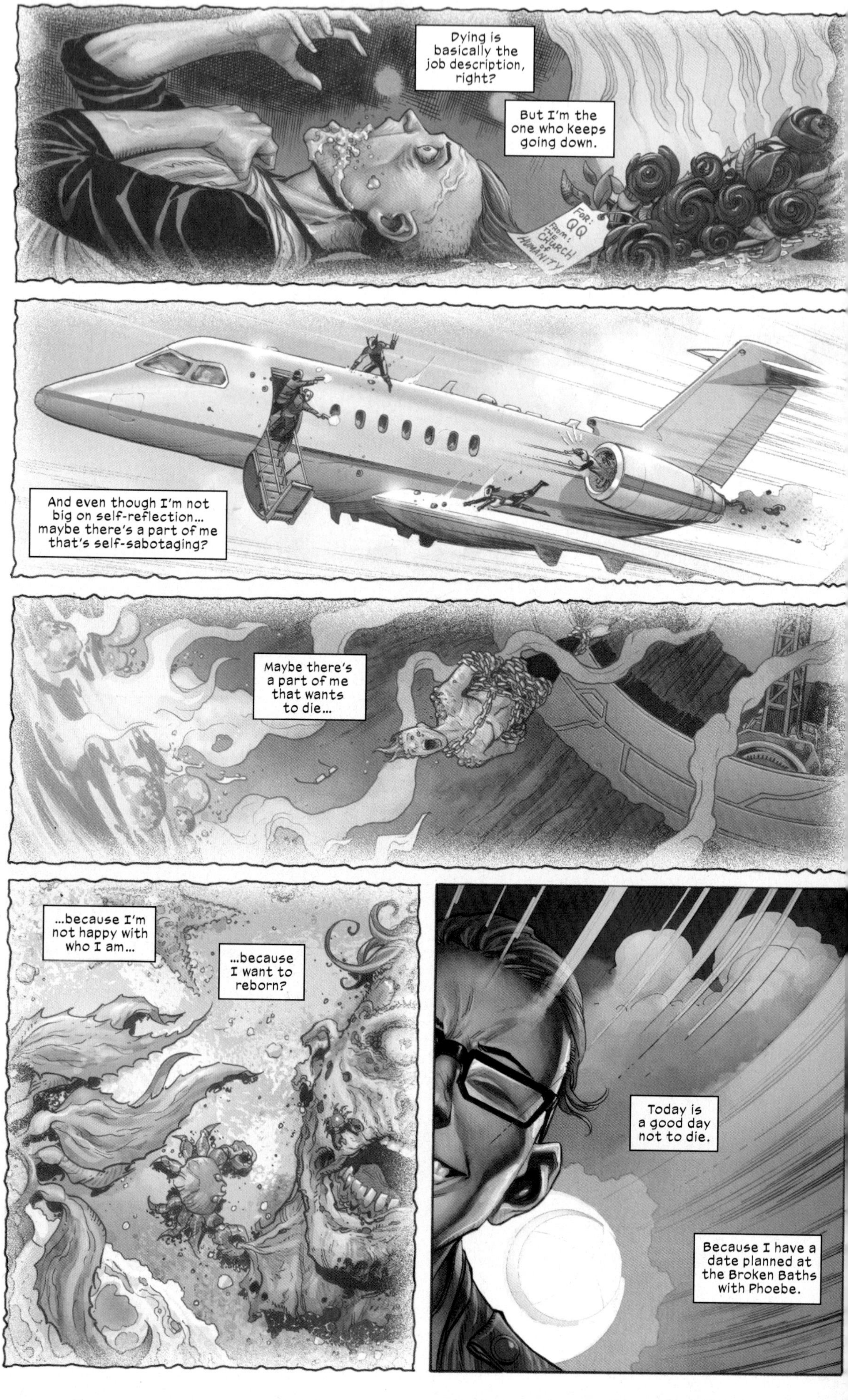

Dying is basically the job description, right?
But I'm the one who keeps going down.
FOR: QQ From: THE CHURCH of HUMANITY
And even though I'm not big on self-reflection... maybe there's a part of me that's self-sabotaging?
Maybe there's a part of me that wants to die...
...because I'm not happy with who I am...
...because I want to reborn?
Today is a good day not to die.
Because I have a date planned at the Broken Baths with Phoebe.

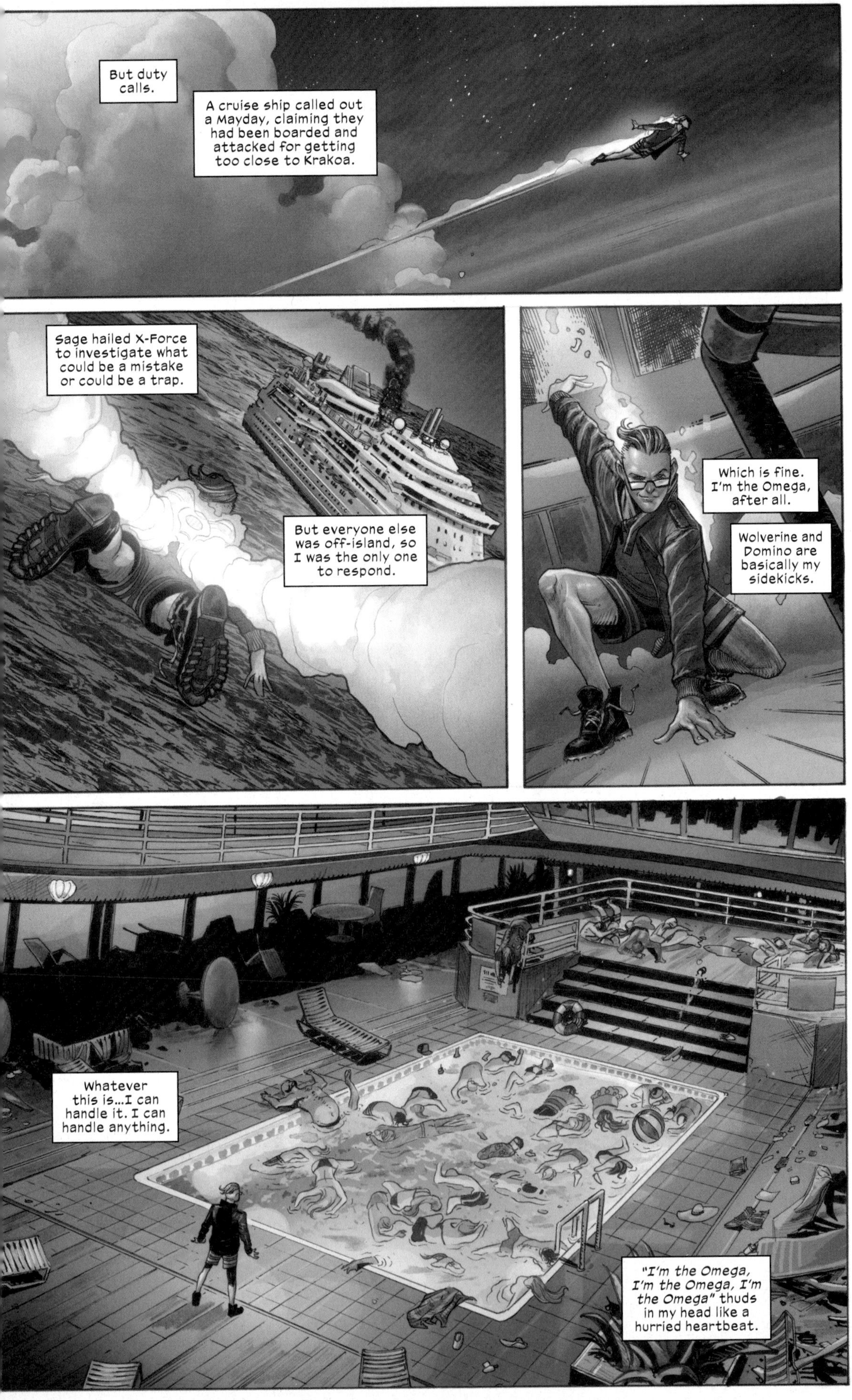
But duty calls.
A cruise ship called out a Mayday, claiming they had been boarded and attacked for getting too close to Krakoa.
Sage hailed X-Force to investigate what could be a mistake or could be a trap.
But everyone else was off-island, so I was the only one to respond.
Which is fine. I'm the Omega, after all.
Wolverine and Domino are basically my sidekicks.
Whatever this is...I can handle it. I can handle anything.
"I'm the Omega, I'm the Omega, I'm the Omega" thuds in my head like a hurried heartbeat.

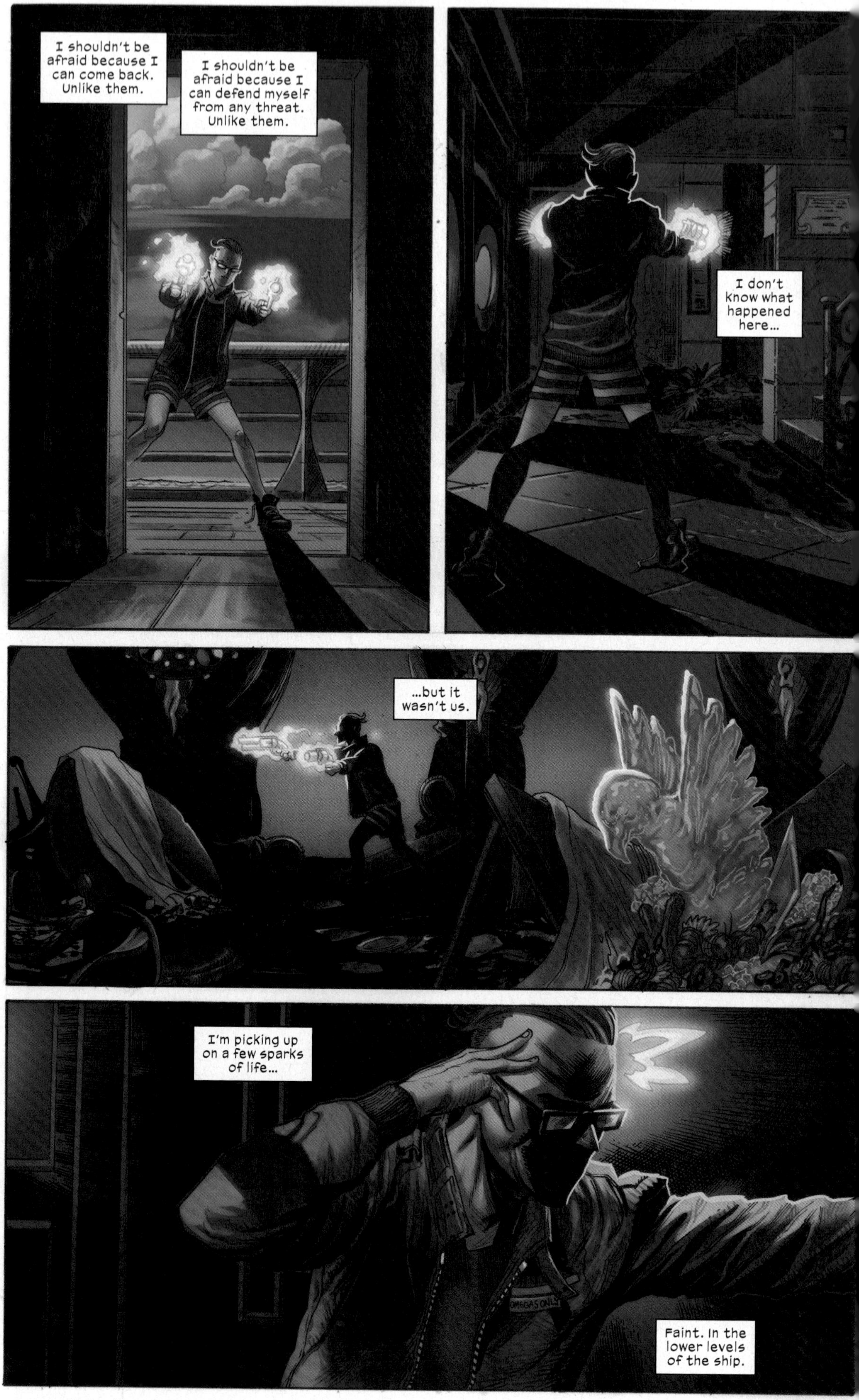
I shouldn't be afraid because I can come back. Unlike them.
I shouldn't be afraid because I can defend myself from any threat. Unlike them.
I don't know what happened here...
...but it wasn't us.
I'm picking up on a few sparks of life...
Faint. In the lower levels of the ship.

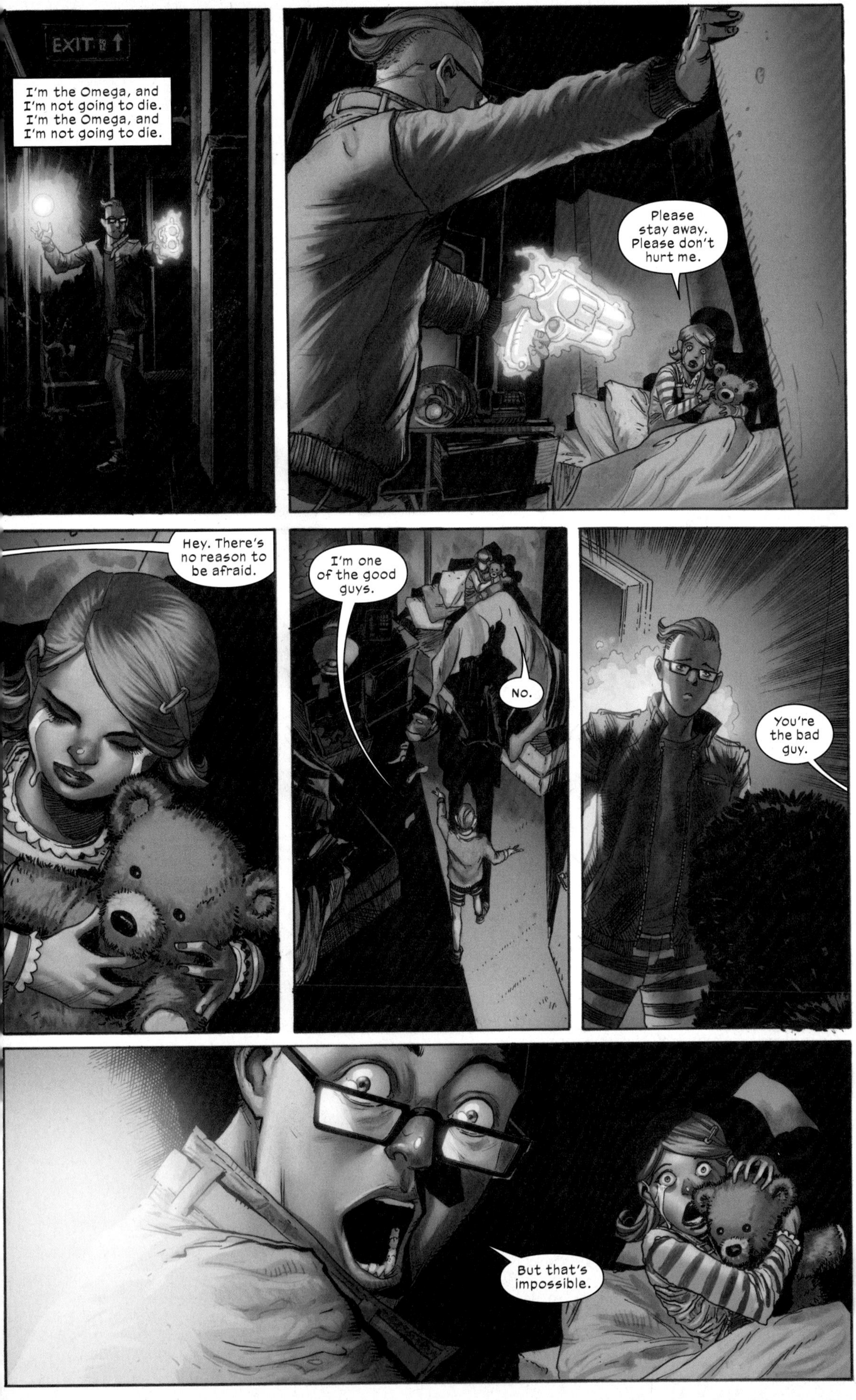
EXIT
I'm the Omega, and I'm not going to die. I'm the Omega, and I'm not going to die.
Please stay away. Please don't hurt me.
Hey. There's no reason to be afraid.
I'm one of the good guys.
No.
You're the bad guy.
But that's impossible.

[00_mutant__espionage]
[00_law_order____X___]

THE THOUSAND DEATHS AND ONE LIFE OF QUENTIN QUIRE

Every member of X-Force is prepared to lay down their life for Krakoa. Even if it means dying over and over and over and over and over again. But practice doesn't make the mental toll easier to bear -- that is, unless you can find something worth living for.

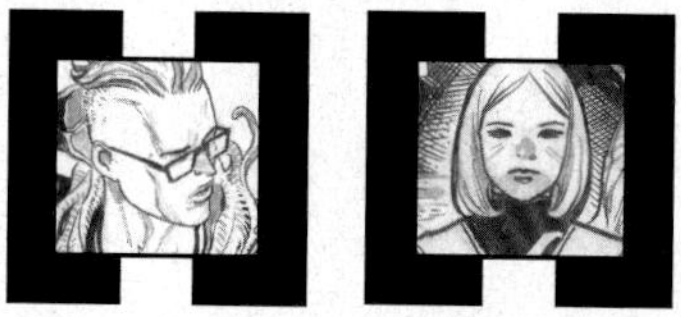

Kid Omega

Phoebe Cuckoo

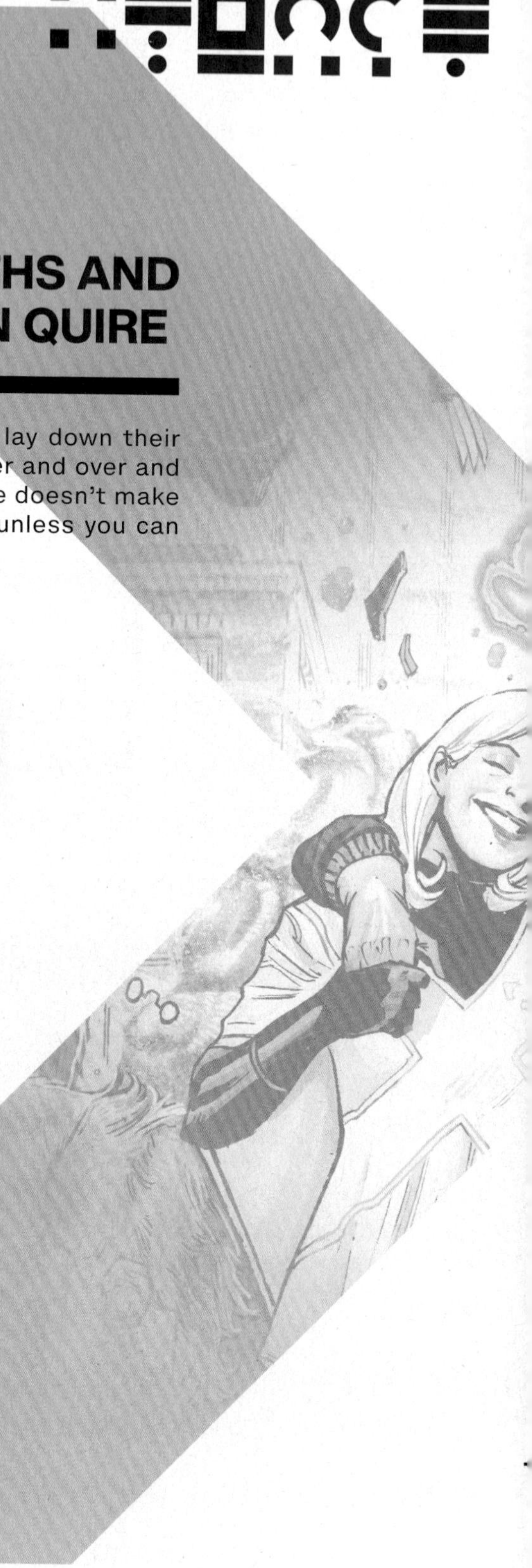

[00_Reign]
[00___ofX]

X-FORCE [X_17]

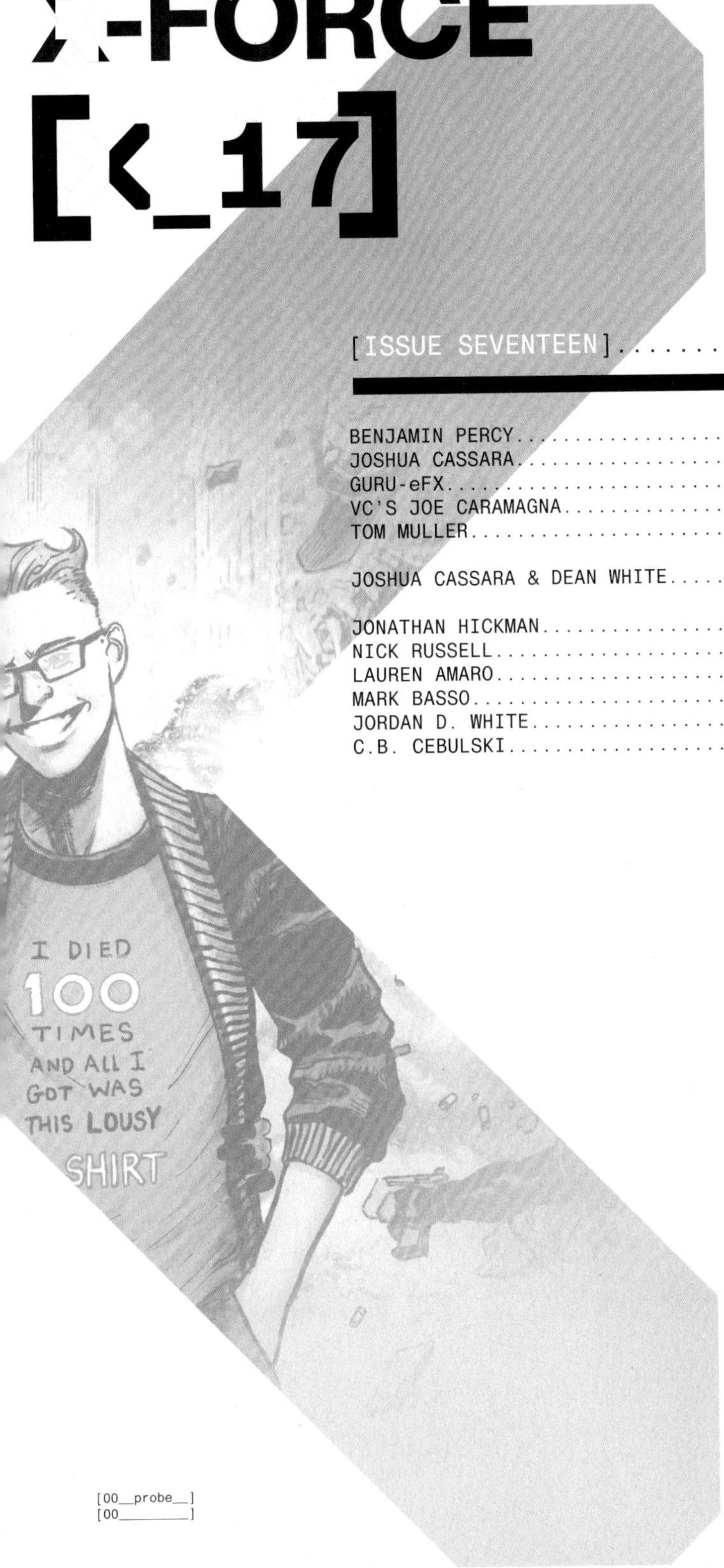
I DIED
100
TIMES
AND ALL I
GOT WAS
THIS LOUSY
SHIRT

[ISSUE SEVENTEEN]........OMEGA, RECONSIDERED

BENJAMIN PERCY....................................[WRITER]
JOSHUA CASSARA....................................[ARTIST]
GURU-eFX....................................[COLOR ARTIST]
VC'S JOE CARAMAGNA..............................[LETTERER]
TOM MULLER..[DESIGN]

JOSHUA CASSARA & DEAN WHITE.................[COVER ARTISTS]

JONATHAN HICKMAN...............................[HEAD OF X]
NICK RUSSELL..................................[PRODUCTION]
LAUREN AMARO............................[ASSISTANT EDITOR]
MARK BASSO..[EDITOR]
JORDAN D. WHITE...........................[SENIOR EDITOR]
C.B. CEBULSKI............................[EDITOR IN CHIEF]

[00__probe__]
[00________]

[00________]

[00________X]

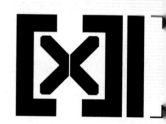

BEAST'S LOGBOOK:
TERROR CAMPAIGN

There have been three unsubstantiated reports of mutant aggression in as many days.

1) The first comes from a propaganda feed -- called SAPIENS -- that has developed a significant following on social media. They recently posted a claim that we put mind-control organics into all our medicines. The article has been shared tens of millions of times, including by politicians. The claim is of course false. Though a) We cannot prove it as such without exposing our bio-technology, and b) We are certainly capable of such measures but would consider it...only in extreme circumstances.

2) Then, the very founder of SAPIENS -- which is dedicated to anti-mutant politics and conspiracies -- flung himself out a window. The news of this -- announced and broadcast via their site -- accuses us of assassination in response to his investigation work.

3) The mass murder of the cruise ship passengers was staged in such a way that its proximity to Krakoa and the profile of the attack itself (which appears at a glance to be a psionic event) implicates us.

//Conclusions//

::: Disinformation and distrust are our greatest enemies :::

::: Civilian loss of life requires immediate response :::

::: Characteristics align with previous XENO campaigns :::

The Hatchery.
Krakoa.

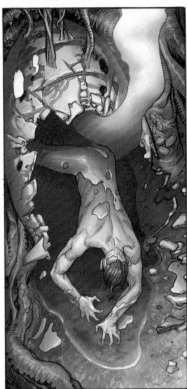

Welcome back.

How did I die this time?

I don't know the details about that.

But I do know this--

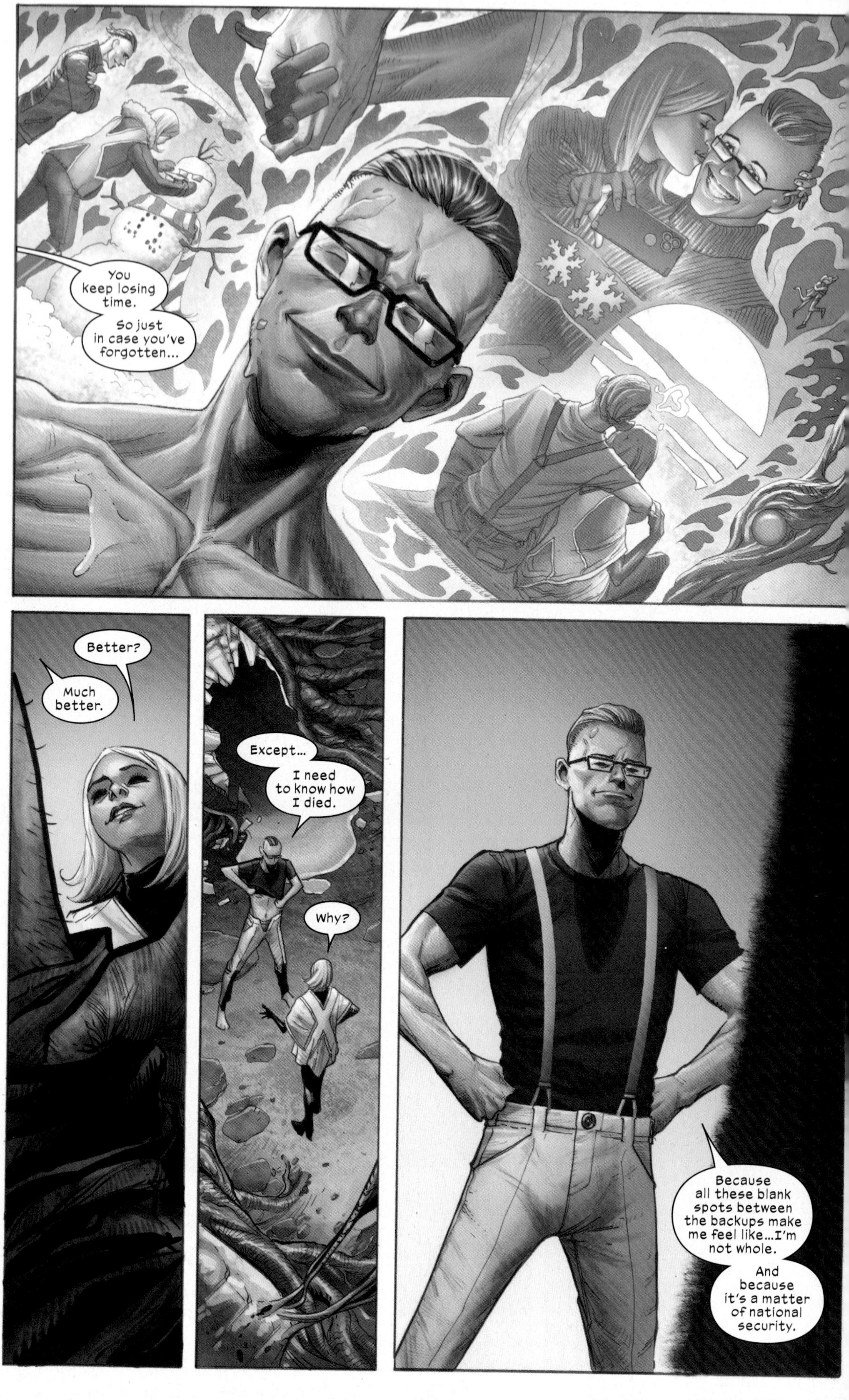
You keep losing time.
So just in case you've forgotten...
Better?
Much better.
Except...
I need to know how I died.
Why?
Because all these blank spots between the backups make me feel like...I'm not whole.
And because it's a matter of national security.

RESURRECTION REPORT

Author: The Five

Subject: Kid Omega / Quentin Quire

Proposal: Bio-editing

Revision #312: Kid Omega has <once again> come to us with a request.

The preliminary oral report reads as follows: "I know, I know, I know. You're annoyed. But perfection takes time. The minute adjustments are like Michelangelo chipping and polishing away at David before the sculpture's display in Florence. Don't you want to be Michelangelo? Don't you believe in art? Of course you do. You should be thanking me for this opportunity. So my problem is my toenails. I would like them to stop growing. I'm considering eliminating them altogether honestly -- because what's the point of toenails? -- but for now I'd like to try an alpha-keratin composition that gives off a glimmer of pearl shellac."

/// Samples from History ///

Recent requests:

310) Coloring his hair rose gold instead of pink
311) Coloring his hair pink instead of rose gold.
   >>>
226) Eliminating hair follicles on face at these precise dimensions (see attached report 2b) so as to avoid shaving.
225) Eliminating hair follicles on sides of head at these precise dimensions (see attached report 2b) so as to avoid shaving.
224) Eliminating hair follicles in armpits, back, chest, and groin at these precise dimensions (see attached report 2b) so as to avoid waxing.
   >>>
14) Adjusting eyes to secure 20/20 vision acuity, making glasses a mere accessory.
13) Adjusting ██████████ to these precise dimensions (see attached report 1a).

Notes: God, he's so annoying. We need to put forward a resolution to the Professor that overrides some of X-Force's power re: resurrection protocols. These cosmetic changes are more than absurd; they're slowing us down.

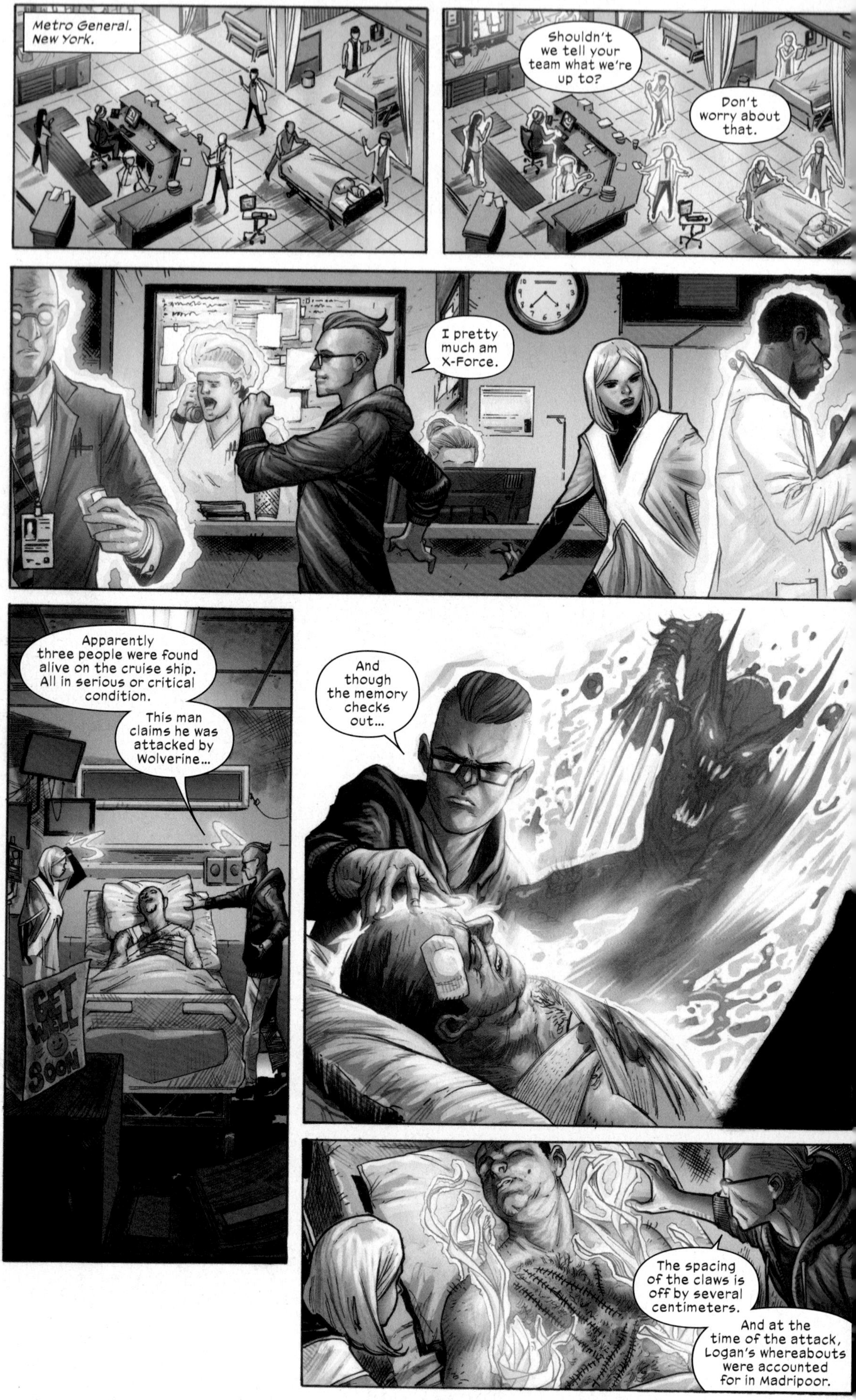
Metro General. New York.
Shouldn't we tell your team what we're up to?
Don't worry about that.
I pretty much am X-Force.
Apparently three people were found alive on the cruise ship. All in serious or critical condition.
This man claims he was attacked by Wolverine...
GET WELL SOON
And though the memory checks out...
The spacing of the claws is off by several centimeters.
And at the time of the attack, Logan's whereabouts were accounted for in Madripoor.

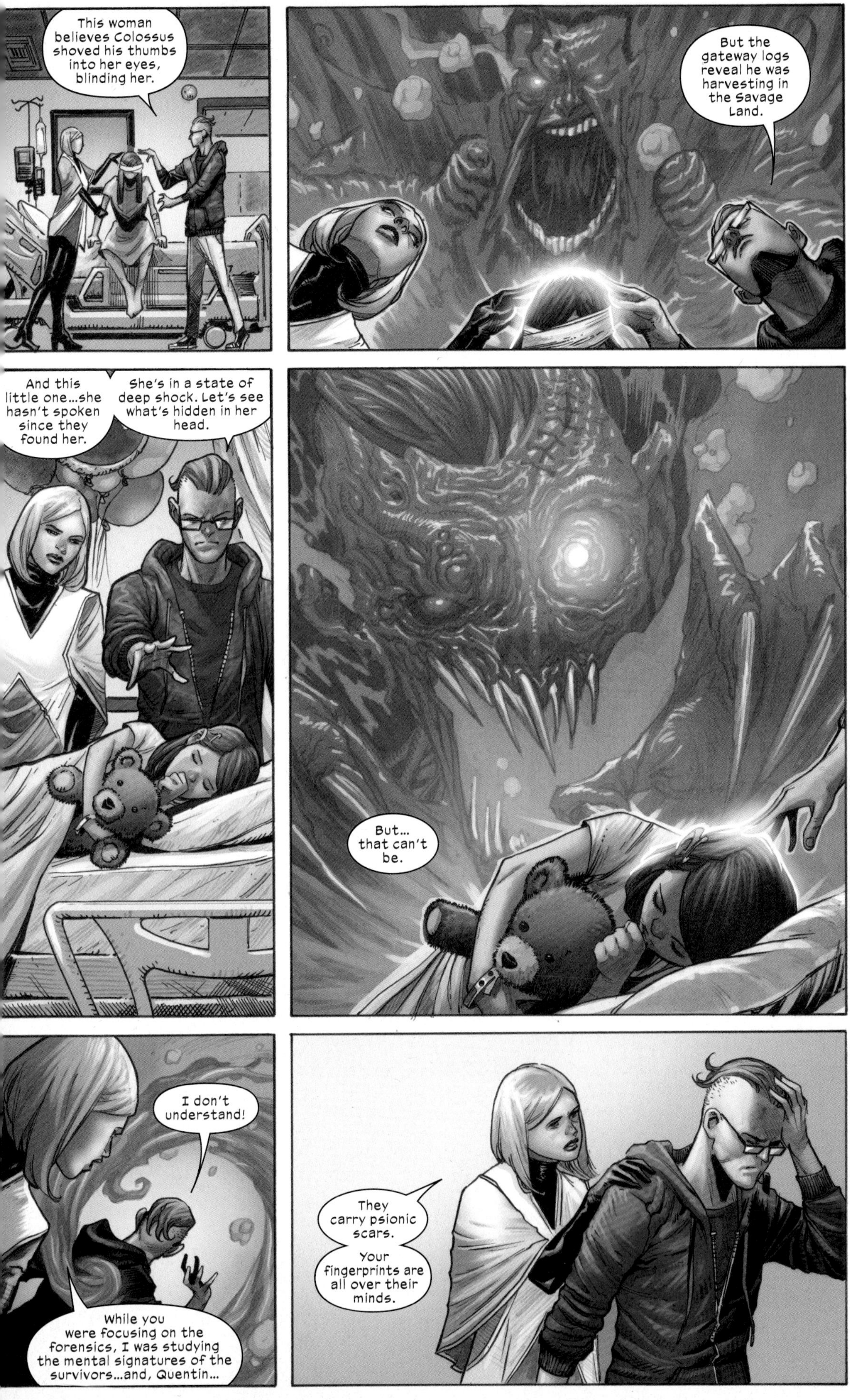
This woman believes Colossus shoved his thumbs into her eyes, blinding her.
But the gateway logs reveal he was harvesting in the Savage Land.
And this little one...she hasn't spoken since they found her.
She's in a state of deep shock. Let's see what's hidden in her head.
But... that can't be.
I don't understand!
While you were focusing on the forensics, I was studying the mental signatures of the survivors...and, Quentin...
They carry psionic scars.
Your fingerprints are all over their minds.

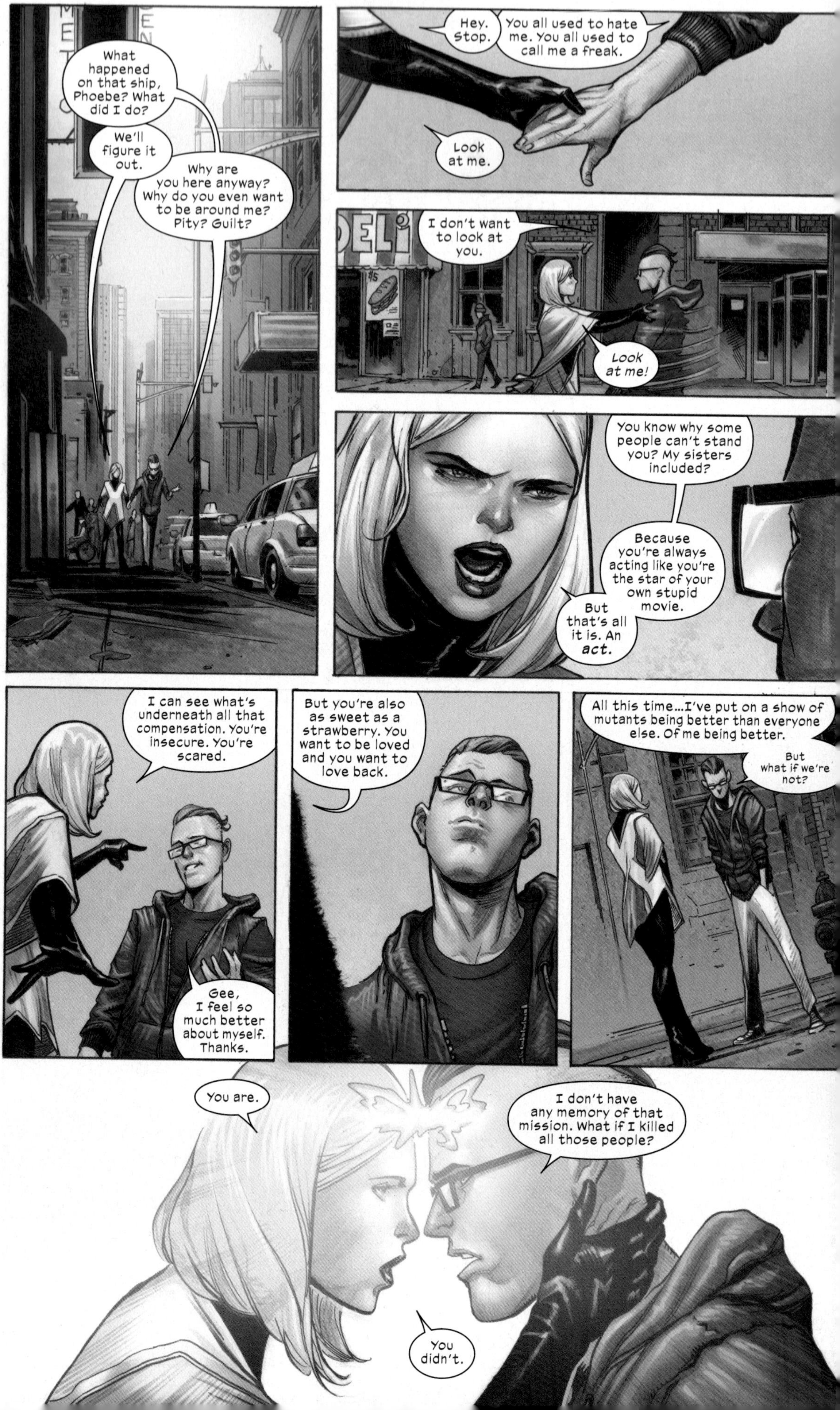
What happened on that ship, Phoebe? What did I do?
We'll figure it out.
Why are you here anyway? Why do you even want to be around me? Pity? Guilt?
Hey. Stop.
You all used to hate me. You all used to call me a freak.
Look at me.
I don't want to look at you.
Look at me!
You know why some people can't stand you? My sisters included?
Because you're always acting like you're the star of your own stupid movie.
But that's all it is. An act.
I can see what's underneath all that compensation. You're insecure. You're scared.
Gee, I feel so much better about myself. Thanks.
But you're also as sweet as a strawberry. You want to be loved and you want to love back.
All this time...I've put on a show of mutants being better than everyone else. Of me being better.
But what if we're not?
You are.
I don't have any memory of that mission. What if I killed all those people?
You didn't.

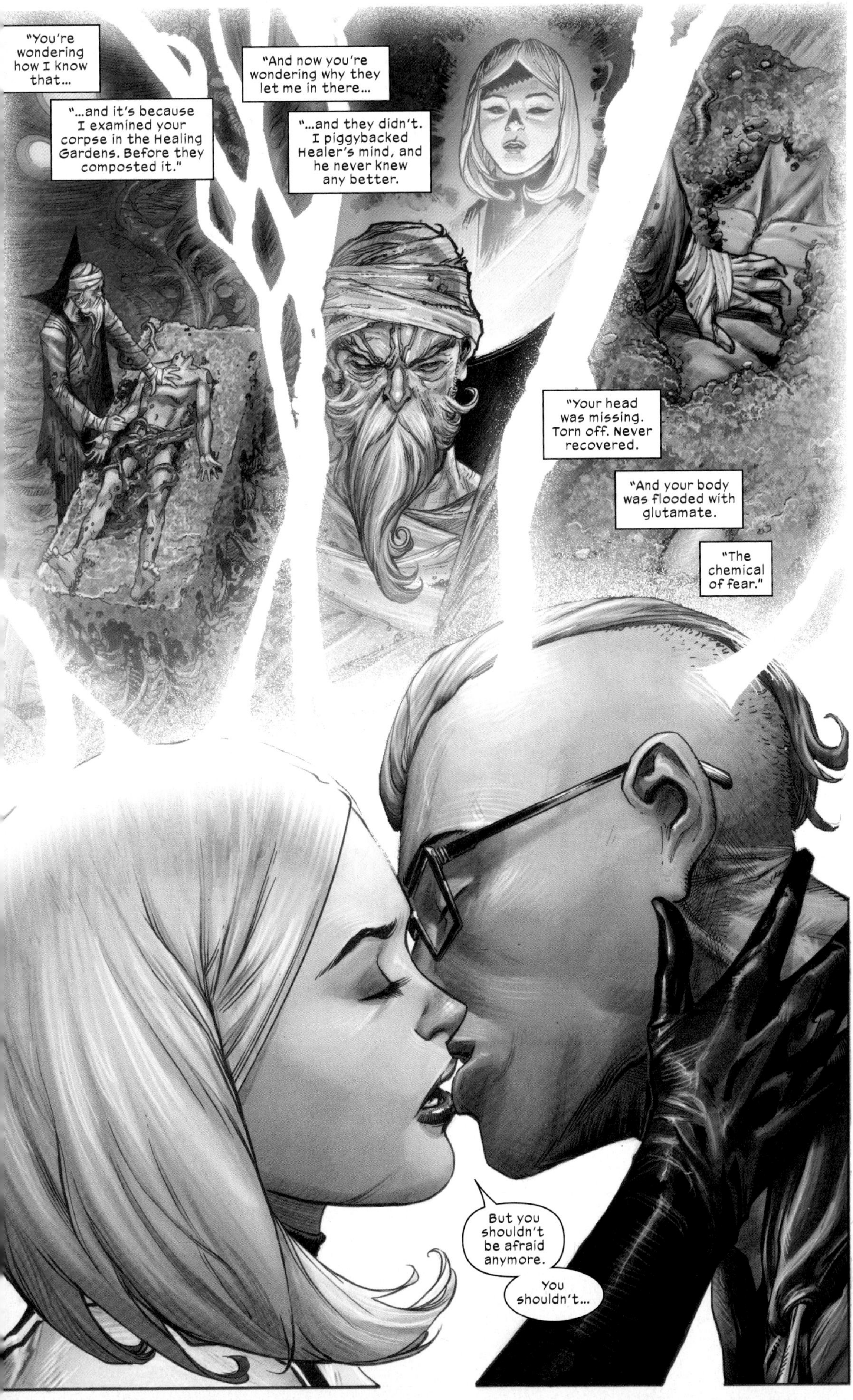
"You're wondering how I know that...
"...and it's because I examined your corpse in the Healing Gardens. Before they composted it."
"And now you're wondering why they let me in there...
"...and they didn't. I piggybacked Healer's mind, and he never knew any better.
"Your head was missing. Torn off. Never recovered.
"And your body was flooded with glutamate.
"The chemical of fear."
But you shouldn't be afraid anymore.
You shouldn't...

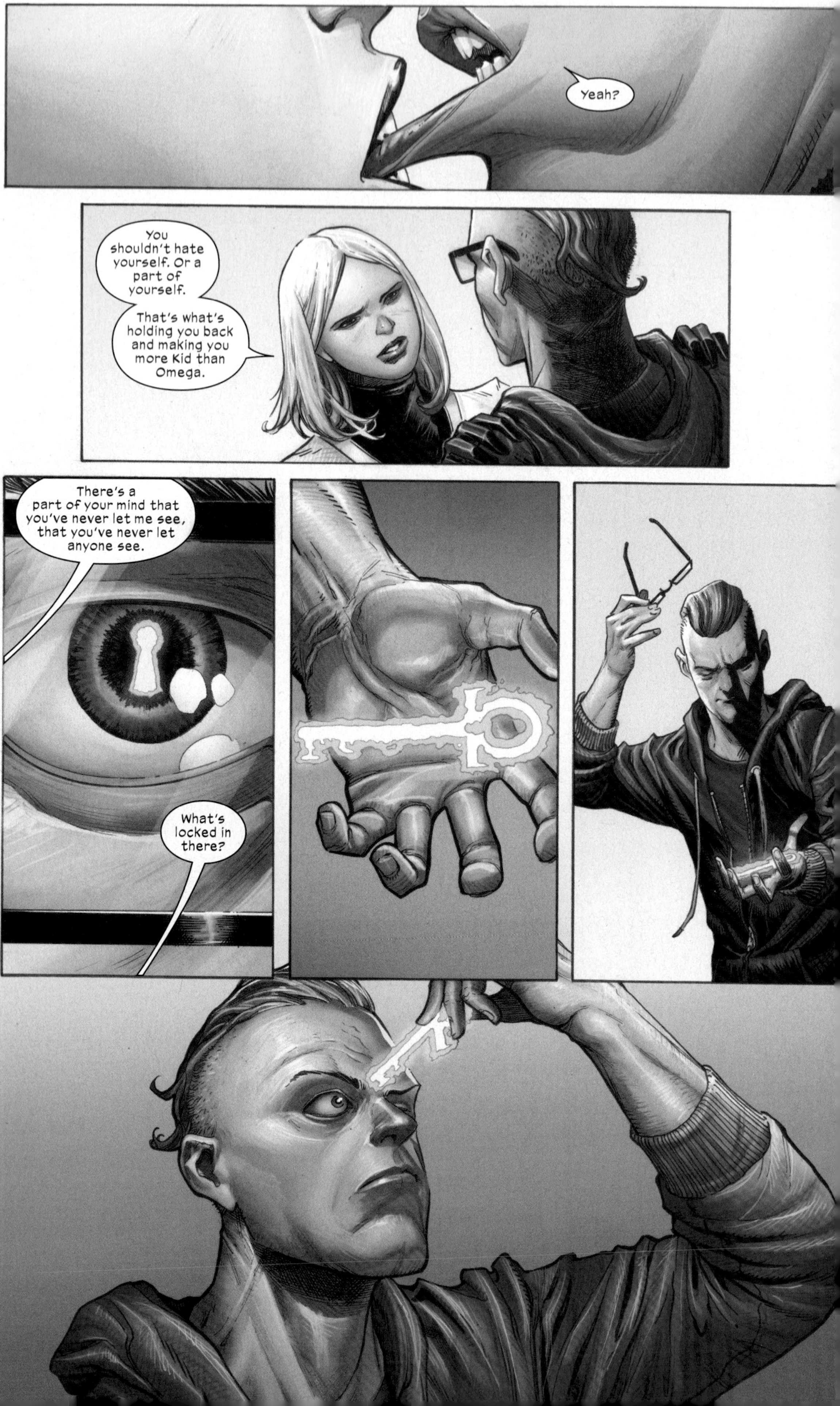
Yeah?
You shouldn't hate yourself. Or a part of yourself.
That's what's holding you back and making you more Kid than Omega.
There's a part of your mind that you've never let me see, that you've never let anyone see.
What's locked in there?

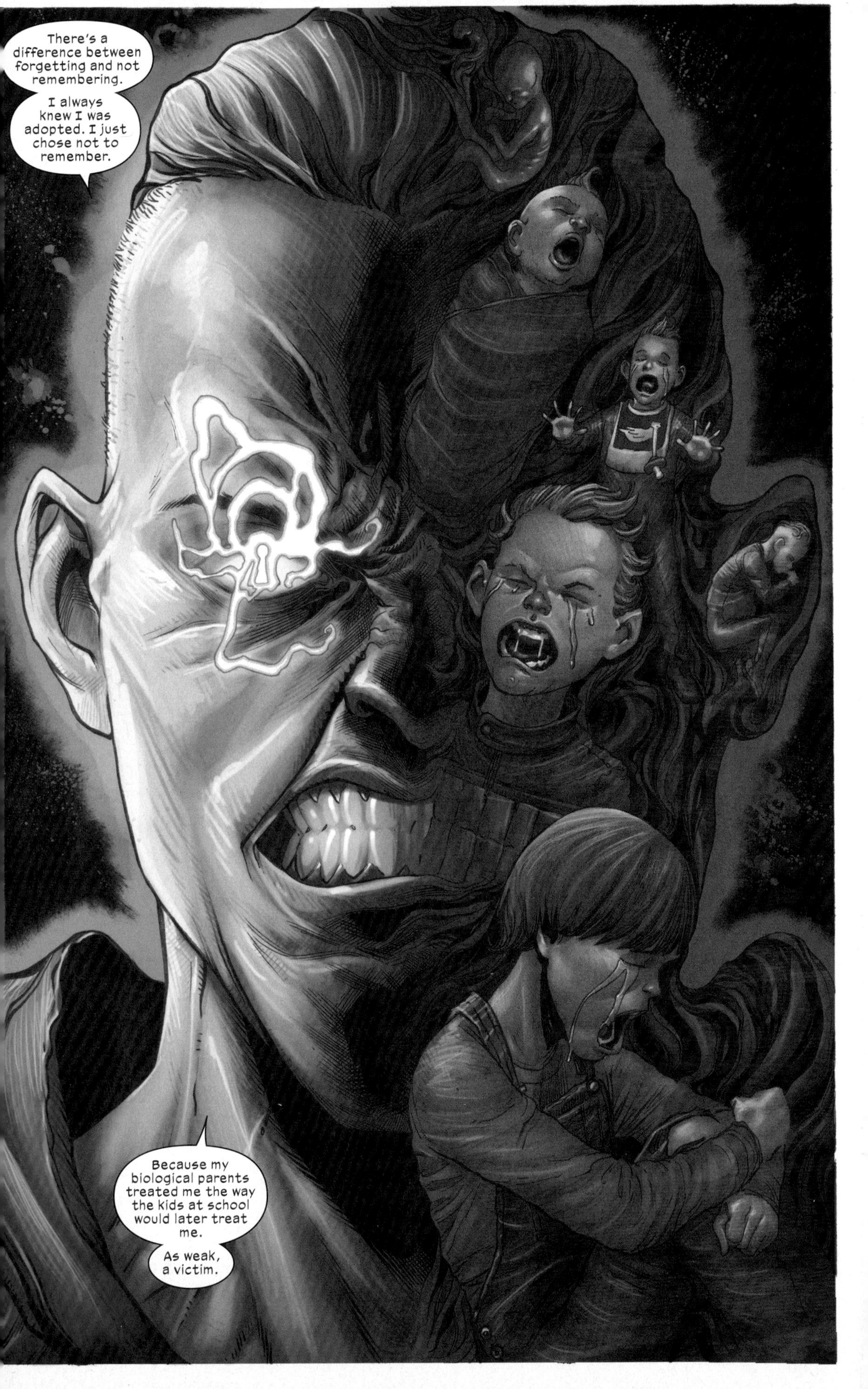
There's a difference between forgetting and not remembering.
I always knew I was adopted. I just chose not to remember.
Because my biological parents treated me the way the kids at school would later treat me.
As weak, a victim.

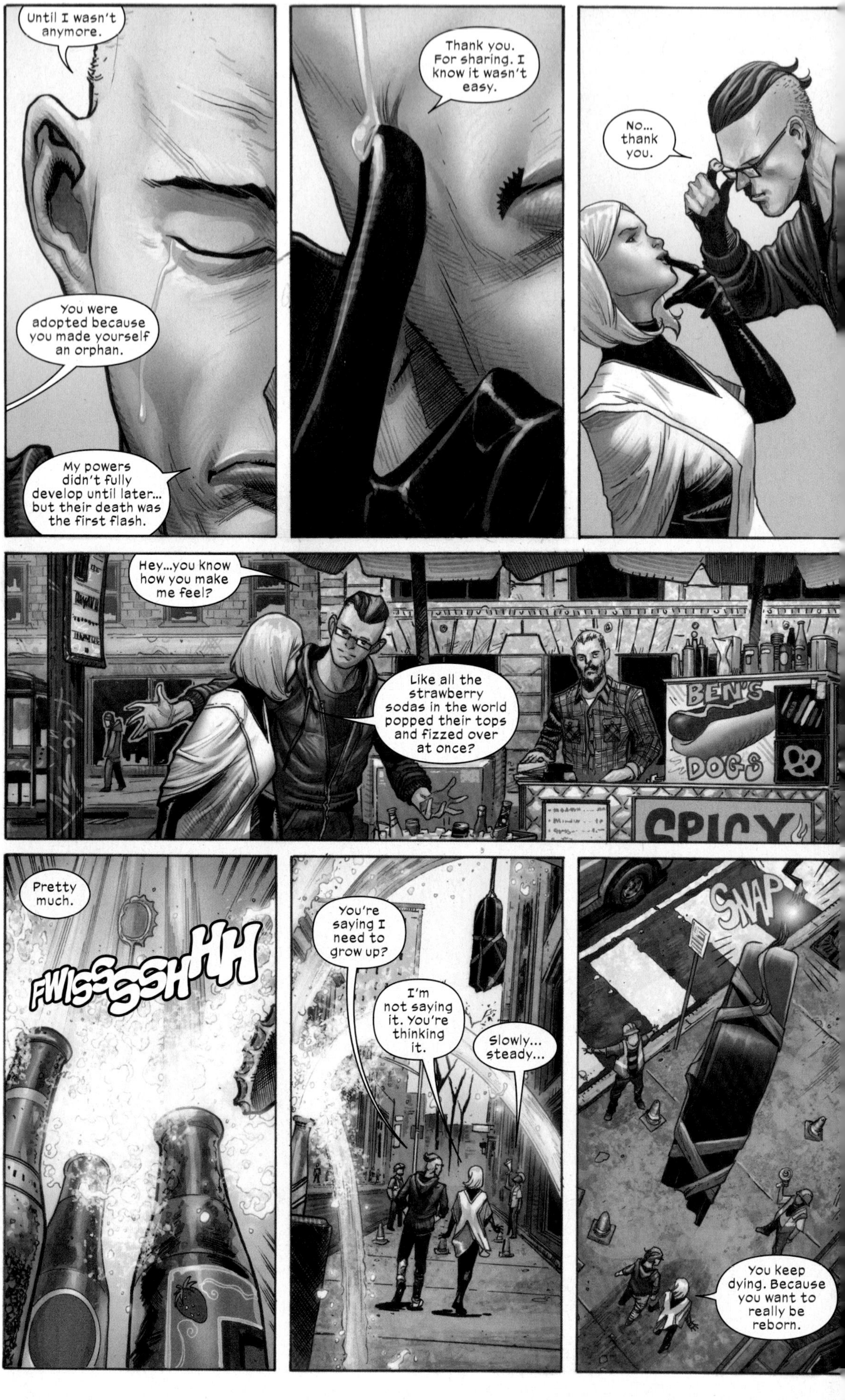
Until I wasn't anymore.
You were adopted because you made yourself an orphan.
My powers didn't fully develop until later... but their death was the first flash.
Thank you. For sharing. I know it wasn't easy.
No... thank you.
Hey...you know how you make me feel?
Like all the strawberry sodas in the world popped their tops and fizzed over at once?
BEN'S
DOGS
SPICY
Pretty much.
FWISSSSSHHH
You're saying I need to grow up?
I'm not saying it. You're thinking it.
Slowly... steady...
SNAP
You keep dying. Because you want to really be reborn.

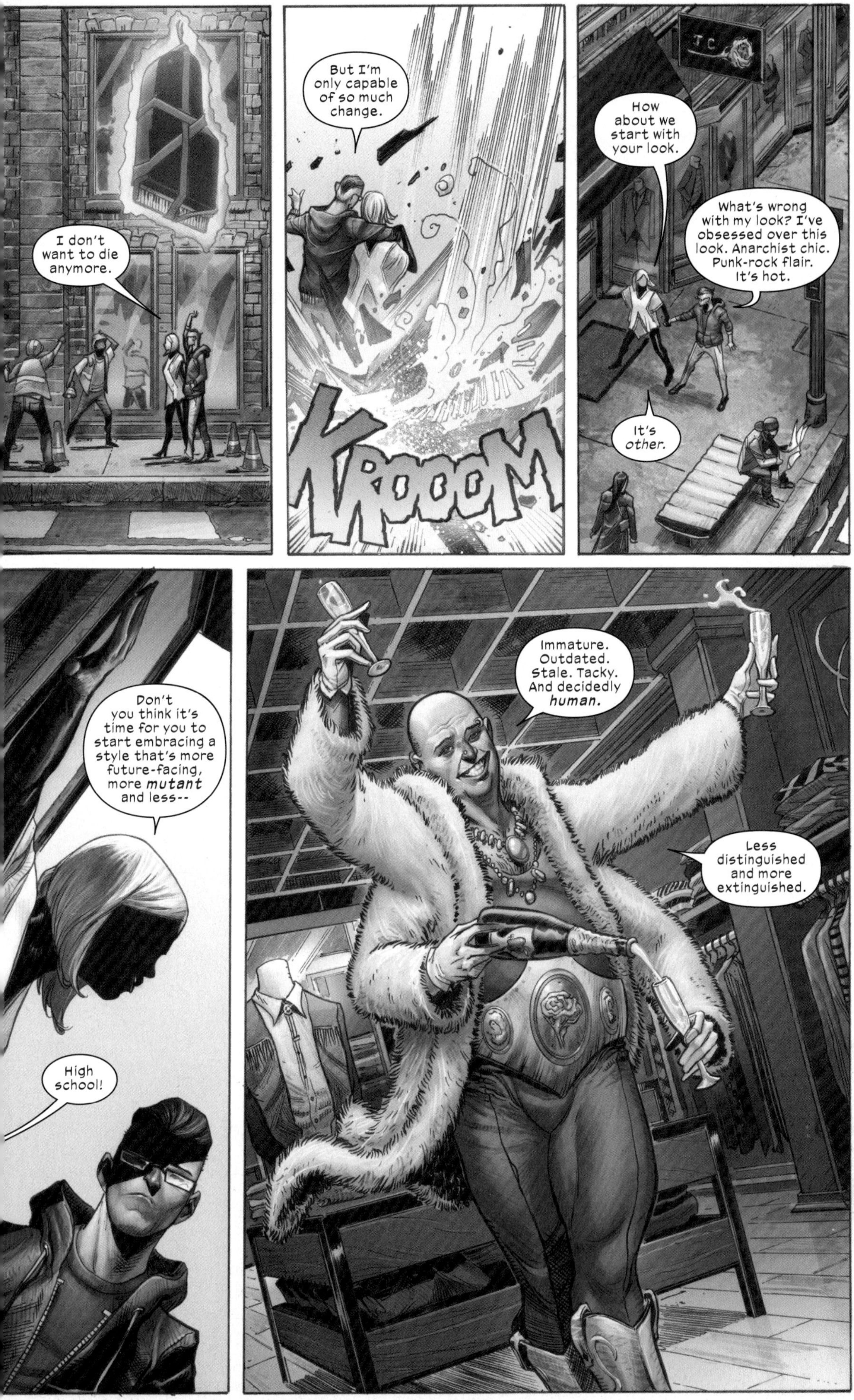
I don't want to die anymore.
But I'm only capable of so much change.
KROOOM
How about we start with your look.
What's wrong with my look? I've obsessed over this look. Anarchist chic. Punk-rock flair. It's hot.
It's *other.*
Don't you think it's time for you to start embracing a style that's more future-facing, more *mutant* and less--
High school!
Immature. Outdated. Stale. Tacky. And decidedly *human.*
Less distinguished and more extinguished.

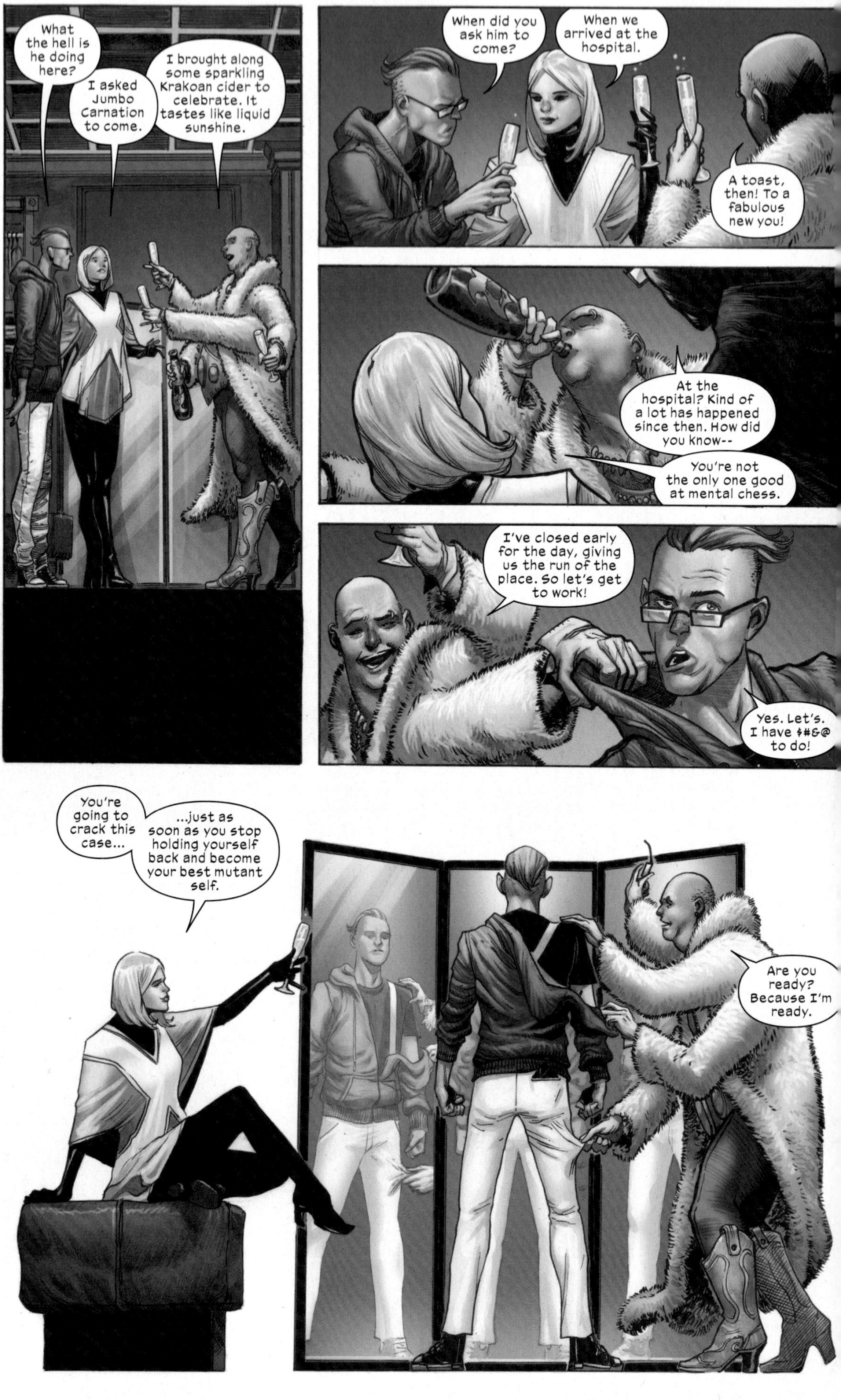
What the hell is he doing here?
I asked Jumbo Carnation to come.
I brought along some sparkling Krakoan cider to celebrate. It tastes like liquid sunshine.
When did you ask him to come?
When we arrived at the hospital.
A toast, then! To a fabulous new you!
At the hospital? Kind of a lot has happened since then. How did you know--
You're not the only one good at mental chess.
I've closed early for the day, giving us the run of the place. So let's get to work!
Yes. Let's. I have $#&@ to do!
You're going to crack this case...
...just as soon as you stop holding yourself back and become your best mutant self.
Are you ready? Because I'm ready.

Too post-apocalyptic?

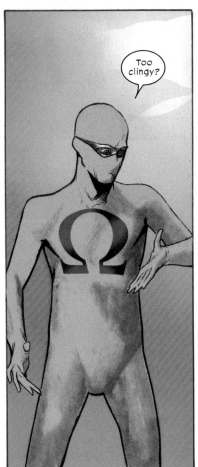

Too clingy?

Too pouchy?

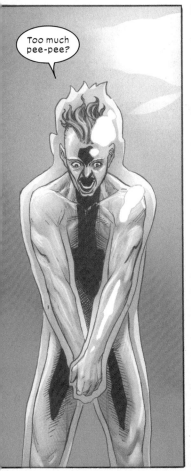

Too much pee-pee?

Too Shi'ar?

Too bad mentor-y?

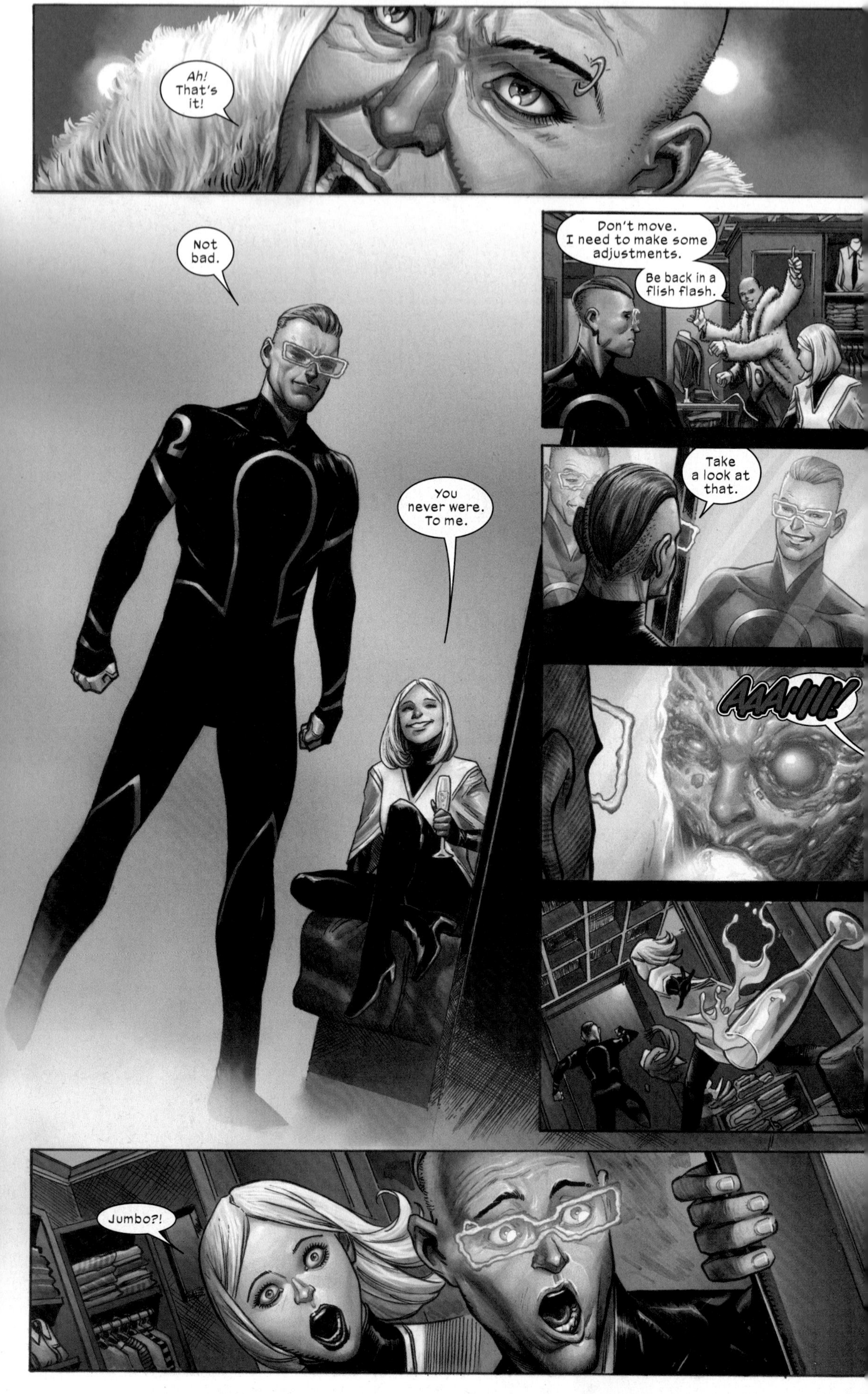
Ah! That's it!
Not bad.
Don't move. I need to make some adjustments.
Be back in a flish flash.
You never were. To me.
Take a look at that.
AAAIIIII!
Jumbo?!

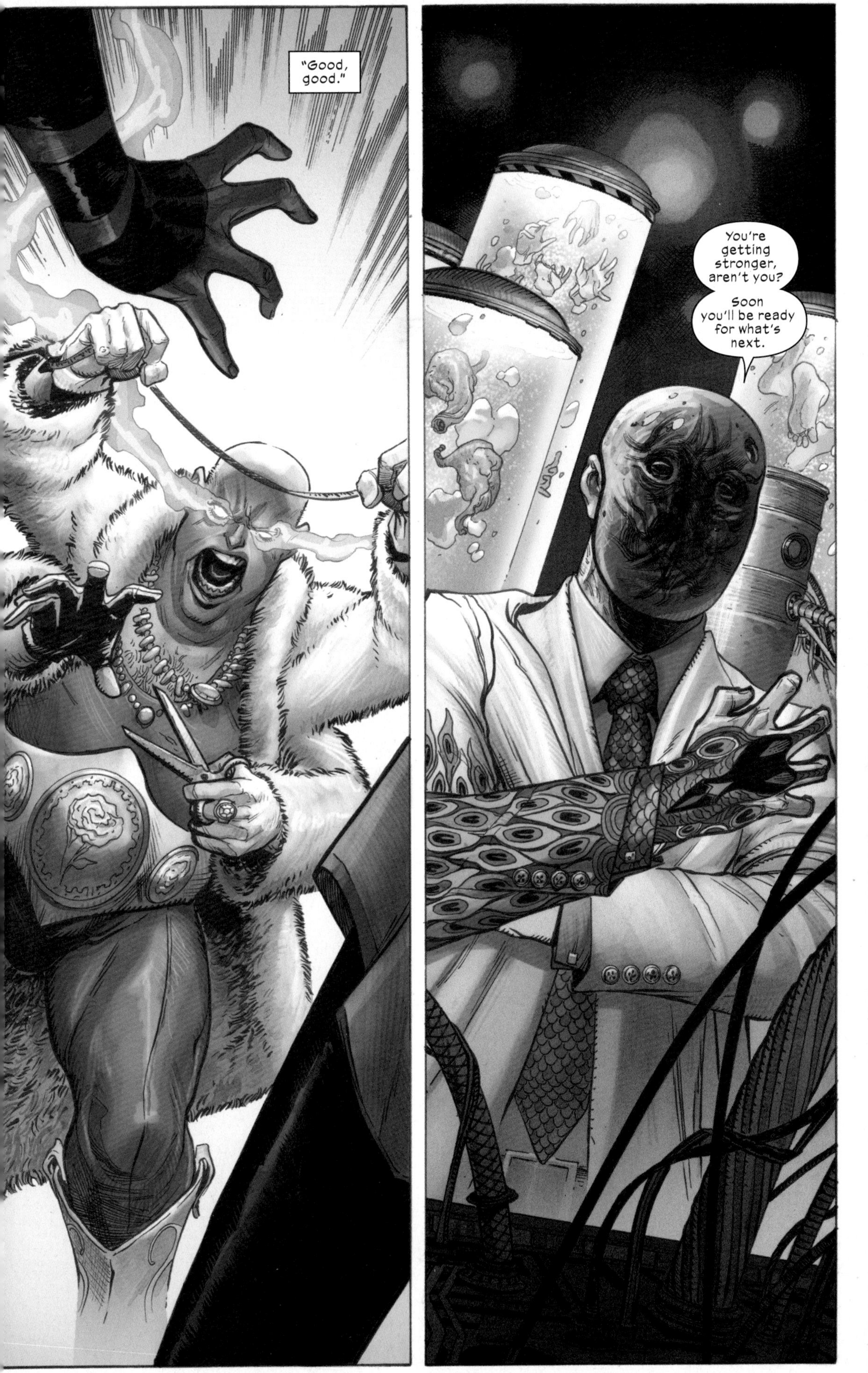
"Good, good."
You're getting stronger, aren't you?
Soon you'll be ready for what's next.

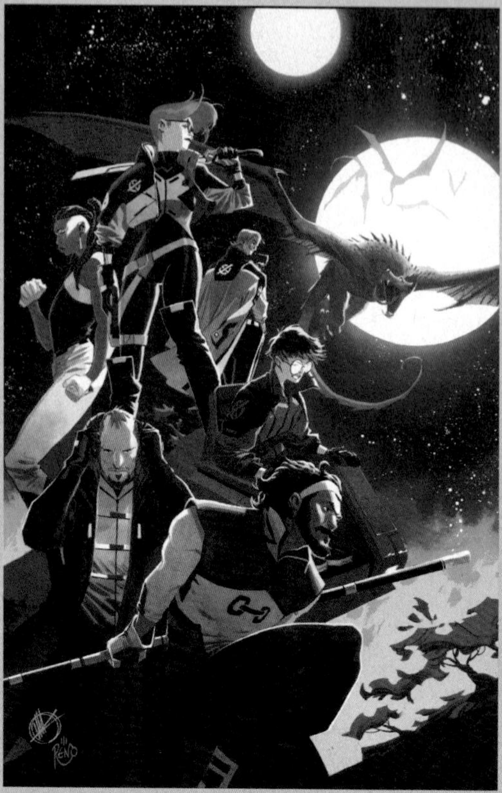

S.W.O.R.D. #4 Variant
by Matteo Scalera & Moreno Dinisio

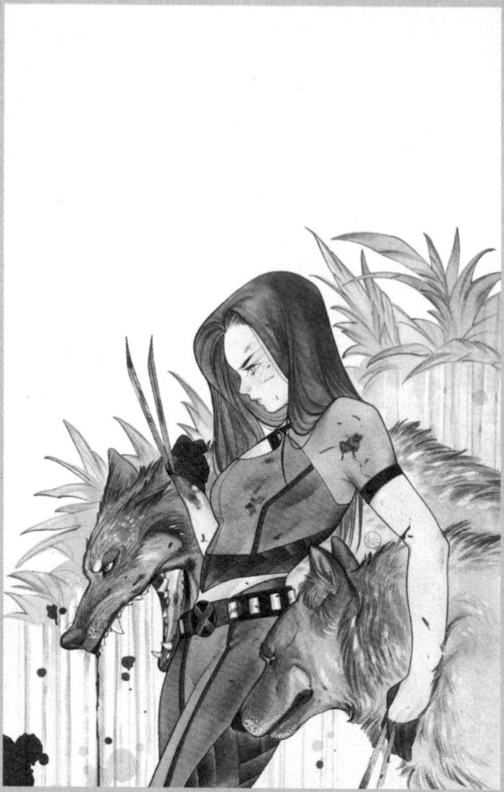

X-Men #18 Variant
by Peach Momoko

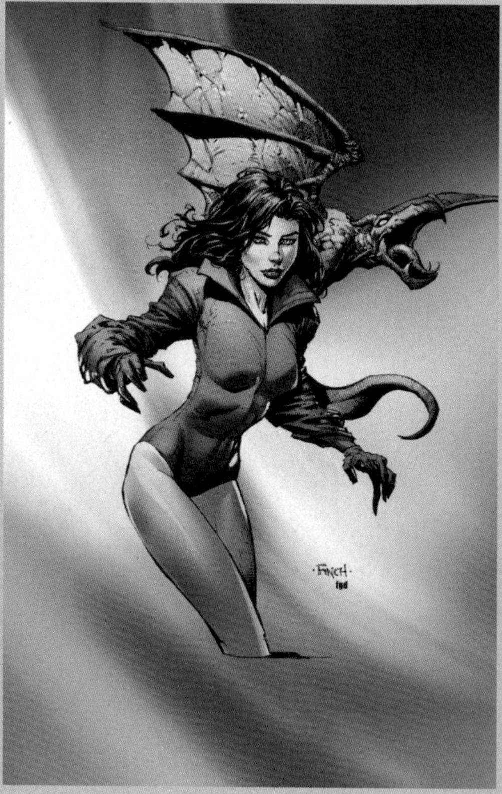

Marauders #19 Variant
by David Finch & Frank D'Armata

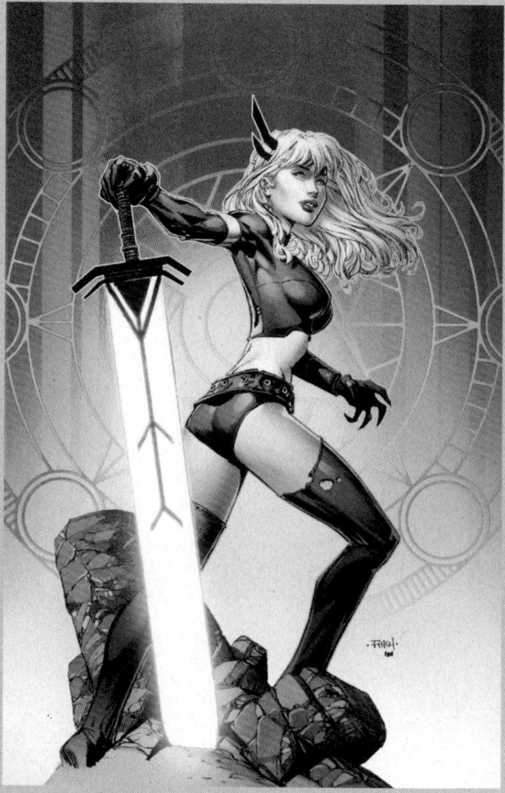

X-Men #19 Variant
by David Finch & Frank D'Armata

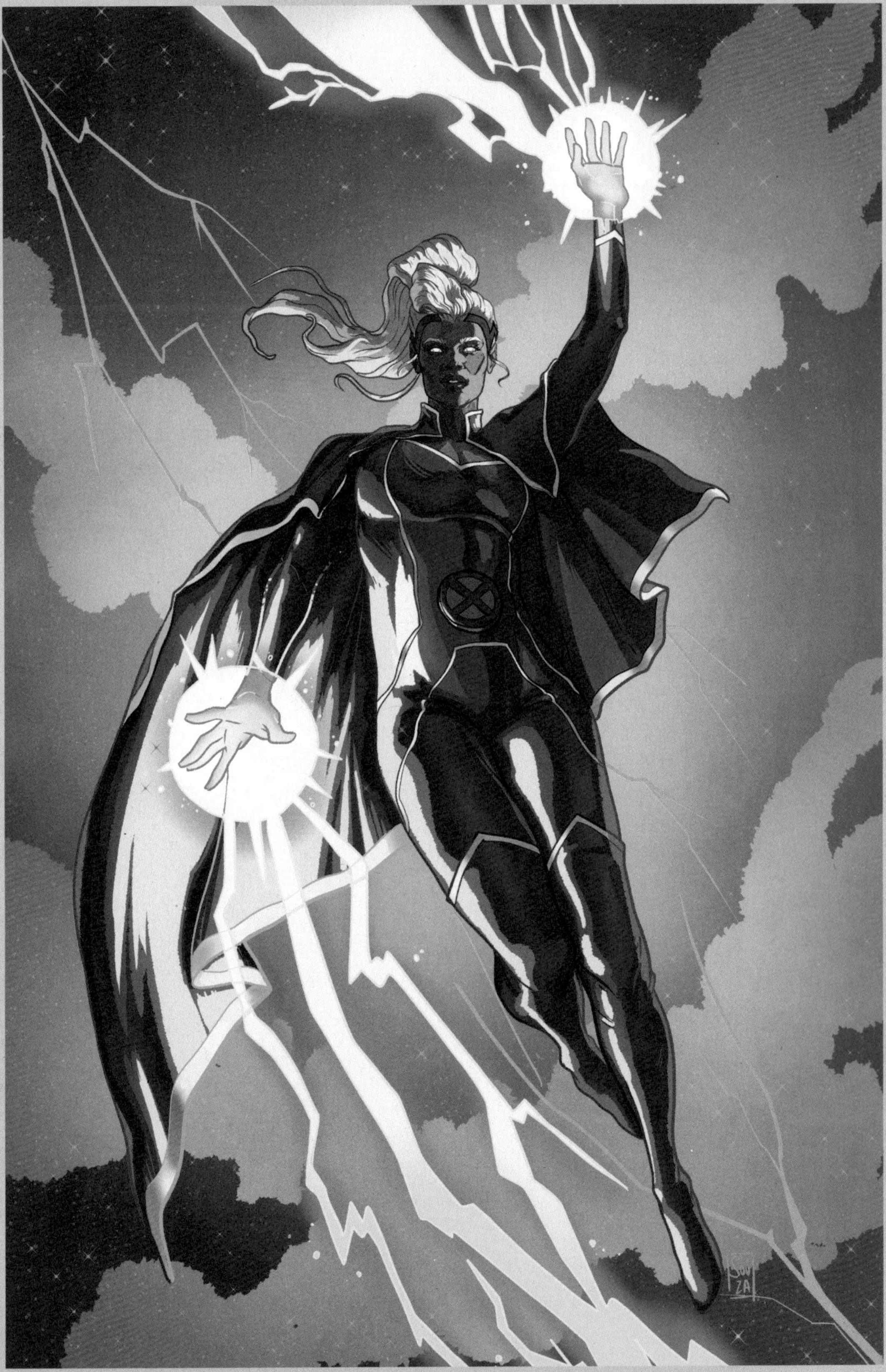

X-Men #18 Black History Month Variant by Ernanda Souza

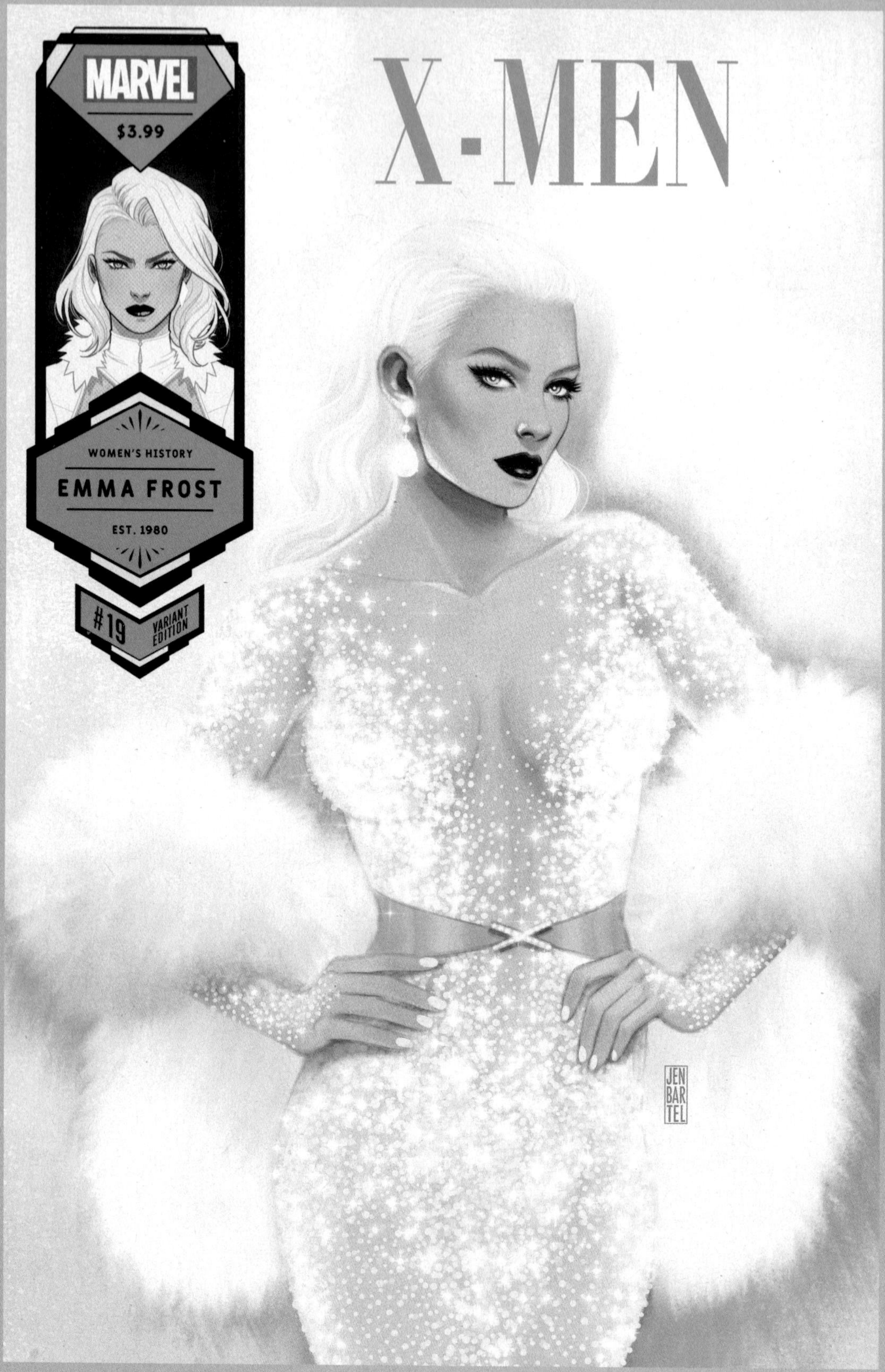
MARVEL
$3.99
X-MEN
WOMEN'S HISTORY
EMMA FROST
EST. 1980
#19
VARIANT EDITION
JEN BAR TEL

X-Men #19 Women's History Month Variant by Jen Bartel